A WORLD BANK COUNTRY STUDY

CHINA

The Energy Sector

Annex 3 to

CHINA

Long-Term Development Issues and Options

The World Bank
Washington, D.C., U.S.A.

Manufactured in the United States of America
First printing September 1985

World Bank Country Studies are reports originally prepared for internal use as part of the continuing analysis by the Bank of the economic and related conditions of its developing member countries and of its dialogues with the governments. Some of the reports are published informally with the least possible delay for the use of governments and the academic, business and financial, and development communities. Thus, the typescript has not been prepared in accordance with the procedures appropriate to formal printed texts, and the World Bank accepts no responsibility for errors. The publication is supplied at a token charge to defray part of the cost of manufacture and distribution.

The designations employed, the presentation of material, and any maps used in this document are solely for the convenience of the reader and do not imply the expression of any opinion whatsoever on the part of the World Bank or is affiliates concerning the legal status of any country, territory, city, area, or of its authorities, or concerning the delimitation of its boundaries or national affiliation.

The most recent World Bank publications are described in the annual spring and fall lists; the continuing research program is described in the annual *Abstracts of Current Studies.* The latest edition of each is available free of charge from the Publications Sales Unit, Department T, The World Bank, 1818 H Street, N.W., Washington, D.C. 20433, U.S.A., or from the European Office of the Bank, 66 avenue d'Iéna, 75116 Paris, France.

Library of Congress Cataloging-in-Publication Data

Main entry under title:

China, the energy sector.

(Annex 3 to China, long-term development issues and options) (A World Bank country study)
1. Energy consumption--China. 2. Energy policy--China. I. International Bank for Reconstruction and Development. II. Series: Annex ... to China, long-term development issues and options ; 3. III. Series: World Bank country study.
HC9502.C62C495 1985 333.79'0951 85-17916
ISBN 0-8213-0602-2

Preface

This report is one of six annexes to a main report entitled China: Long-Term Development Issues and Options. The complete list of annex volumes is:

Volume 1 - China: Issues and Prospects in Education
Volume 2 - China: Agriculture to the Year 2000
Volume 3 - China: The Energy Sector
Volume 4 - China: Economic Model and Projections
Volume 5 - China: Economic Structure in International Perspective
Volume 6 - China: The Transport Sector

(Note: Throughout this volume references to Annexes A, B, C and so on refer in that same order to Annex Volumes 1, 2, 3 etc.)

The main report and annex volumes were prepared principally by members of an economic mission that visited China twice in 1984, for four weeks in February/March and for five weeks in April/May. In addition to Beijing, the mission went to three provinces: one coastal and relatively high-income (Jiangsu); one inland and average-income (Hubei); and one interior and low-income (Gansu). It received a lot of information, as well as numerous valuable comments and suggestions, from officials and others in these provinces, as well as from those in many central agencies and institutions, including: the State Planning and State Economic Commissions; the Ministries of Finance, Agriculture, Coal, Communications, Education, Foreign Economic Relations and Trade, Labor and Personnel, Petroleum, Railways, Urban and Rural Construction, and Water Resources and Electric Power; the State Statistical Bureau; and various universities and research institutes of the Chinese Academy of Social Sciences. A series of seminars was organized by the Technical-Economic Research Center under the State Council. The generous and thoughtful assistance of all these people in China contributed greatly to the preparation of the reports.

The Bank mission was led by Edwin Lim (mission chief) and Adrian Wood (deputy mission chief), and also consisted of William Byrd (economist), Mats Hultin (senior education adviser), Erh-Cheng Hwa (senior economist), Timothy King (senior economist), Jacques Yenny (senior transport economist), Umnuay Sae-Hau (research assistant), Betty Ting (interpreter), Luc De Wulf (senior economist, International Monetary Fund), Benjamin King (consultant on statistics), Wouter Tims (consultant on planning and agriculture); and the following teams:

Agriculture: J. Goering (team leader, April/May), Tom Wiens (team leader, February/March), Lang-Seng Tay (irrigation specialist), Lo-Chai Chen (fishery consultant) and Fred Bentley (consultant on arid agriculture);

Energy: Roberto Bentjerodt (senior economist, coal projects), Weigong Cao (power engineer), Abdel El-Mekkawy (engineer, petroleum projects), Robert Taylor (energy economist), and Darrel Fallen-Bailey (consultant); D.C. Rao (Assistant Director, Energy Department) led the team in the field;

Industrial Technology: Gene Tidrick (team leader), Anupam Khanna (industrial economist), Reza Amin (industrial specialist), and Josephine Woo (research assistant);

Location and Trade: Ian Porter (team leader), Vernon Henderson (consultant on urbanization), John Sheahan (consultant on industrial location and trade) and Samuel Ho (consultant on rural nonfarm activities).

The following also contributed to the preparation of the reports: Wlodzimierz Brus (consultant on socialist economies), Gerhard Pohl (energy and transport), Robert Drysdale (Annex Vol. 1); Helena Ribe, Nikhil Desai (Annex Vol. 3); Shujiro Urata (Annex Vols. 4 and 5); and Lily Uy (Annex Vol. 6). Larry Westphal, Carl Dahlman and Bruce Ross-Larson organized background work on technology. Behrouz Guerami-N, Tejaswi Raparla, and Kong-Yam Tan helped with the multisectoral model, the input-output table and data for international comparisons. Ann Orr, Kenneth Hill, Moshe Syrquin, J.V.S. Sarma, Kenneth Cochran, Chang Hsin, Liu Ying and Cai Jinyong undertook research. Linda Mitchell and Terrice Bassler edited the reports; and Helen Kung assisted in their processing.

The reports also benefited from comments of a review panel consisting of Anne O. Krueger, Luis de Azcarate, Kemal Dervis, Janos Kornai (consultant) and managers of the East Asia and Pacific Regional Office.

In addition to the main report and annex volumes, the following background papers have been prepared and are being issued as World Bank Staff Working Papers:

1. "The Asian Experience in Rural Nonagricultural Development and its Relevance for China"
2. "International Experience in Urbanization and its Relevance for China"
3. "Alternative International Economic Strategies and their Relevance for China"
4. "International Experience in Budgetary Trends during Economic Development and their Relevance for China"
5. "Productivity Growth and Technological Change in Chinese Industry"
6. "Issues in the Technological Development of China's Electronics Sector"
7. "The Environment for Technological Change in Centrally Planned Economies"
8. "Managing Technology Development: Lessons from the Newly Industrializing Countries"
9. "Growth and Structural Change in Large Low-Income Countries"

The main report, other annex volumes and background papers are available from World Bank Publications, P.O. Box 37525, Washington, D.C., 20013 or from World Bank distributors listed on the last page of this volume. Prices will be furnished upon request.

Table of Contents*

Page No.

---

* Chapter 4 of the Main Report summarizes the main findings and conclusions in this Annex.

APPENDICES

MAPS

LIST OF TABLES IN THE TEXT

Page No.

Page No.

LIST OF APPENDICES

Page No.

Page No.

CURRENCY EQUIVALENTS

The Chinese currency is called Renminbi (RMB). It is denominated in Yuan (Y). Each Yuan is

1 Yuan = 10 jiao = 100 fen

In early 1984 the official exchange rate of the Yuan to the US dollar was around Y 2 = US$1. The internal settlement rate (ISR) of Y 2.8 = $1, however, was used in most merchandise transactions. The offical exchange rate is now about Y 2.8 = $1. On January 1, 1985, the Government abolished the ISR.

FISCAL YEAR

January 1 - December 31

ABBREVIATIONS AND ACRONYMS

AIC	-	Average incremental cost
bcm	-	Billion cubic meters
CIC	-	Coal Industry Company
CINOPEC	-	China Petro-Chemical Corporation National
CMA	-	Coal Mine Administration
CNOOC	-	China National Offshore Oil Corporation
ctkm	-	Converted ton-kilometer
EOR	-	Enhanced oil recovery
gcal	-	Giga-calorie
GVAO	-	Gross value of agricultural output
GVIAO	-	Gross value of industrial and agricultural output
GVIO	-	Gross value of industrial output
kcal	-	kilo-calorie
IOC	-	International oil companies
LPG	-	Liquid petroleum gas
MOC	-	Ministry of Communications
MOCI	-	Ministry of Coal Industry
MOG	-	Ministry of Geology
MOPI	-	Ministry of Petroleum Industry
MOR	-	Ministry of Railways
mtpy	-	million tons per year
MWREP	-	Ministry of Water Resources and Electric Power
pkm	-	passenger-kilometer
SEC	-	State Economic Commission
SPC	-	State Planning Commission
TCE	-	Tons of coal equivalent
tkm	-	ton-kilometer
tpd	-	Tons per day

ENERGY CONVERSION FACTORS

1 ton of coal equivalent	=	7 million kilocalories
1 ton of oil	=	10.2 million kilocalories
1 ton of coal (run-of-mine average)	=	5.0 million kilocalories
(export)	=	6.5 million kilocalories
1,000 cubic meters of natural gas	=	9.31 million kilocalories
1,000 kWh of electricity	=	2.89 million kilocalories
(unless specified otherwise)		(1980 Thermal replacement value)

Table 1.2: CHINA: ENERGY BALANCE, 1980
(Millions of tons of coal equivalent)

	Oil	Coal	Natural gas	Electricity	Total commercial energy	Biomass	Total
Primary Supply							
Production	154.3	443.0	19.0	24.0	640.3	219.1	859.4
Exports	25.5	5.9	-	-	31.4	-	31.4
Stock changes	-	4.3	-	-	4.3	-	4.3
Domestic supply	128.8	432.8	19.0	24.0	604.6	219.1	823.7
Energy Industry Conversion, Losses and Use							
Power industry							
Thermal power production	28.3	78.2	6.0	(100.1)/a	12.4/a	-	12.4/a
Heat supply credit /b	(4.7)	(3.9)	(3.3)	-	(11.9)	-	(11.9)
Station and T&D losses	-	-	-	18.4	18.4	-	18.4
Subtotal	23.6	74.3	2.7	(81.7)	18.9	-	18.9
Petroleum industry							
Extraction	6.0	0.4	2.1	2.4	10.9	-	10.9
Refineries	13.1/c	-	-	1.2	14.3	-	14.3
Subtotal	19.1	0.4	2.1	3.6	25.2	-	25.2
Coal industry	0.7	29.0	-	7.9	37.6	-	37.6
Final Consumption							
Transportation	21.0	19.0	-	0.6	40.6	-	40.6
Residential/commercial	1.9	90.2	0.3	10.6	103.0	219.1	322.1
Agriculture /d	13.1	21.5	-	10.8	45.4	-	45.4
Industry	42.4	189.4	13.9	70.1	315.8	-	315.8
Other /e	7.0	9.0	-	2.1	18.1	-	18.1
Total	85.4	329.1	14.2	94.2	522.9	219.1	742.0

/a Electricity is calculated at a thermal replacement value net of the heat supply credit. Nevertheless, a statistical discrepancy of 0.5 MTCE exists as the standard thermal replacement value used for electricity in China for 1980 (and here also) does not quite match the reported net energy consumption in thermal power production.

/b Fuel which is consumed in the production of heat which is eventually supplied to consumers outside of the power industry.

/c Includes 3.8 MTCE of unallocated consumption.

/d Excludes township and village industries (formerly referred to as commune and brigade industries) outside of the agricultural processing field.

/e Includes construction and other nonspecified sectors.

Source: Appendix A.

Table 1.3: CHINA - PERCENTAGE SHARES OF FINAL ENERGY CONSUMPTION, 1980

Sector	Oil	Coal	Natural gas	Electricity	Total commercial energy	Biomass	Total energy
			A. Energy Composition (%)				
Agriculture	28.8	47.4	-	23.8	100.0	-	100.0
Transportation	51.7	46.8	-	1.5	100.0	-	100.0
Industry	13.4	60.0	4.4	22.2	100.0	-	100.0
Other	38.7	49.7	-	11.6	100.0	-	100.0
Residential/commercial							
Commercial energy	1.8	87.6	0.3	10.3	100.0	-	-
Total energy	0.6	27.9	0.1	3.3	31.9	68.1	100.0
Total							
Commercial energy	16.3	63.0	2.7	18.0	100.0	-	-
Total energy	11.5	44.3	1.9	12.7	70.4	29.6	100.0
			B. Sectoral Shares (%)				
Agriculture	15.3	6.5	-	11.5	8.7	-	6.1
Transportation	24.6	5.8	-	0.6	7.8	-	5.5
Industry	49.7	57.6	97.9	74.4	60.4	-	42.6
Other	8.2	2.7	-	2.2	3.4	-	2.4
Residential/commercial	2.2	27.4	2.1	11.3	19.7	100.0	43.4
Total	100.0	100.0	100.0	100.0	100.0	100.0	100.0

Source: Table 1.2.

A. The Mix of Energy Sources

1.04 A unique feature of energy consumption in China is the high share of coal in both commercial and total energy consumption. In 1980, coal accounted for approximately three-quarters of primary commercial energy consumption and one-half of total primary energy consumption -- the highest shares in any major country. Even in India, where it is also a major energy source, coal accounted for only 54% and 32% of primary commercial and total primary energy use, respectively, in 1980.

1.05 China's heavy reliance on coal is due primarily to the existence of large, low-cost reserves. There are coal deposits of varying quantities in every major region of the country. Before the relatively recent development of China's petroleum industry, the role of coal was even larger: in 1965, it accounted for almost 90% of primary commercial energy use. The share of coal consumption today is high in all major economic sectors -- even in transport, where railway consumption brings the share of coal to almost one half of the sector total.

1.06 Biomass fuels are China's second most important energy source, accounting for over one-quarter of primary consumption and an estimated 30% of final consumption. Small quantities are consumed in some urban areas and in some rural industries, particularly in the Southwest, but the lion's share of biomass fuel use is in rural households. Although actual consumption levels in other countries are as difficult to determine as in China, biomass fuels appear generally to account for higher shares of energy consumption in other low-income developing countries. Estimates in OECD sources place biomass fuel consumption in India at 46% of final energy use.

1.07 One feature of energy consumption in China that is not commonly recognized is the low share of electricity consumption compared with that of other countries. The share of electricity consumption in China has been increasing since 1970 despite serious supply constraints in the power sector, rising from some 13% of final commercial energy use to almost 15% in 1975 and to 18% in 1980. This share is still lower, however, than in any of the five major developing countries reviewed[3/] (see Appendix B, Table B.1). In India, for example, electricity provided 30% of final commercial energy in 1980. One factor that helps explain China's consumption figures is the relatively low electricity use in the residential and commercial sectors. On a per capita basis, 1980 consumption in these sectors was 26 kWh in China, compared with about 60 kWh in India, 250 kWh in South Korea, and 400 kWh in Brazil. Perhaps more important, however, is the low share of power use by industry in China relative to other countries with substantial industrial sectors. A key element in this difference is the relative inefficiency of fuel consumption in Chinese industry, which serves to decrease the relative share of electricity in total industrial energy consumption.

3/ Electricity consumption is calculated at a thermal replacement value of 2,900 kcal/kWh for all countries.

1.08 Oil accounted for about 21% of primary commercial energy consumption in 1980. Petroleum product demand is met through domestic refinery production. More than 10 million tons of crude oil was burned as a direct fuel in the power and industrial sectors in 1980, although use of crude oil as a direct fuel has fallen sharply in recent years. This practice resulted largely from the characteristics of the crude and transport and refining constraints in certain locations. In 1980, fuel oil and direct crude consumption accounted for just about one-half of oil consumption outside of the petroleum production and refinery sectors. Another unusual feature of petroleum product use is that gasoline is the dominant fuel for trucks. Thus, while consumption of gasoline in automobiles is almost negligible, the transport sector still accounts for over 90% of gasoline consumption (see Table 1.4). Natural gas represented only 2.7% of primary commercial energy consumption in 1980.

B. The Sectoral Structure of Consumption

1.09 China's industrial sector dominates final commercial energy consumption, accounting for some 60% of the total in 1980. Industry also accounts for at least half of final consumption of each of the commercial fuels and three-quarters of final electricity consumption. While the share of industrial energy use in China is high, it is not extraordinary by comparison to other countries with major industrial sectors, particularly when all forms of energy are considered (see Table 1.5).

1.10 As of 1980, China's metallurgy, chemical, and building materials industries accounted for 65% of final industrial energy consumption (see Table 1.6). This pattern is similar to that of other major countries. The structure of energy use in these three energy intensive industrial subsectors, however, has several special characteristics. In the chemical industry, coal accounts for 45% of energy use -- a far higher share than in any other major country. A key reason is that synthetic ammonia production accounts for an unusually high share of energy use in China's chemical industry -- about one half -- and coal and coke provide about three-quarters of the total fuel and feedstock used in the ammonia industry. In metallurgy, the iron and steel industry dominates the subsector, accounting for 87% of energy consumption in 1980. In the building materials subsector, brick manufacturing dominates. In 1980, China produced some 150 billion bricks, 110 billion of which were produced by rural collective industries. Brick and tile production accounted for almost one-half of energy use in the building materials industry, and consumed approximately 50% more energy than the cement industry.

Table 1.4: CHINA: PETROLEUM PRODUCT CONSUMPTION, 1980 /a
(Millions of tons)

	Gasoline	Diesel oil	Kerosene/ jet fuel	LPG	Fuel oil/ crude /b	Other	Total
Power industry	-	0.5	-	-	18.9	-	19.4
Transportation /c	8.9	4.2	0.3	-	1.0	-	14.4
Residential/commercial	-	-	1.0	0.3	-	-	1.3
Agriculture	0.8	8.2	-	-	-	-	9.0
Industry/other	-	3.8	2.3	0.9	18.3	5.9/d	31.2
Total	9.7	16.7	3.6	1.2	38.2	5.9	75.3

/a Excludes consumption and losses in the petroleum industry and refineries.

/b Includes 10.5 million tons of crude oil which is directly burned.

/c Includes own-account trucks.

/d Includes lubricants (2.0 million tons), some of which are consumed in other sectors, but data on sectoral breakdowns are not available.

Source: Mission estimates.

Table 1.5: INTERNATIONAL COMPARISONS OF SECTORAL ENERGY CONSUMPTION, 1980 (%)

	Share in final commercial energy consumption (A)			Share in final total energy consumption /a (B)		Share of transport in final oil consumption (C)
	Industry	Transport	Res/com/pub/b	Industry	Res/com/pub	
Developing Countries						
China	60.4	7.8	19.7	42.6	43.4	24.6
Argentina	35.0	30.6	22.9	36.7	25.6	55.2
Brazil	47.3	26.0	20.0	42.8	25.7	46.4
Mexico	37.4	33.9	18.9	39.2	17.7	56.4
India	55.1	22.2	13.7	30.6	52.5	44.1
South Korea	43.3	12.3	42.8	40.8	46.2	27.7
Developed Countries						
US	31.0	25.2	36.2	-- same as in A --		62.0
Canada	38.4	20.2	35.9	"		51.2
Japan	54.3	14.1	27.0	"		28.6
France	42.8	18.4	33.0	"		34.8
West Germany	41.0	15.7	38.4	"		34.4
Italy	44.7	18.5	30.8	"		35.8
UK	33.3	18.6	43.6	"		52.2

/a Includes biomass.

/b Residential, commercial and public services sectors.

Source: OECD. Biomass consumption figures for South Korea were revised using World Bank sources.

Table 1.6: CHINA: FINAL ENERGY CONSUMPTION IN INDUSTRY, 1980
(Millions of tons of coal equivalent)

	Oil	Coal	Natural gas	Electricity	Total
Basic metallurgy	6.6	54.2	1.3	19.1	81.2
Chemicals	12.4	34.3	7.6	21.7	76.0
Building materials	2.0	42.3	0.1	4.7	49.1
Machine building	3.5	14.4	0.7	9.4	28.0
Pulp and paper	0.6	5.4	0.1	2.3	8.4
Textiles	6.0	10.0	0.4	5.4	21.8
Food, beverages and tobacco	0.6	9.7	0.3	2.5	13.1
Other /a	3.0	9.3	0.1	5.0	17.4
Unallocated /b	7.7	9.8	3.3	-	20.8
Total	42.4	189.4	13.9	70.1	315.8

/a Forestry industry, clothing, leather goods and cultural articles (including printing).

/b Includes power industry heat supply credit (see Table 1.2) and any consumption not specified for other sectors.

Source: Appendix A.

1.11 China's residential and commercial sector [4] accounted for some 20% of final commercial energy consumption in 1980. Including biomass, the sector accounted for approximately 43% of final energy use -- the same share attributable to industry. Measured on this basis, the consumption share of the sector is significantly lower than in India and higher than in most developed countries. On a per capita basis, consumption is significantly higher than in India, but less than one-half of that in South Korea and less than one-third of the level in Japan, where space heating requirements are somewhat comparable (see Appendix B, Table B.2).

1.12 The share of the transport sector in both total final commercial energy consumption and final petroleum consumption in China is exceptionally low relative to developed countries and other major developing countries. In 1980, China's transport sector accounted for just 8% of final commercial energy use, while the share in most other major developing countries was at least twice as high (see Table 1.5). The fundamental reason is that road transport, which is far more energy-intensive than other modes,[5] is underdeveloped in China. In 1980, for example, road transport accounted for just 9% of total net freight transportation, compared with 32% in India (1977), 35% in South Korea (1981), and 59% in Brazil (1980) (see Appendix B, Table B.4). The share of fuel consumption by passenger sedans is almost negligible.

C. The Energy Intensity of China's Economy

1.13 Comparisons with other countries reveal an exceptionally high energy intensity in the Chinese economy, particularly in the industrial sector. The analysis below is based on a variety of analytical methods, including comparisons of energy consumption per unit of output value and per physical unit of output, and comparisons of end-use efficiencies for various energy applications. While the actual comparisons shown indicate the degree of current energy intensities in China, they should by no means be interpreted as representing the actual potential for energy conservation, which can be accurately analyzed only in a case-by-case evaluation that considers actual conditions in China.

4/ Consumption in the residential and commercial sector is defined according to the Chinese term, minyong, or "use by the people." It includes consumption by urban and rural households, commercial enterprises (shops, restaurants, etc.), government offices, and some municipal services, such as recreation facilities and street lighting.

5/ Road transport in China consumes about nine times as much energy per payload ton-kilometer as rail transport. In India and the USA, road freight transport is about 10 and 4 times as energy intensive as rail transport, respectively.

Energy Consumption Per Unit of Output Value

1.14 Cross-country comparisons of energy use per unit of output value can provide only a rough picture of relative energy intensities in different countries, owing to factors such as different methods of calculating output value statistics, different relative prices, and problems resulting from use of official exchange rates to convert monetary statistics to comparable units. Such comparisons can, however, be useful in that they provide aggregate measures that reflect differences in energy demand caused by differences in economic structure.

1.15 Consumption of both commercial and total primary energy per unit GDP in China is well above that of any other major developing countries reviewed (see Table 1.7).[6/] Compared with Germany, France, Italy, and Japan, commercial energy intensities in China are more than four times higher, while total energy intensities are about six times higher.

1.16 One factor contributing to China's high level of energy use relative to GDP is a high share of industrial output in GDP. While industry and infrastructure typically account for less than 20% of GDP in other low-income countries, these sectors currently account for almost one-half of GDP in China -- a share that surpasses average levels in both middle-income and industrialized market economies. Only the developed, centrally planned economies have, on average, higher shares of industrial output.

1.17 More typical of energy use patterns in low-income countries, however, is China's high ratio of residential/commercial energy consumption to GDP (or residential/commercial energy consumption per capita relative to GDP per capita). This ratio usually decreases as development proceeds, because per capita household energy use grows more slowly than GDP per capita over the long run (partly owing to end-use efficiency improvements). Another important contributing factor in China, compared with most other developing countries, is the existence of substantial winter heating requirements in many parts of the country.

1.18 Economic development of a low-income country typically brings an increase in the share of industrial output in GDP, which tends to increase energy intensities. At the same time, residential/commercial sector consumption tends to rise more slowly than GDP. In China, however, both the exceptionally high share of industrial output and the high aggregate demand for basic household energy requirements relative to GDP serve to increase energy intensities.

1.19 These factors alone do not explain China's high energy intensity relative to GDP. Total energy consumption per unit of gross output value in the industrial sector is also exceptionally high compared with most other

---

6/ This apparently cannot be explained to any great extent by underestimation of China's GDP in 1980 (due to possible noncomparability of price levels and/or exchange rates). See Annex E of the Main Report.

Table 1.7: INTERNATIONAL COMPARISONS OF PRIMARY ENERGY CONSUMPTION RELATIVE TO GDP, 1980

	Primary commercial energy consumption per unit GDP	Total primary energy consumption per unit GDP /a	Residential/commercial energy consumption per unit GDP /a	Share of industry & infrastructure in GDP/b
	(kgce/US$)			(%)
Developing Countries				
China	2.13	2.90	1.14	48
Argentina	0.44	0.49	0.10	n.a.
Brazil	0.61	0.88	0.19	37
Mexico	0.80	0.84	0.11	38/c
India	1.05	1.77	0.83	26
Korea, Rep.	1.06	1.12	0.48	41
Developed Countries				
Canada	1.39	1.39	0.45	33
France	0.45	0.45	0.14	36
Germany, Fed. Rep.	0.49	0.49	0.18	n.a.
Italy	0.53	0.53	0.16	43
Japan	0.51	0.51	0.13	41/c
UK	0.57	0.57	0.22	35
US	1.05	1.05	0.35	34

/a Includes biomass.

/b Includes all industry, construction and transport.

/c 1979.

Sources: Energy consumption data: China: Table 1.2.

Others: OECD, Energy Balances of OECD Countries, 1970-82; Energy Balances of Developing Countries, 1971-82. Biomass consumption estimates for South Korea were revised, based on World Bank sources.

GDP data: China: IBRD, China: Recent Economic Trends and Policy Developments (March 1983).

Others: IBRD, World Development Report, 1982.

countries (Table 1.8). While the energy intensity of industrial production is similar to that in India, it is over twice the levels in South Korea and the US, almost three times the level in Brazil, and over three times the current level in Japan. The relative intensity of fuel and feedstock use in Chinese industry is particularly striking -- exceeding that in Japan by more than five times. Electricity intensities, on the other hand, are more in line with those of other countries.

1.20 Energy intensities in industry are of course highly dependent upon the structure of industrial output. Although comparisons of China's industrial output structure with that of other countries are clouded by differences in relative prices, it appears from available statistics that the structure of Chinese industrial output between major subsectors is not radically different from that of other developing countries with substantial industrial output (Appendix B, Table B.6). Indeed, the share of output from the three most energy-intensive major industrial subsectors -- basic matallurgy, chemicals, and building materials -- is surprisingly similar in China, Japan, and South Korea. However, within each industrial subsector -- and particularly within the chemical industry -- there are major differences in output structure (see para. 1.10).

Energy Consumption per Physical Unit of Output and End-Use Efficiencies

1.21 The available data on energy consumption per physical unit of output and on end-use efficiencies in China suggest that, compared with other countries, several factors contribute to China's exceptionally high energy intensities in industrial production. These factors include the scale of industrial plants, the technology employed in industrial production, the raw materials used, industrial organization, and factory operating practices. In the past the efficiency of energy use, particularly fuel use, received little emphasis in China's industrial development policy, and little regard had been given to providing incentives for enterprises to use energy efficiently. In addition, the dominance of coal as an energy source and the use of coal as a feedstock have contributed to inefficiencies, as it is difficult to use coal as efficiently as oil or gas.

1.22 Although data are only available for a handful of major industrial commodities, the generally higher levels of unit energy consumption in China do not, however, fully account for the comparatively high degree of energy intensity in industrial production suggested by output value comparisons. Statistical distortions and differences in the structure of output within major industrial subsectors also appear relevant.

1.23 At an aggregate level, one of the most important factors underlying high levels of unit energy consumption in Chinese industry is the preponderance of small-scale enterprises in energy-intensive industries. As Table 1.9 shows, unit energy consumption in these small-scale plants tends to be well above levels in large plants, owing primarily to both the inability to realize economies of scale and the use of less advanced technology. Moreover, the quality of commodities produced is usually lower in small plants. In some cases, nevertheless, small plant production may offer significant advantages, including reduced transport requirements, use of labor-intensive methods, and

Table 1.8: ENERGY CONSUMPTION IN INDUSTRY PER UNIT GROSS VALUE OF INDUSTRIAL OUTPUT IN SELECTED COUNTRIES

Country	Year	Energy consumption per unit output value (kilograms of coal equivalent per 1980 US$)		
		Fuel and feedstock	Electricity/a	Total/b
China	1980	0.82	0.23	1.06
France	1980	0.17	0.13	0.30
Germany, F.R.	1980	0.15	0.11	0.26
Japan	1980	0.16	0.15	0.30
UK	1980	0.13	0.09	0.23
US	1980	0.29	0.17	0.47
Brazil/b	1978	0.26	0.14	0.40
India/b	1978	0.71	0.33	1.04
S. Korea	1980	0.30	0.17	0.48
Philippines/b	1979	0.49	0.18	0.66
Turkey	1979	0.24	0.21	0.44

/a Electricity consumption is calculated at a thermal replacement value of 2,900 kcal/kWh for all countries.

/b Includes biomass consumption.

Source: Appendix B, Table B.5.

Table 1.9: CHINA: PRODUCTION AND ENERGY CONSUMPTION IN SMALL AND LARGE PLANTS, 1980

Industrial product	Small plant share of total production (%)	Energy consumption per ton produced (tons of coal equivalent)	
		Small plants	Large plants
Crude steel	24/a	1.57/b	1.20/b
Synthetic ammonia	55	3.00	1.45/c
Cement	68	0.18/d	0.21/d
Plate glass	n.a.	0.87/e	0.30/e
Coke	n.a.	2.60	1.96

/a Estimate for small- and medium-sized plants under local control, as a percentage of total iron and steel company production.

/b Figures denote "comparable energy consumption" which includes only energy used for the production of iron and steel, and not other types of energy, such as energy consumed in mining, equipment manufacturing, etc.

/c Excludes medium-sized plant production.

/d Comparisons of energy consumption are misleading in that the quality of cement produced in small plants is far lower than that in large plants.

/e Refer to tons of coal equivalent per standard case.

Sources: Mission estimates, based on a variety of Chinese sources.

-- at times -- the use of locally available, relatively low-cost energy and raw materials.

1.24 Currently, boiler fuel for industry and space heating accounts for more than 35% of total final commercial fuel consumption.[7] Nearly 200,000 boilers are currently used in China, of which some 70% have steam production capacities of less than two tons per hour. According to Chinese estimates, average thermal efficiencies are roughly 55%, compared with averages of some 70% abroad. The dominance of coal helps explain this difference, but the preponderance of small unit sizes, technology dating to the 1930s and 1940s, lack of mechanization, and inefficient operating practices all contribute to high consumption rates in China.

Energy Consumption in Major Industrial Sectors

1.25 Iron and Steel. As shown in Appendix B (Table B.8) 1980 energy consumption per ton of crude steel in China was approximately double the level in Japan, and more than double the levels achieved in Italy and Spain, where electric arc furnaces, largely based on scrap inputs, account for about one-half of steel production.[8] Compared with rates in other developing countries, unit consumption was some 60% higher than in Brazil, about the same as in Egypt, and some 20% lower than in India.

1.26 Compared with the most advanced iron and steel industries (i.e., in Japan), one of the key factors underlying the relatively high unit energy consumption in China is a lack of full production integration, resulting in large energy requirements for reheating pig iron and cold steel. In addition, some integrated plants have suffered from a lack of effective integration of production and production capacities in the various links of the production chain, resulting in energy wasted through below-capacity operation of energy-intensive equipment.

1.27 Locally operated small and medium-scale plants apparently contributed 20-25% of steel production in 1980, with energy consumption rates per ton of steel approximately 30% higher than rates in China's large, key plant sector.

7/ Final commercial fuel consumption includes final consumption of crude oil, fuel oil, coal and natural gas, used as direct fuel. Thermal power plant boilers are excluded.

8/ Refers to "comparable" energy consumption, that is, energy used in crude steel production (coke, sinter, pellet, iron, and steel production; rolling; plant transport of equipment and processed raw materials; and losses). Total energy consumption in the iron and steel industry is referred to in Chinese sources as "comprehensive" consumption, and includes consumption in the production of pig iron not used in steel production, mining and beneficiation of ore, refractory production, alloy production, workers' residences, some equipment manufacturing, and any sideline activities pursued by iron and steel companies.

1.28 Open-hearth furnaces accounted for some 32% of steel production, a much higher percentage than in most developed countries. In 1980, only 6.6% of steel production was cast using continuous casting machines -- one of the lowest percentages in the world. While not as low as in Japan, blast furnace fuel rates in China's key plants are comparable to rates in the US and UK (4.3-4.5 gcal/ton pig iron), and far lower than in India (over 6.0 gcal/ton pig iron).

1.29 Chemical Industry. Striking disparities exist in the unit energy consumption levels of different plants within China's chemical subsector, owing primarily to differences in levels of technology and in plant scale. Large, modern plants based on imported, state-of-the-art technologies of the 1970s exist alongside smaller, less efficient plants, using designs which often incorporate outdated technologies.

1.30 Thirteen large (1,000 tpd) synthetic ammonia plants, which use natural gas or naphtha feedstocks, were imported during the 1970s. In 1980, these plants accounted for 21% of synthetic ammonia production, consuming an average of 10.1 gcal per ton -- a level typical of new plants constructed abroad during the 1970s. However, small-scale plants (30-100 tpd) producing ammonia bicarbonate from coke or anthracite accounted for 55% of synthetic ammonia production in 1980, and consumed twice as much total energy per ton as the large plants, and one-hundred times as much electricity per ton.[9/] Medium-sized plants of domestic manufacture based on coal, fuel oil, and natural gas feedstocks accounted for the balance of production, with unit energy consumption levels in the neighborhood of 17.5 gcal/ton. Taken together, unit energy consumption in the synthetic ammonia industry was about 18.0 gcal/ton -- about 2½ times the lowest level for new plants abroad.

1.31 Feedstock inputs for ethylene production range from more than eight tons of crude oil per ton of ethylene (in the case of one plant constructed during the 1960s) to approximately four tons of gas oil per ton (in a recently imported plant). Unit energy consumption in calcium carbide production is 10-15% higher in China's key plants than in the most advanced plants abroad.[10/]

1.32 Building Materials Industry. In 1980, unit energy consumption in China's cement industry averaged about 1.3 gcal/ton - a rate lower than in many countries where modern dry processes are still not dominant (see Appendix B, Table B.9). However, 68% of production was in small-scale cement kilns, where unit energy consumption levels are relatively low (1.24 gcal/ton) but the quality of cement produced is far lower than international standards. More than 90% of the small kilns are vertical kilns, and clinker contents

---

9/ Small plants consumed about 1,500 kWh/ton, compared to 14.4 kWh/ton in large plants.

10/ In 1982, key plants in China consumed 575 kg of coke and 3,518 kWh of electricity per ton, compared to about 500 kg and 3,300 kWh per ton, respectively, in advanced plants abroad.

average at 70-75%. Unit energy consumption (and cement quality) is higher in China's medium and large-scale kilns (about 1.44 gcal/ton), where cement produced through the wet process accounted for 63% of production in 1980.

1.33 Brick production currently consumes more energy than the cement industry. In 1980, commune and brigade enterprises, which rely on traditional kiln technologies, accounted for about three-quarters of total brick production. Although firm data are not available, the most backward rural kilns are believed to consume four times as much energy as modern domestic kilns per unit of production.

Energy Consumption in the Transport Sector

1.34 While the relatively low share of road transport in total transportation in China leads to relatively low levels of energy consumption in the sector as a whole (para. 1.12), energy consumption levels per ton-kilometer (tkm) within both the rail and road subsectors are relatively high, particularly when compared with developed countries.

1.35 Currently, coal-fired steam locomotives account for about 80% of the total gross converted ton-kilometers (ctkm) 11/ of rail transport, followed by diesel traction at 18% and electric traction at 2%. Unit consumption of diesel locomotives in China compares favorably with most other countries, but steam locomotives consume about 17.3 kg of coal equivalent per 1,000 ctkm of haulage, or more than three times as much energy per 1,000 ctkm as diesel or electric locomotives.

1.36 Available data on road freight transport suggests that average fuel consumption per tkm in China is exceptionally high compared with France and the US (Table 1.10). Much of the difference can be attributed to China's own-account trucking sector. Own-account trucks currently consume roughly twice as much fuel per payload tkm as trucks run by state transport departments, and they account for 89% of China's truck fleet and about two-thirds of the total tkm of road freight moved. Although own-account trucks are on average older and in poorer condition than trucks operated by state transport departments, the most important factor underlying the different unit consumption rates between own-account and state transport department trucks is a difference in average load factors. 12/ According to the Ministry of Communications (MOC), the average load factor for trucks in state transport departments currently exceeds 62%, which is only slightly lower than that for trucks on the

---

11/ Refers to the gross tailing weight of cars, freight, and passengers transported times distance. One passenger-kilometer is assumed to equal one gross ton-kilometer of freight transport following the practice of the Ministry of Railways.

12/ Average load factor = $\frac{\text{Payload ton-km per year}}{\text{vehicle payload capacity x vehicle-km per year}}$

Table 1.10: COMPREHENSIVE ENERGY CONSUMPTION IN TRUCK TRANSPORT: US, FRANCE AND CHINA

	Energy consumption per 100 actual payload ton-kilometers /a	
	Liters of fuel	1,000 kilocalorie
US, 1978		35
France, 1973: /b		
0- 50 km		71
150-300 km		47
Over 500 km		29
China, 1980:		
State transport departments	8.2/c	65
Own-account trucks	17.5	137
National average	14.4	113

/a Actual payload ton-kilometers denote the actual net tonnage of freight moved times the distance moved. Energy consumption rates are therefore influenced by a variety of factors such as road conditions and load factors, in addition to the rated fuel consumption characteristics of different trucks.

/b Key factors which account for the different fuel consumption rates for different haulage distances probably include truck size, load factors, road conditions, and operating speeds.

/c Assumes 80% gasoline and 20% diesel oil.

Sources:

US: G. Kulp, et. al., Transportation Energy Conservation Data Book (Oak Ridge National Laboratory, 1980); p. 1-28.

France: Pierre Merline, "Comment economiser l'energie dans les transports" (cited in TWD, the World Bank, Energy and Transport in Developing Countries, 1983).

China: 1981 Statistical Yearbook of China; Ministry of Communications; mission estimates.

interstate highway system in the US. 13/ Own-account trucks in China, however, are believed to have an average load factor in the neighborhood of 30%.

1.37 Other factors contributing to high fuel consumption rates in both state transport departments and own-account trucks include prevailing truck sizes, engine efficiencies, road conditions, fuel quality, and operating standards. As shown in Appendix B (Table B.10) rated fuel consumption per payload tkm drops sharply as truck sizes increase. Unlike most developed countries, road conditions in China are not appropriate for trucks with payloads over 20 tons. While several models in the 8-ton range have been developed and used, the vast majority of freight is moved by trucks in the 4-5 ton range. This brings a major penalty in energy efficiency. Most Chinese gasoline truck engines also operate with compression ratios of 6 to 7, compared to averages of about 8.5 abroad. This is primarily due to the low octane content of the bulk of the gasoline currently produced for the domestic market (about 70 MON) and to the old design of the engines. Moreover, less than 20% of China's highway network is paved with asphalt. Poor road conditions and low average operating speeds (resulting from these conditions and from congested, slow-moving traffic) further contribute to high consumption. All of these factors combined result in the fuel efficiency differentials between Chinese trucks and modern trucks operating abroad under ideal conditions -- as illustrated in Appendix B (Table B.10).

Energy Consumption in the Residential/Commercial Sector

1.38 Although the residential/commercial sector includes consumers such as shops, restaurants, and government office buildings, the greatest share of energy consumption is for household cooking and heating. In urban areas, coal is the dominant fuel. Although use of honeycomb briquettes (using compressed raw coal) is common in household stoves with thermal efficiencies of about 25%, coal balls or cakes are used more often, resulting in thermal efficiencies closer to 10%. (In addition, household coal stoves represent the single most important cause of street-level urban air pollution.)

1.39 End-use efficiencies for cooking are higher in households using gas. In 1980, 16.4 million people had gas service, representing about 9% of the total urban population. Although almost 1 million TCE of LPG and natural gas were consumed in the sector in 1980, most gas is manufactured -- including coke-oven gas, low-BTU water gas made from coal, medium-BTU gas made from coal using adaptations on the Lurgi process, and gas made from heavy oil. Except for by-product gas, major penalties in energy efficiency result from conversion processes.

13/ In 1976, empty truck capacity miles (including the empty truck capacity miles of partially loaded trucks) accounted for 27.1% of total truck capacity miles. Interstate Commerce Commission, Empty/Loaded Truck Miles on Interstate Highways During 1976 (April 1977).

1.40 In northern cities, an estimated one-half of the population uses small coal stoves for heating, while most of the remainder rely on central, hot-water heating systems based on small coal-fired boilers. District heating from cogenerating power plants - a particularly efficient method for heat supply - is used for only 2% of total urban household living space.

1.41 In rural areas, end-use efficiencies tend to be even lower than in the cities. Average thermal efficiencies of biomass-fueled stoves are estimated at about 10% (see Chapter 7 for full discussion).

2. FUTURE COMMERCIAL ENERGY DEMAND

2.01 While Chinese goals for economic development imply growth rates during 1980-2000 that are at least as high as those of the last two decades, total energy production is expected to grow substantially slower than in the past. In a very real sense, therefore, the extent to which the intensity of energy use relative to economic output can be decreased, without compromising goals to improve standards of living, will play a critical role in China's development prospects.

2.02 Although there is little doubt that the intensity of energy use in China could decrease substantially in the future, the sheer speed of economic growth currently envisioned implies that balancing energy supply and demand will continue to be a key problem. Hence, formulation and implementation of a comprehensive and long-term energy development and utilization strategy will be critical. At the macro level, explicit consideration must be given to the impact of broad aspects of China's economic development strategy on energy demand (i.e., the role of industry in economic growth, the direction of industrial development, the structure of foreign trade, and the level and structure of household consumption) and corresponding requirements for increasing energy supply. At the micro level, policies must promote changes in technology and management that result in improved efficiency in utilization of both energy and energy-intensive materials. Success in strengthening incentives for improving efficiency in existing plants and for improving efficiency in new capacity and equipment will be critical. Further success must also be achieved in strengthening the institutional infrastructure needed to support such efforts.

2.03 Adding to the energy challenge is the need to minimize the potential adverse environmental impacts associated with use of China's two chief fuels: coal and biomass. Environmental problems created by coal use stem from the ways in which it is consumed, while problems with biomass result primarily from the ways in which it is supplied.

2.04 Because decisions made over the short and medium terms regarding energy development and use will in many ways determine the long-term balance between energy supply and demand, analysis of possible future energy demand trends -- and the factors that determine them -- has a major role to play in energy sector planning. Future energy demand cannot be predicted accurately, however, and in the case of China, uncertainties are compounded by a lack of knowledge concerning the energy demand impacts of system reform. Contingency planning is therefore critical, and achieving maximum flexibility is an important objective.

2.05 This chapter presents a variety of scenarios of future commercial energy demand, in the aggregate and by fuel and sector. The purpose of the analysis is to identify possible ranges of future demand, analyze the key factors determining demand trends, and discuss some of the issues and options raised. Particular emphasis was given to the manufacturing and transportation sectors. Achievements in reducing energy intensities in recent years, and issues regarding incentives and institutional support for energy conservation are discussed in Chapter 3. Issues relating to the supply and demand for biomass fuels are discussed in Chapter 7.

2.06 A discussion of the methodology used in the analysis is presented first, followed by a presentation and discussion of the aggregate results, the major issues raised, and possible alternative scenarios for balancing supply and demand. Later sections detail the trends and issues concerning different types of energy. Final sections discuss trends and issues in energy demand in the manufacturing and transportation sectors.

A. Methodology

2.07 Scenarios of future commercial energy demand were generated with the use of a multi-sectoral macro model.[1/] The macro model provided scenarios of both aggregate economic growth and growth of output value for 20 major economic subsectors. (In manufacturing, the major subsectors included basic metallurgy, chemicals, building materials, machine building, food and related products, textiles, and other.) Subsector output value projections were then multiplied by subsector unit energy consumption coefficients to provide the series of scenarios of energy demand.

2.08 The macro model uses an input-output framework that provides internally consistent projections of subsector output. The model thereby accounts for changes in direct and indirect intermediate flows as well as changes in final demand and foreign trade. Changes in the most important input-output relationships between manufacturing subsectors were incorporated exogenously in the model, based on a review of available data on such changes in other countries. Thus, use of the macro model for energy projections allowed analysis of the impact of changes in the structure of output between major subsectors on energy demand, as well as the energy demand implications of different rates of aggregate economic growth.

2.09 The macro model was used to project a basic triad of scenarios, labelled the QUADRUPLE, MODERATE, and BALANCE macro cases. The first two cases imply a continuation of growth with industry contributing an unusually large share by international standards. In the QUADRUPLE case, the Chinese target to quadruple the gross value of industrial and agricultural output (GVIAO) during 1980-2000 is attained. The MODERATE case maintains most of the same assumptions, but takes a less optimistic view of the future efficiency of China's economy, and hence the economy grows slower. The BALANCE case represents an alternative way of achieving the same growth rate of per capita GDP as in QUADRUPLE, under which the commerce and service sectors contribute an increased share to GDP, while the share of industry in GDP is slightly lessened. Production in individual subsectors in the BALANCE case becomes more service-intensive, and less materials-intensive, than in the other two

---

1/ For full discussion of the assumptions and results of the multi-sectoral macro model, see the Main Report, Chapter 2 and <u>Annex D: Models and Projections</u>.

cases. This shifts the structure of China's economy away from the past pattern and toward the pattern of Japan and most other countries at a comparable stage of development.

2.10 Changes in unit energy consumption coefficients (energy input-subsector output coefficients) were built into the macro model for every subsector. Coefficients were estimated for three broad categories of energy inputs -- fuel, oil distillates, and electric power -- to yield distinctions according to end use. Coefficients in the fuel category were further divided into categories representing petroleum (crude oil and natural gas), residual oil, and coal.[2/]

2.11 Projected unit energy consumption coefficients consider changes in subsector energy intensities caused by (1) changes in technical energy efficiency (from changes in the technology and raw materials used, operating practices, and plant sizes) and (2) changes in the structure of output within subsectors (i.e., between chemical products in the chemical industry). In the metallurgy, chemical, and building materials subsectors, consumption coefficients were estimated through a further breakdown of production to more disaggregate levels, and -- where feasible -- unit energy consumption for key energy-intensive products was projected in physical terms (e.g., tons). This was possible for iron and steel, aluminum, synthetic ammonia, cement, plate glass, and bricks and tiles. In 1980, production of these commodities accounted for nearly one-half of energy consumption in manufacturing. Future production was broken down among existing and new plants and also among large, medium-sized, and small plants (where relevant and feasible) -- with different consumption coefficients applied to each. Unit consumption in the energy industries was also projected on a physical basis.

2.12 For many subsectors (e.g., machine building or the various light industries) or components of subsectors (e.g., the chemical industry excluding synthetic ammonia), consumption coefficients were related only to gross output value. Projections were formulated after a review of historical trends in other countries, both developed and developing.[3/]

2/ For most subsectors, assumptions regarding interfuel substitution were made at an aggregate level and then applied to individual subsectors.

3/ While data on trends in energy consumption per unit gross output value in other countries reflect changes in technical efficiency and structure, it is not possible to differentiate between the impacts of each. Assessment of the relevance for China of available data on international trends in consumption per unit output value was probably the most difficult topic encountered in formulating the consumption coefficients. Complications include differences in levels of development, particularly mechanization, and in output structures, which are often heavily influenced by foreign trade. The reliability of available data is also often questionable. Hence, the ranges adopted for China were often wide.

2.13 In the transportation sector, projections of total ton-kilometers -- related to GVIAO growth -- and passenger-kilometers -- related to growth in GDP per capita -- were broken into various modes and then projected through application of physical unit consumption coefficients. Residential consumption was also projected on a physical basis, considering different levels of growth in useful energy consumption and improvements in energy efficiency. Unit consumption coefficients in all other sectors were related to output value. Energy consumption in rural areas was divided among the manufacturing, agricultural and residential/commercial subsectors -- figures on agriculture refer to energy used in agricultural production and agricultural processing only.

2.14 For each subsector, and relevant subsector components, three sets of unit consumption coefficients were projected -- designated as HIGH, BASE, and LOW coefficients. The difference between the HIGH and LOW coefficients expresses the probable range of unit energy consumption, given continued efforts to promote conservation. Where coefficients were related to physical output, LOW coefficients incorporated very optimistic assumptions for renovating existing equipment and employing the most energy-efficient new technology available abroad in new industrial plant and transportation equipment (except in cases where conditions in China were considered to make achievement of state-of-the-art efficiency levels highly improbable).[4/] The HIGH coefficients related to physical output assume less success (but continuing improvement) in improving energy efficiency and imply a substantial shortfall between actual and potential energy savings. Where coefficients were related to output value, LOW coefficients expressed the most optimistic view, given available data on the spectrum of international experience considered relevant for China. The HIGH coefficients were more pessimistic in projecting the impact of conservation and intra-sectoral structural change, but still reflect favorable impacts in both areas.

2.15 The BASE coefficients represent mid-points in the probable range of unit energy consumption. The midpoints are not always arithmetic mid-points; they depend upon judgements concerning the relative probability of the LOW and HIGH coefficients. The BASE coefficients were used to test sensitivity to change of various factors while unit consumption variables were fixed.

2.16 Appendix C shows a matrix of nine scenarios of energy demand in the year 2000 derived by pairing each of the three macro cases (QUADRUPLE, MODERATE, BALANCE) with the three unit consumption cases (HIGH, BASE, LOW).

4/ One example of such a case is in brick manufacturing, where continued construction of small-scale, rural up-draft kilns is expected to continue, and hence modern, large-scale and mechanized brick production is expected to comprise only a portion of new plant output. Another example is in road transport, where widespread use of the most efficient trucks -- those with payload capacities in excess of 20 tons -- was considered highly improbable, due to road conditions.

B. Aggregate Energy Demand and the Problem of Adequate Fuel Supply

2.17 The projected scenarios of total primary commercial energy demand by the year 2000 range from 1,180 to 1,765 million TCE depending on macroeconomic and unit energy consumption assumptions:[5/]

Table 2.1: PRIMARY COMMERCIAL ENERGY DEMAND, YEAR 1980-2000

MACRO CASE	GDP Growth 1980-2000, % p.a.	Energy Demand (million TCE) 1980	2000 LOW	2000 BASE	2000 HIGH
QUADRUPLE	6.6	605	1,385	1,555	1,765
MODERATE	5.4	605	1,180	1,320	1,500
BALANCE	6.6	605	1,270	1,420	1,610

In early 1984, official targets for primary commercial energy production in the year 2000 included 1,200 million tons of raw coal, 200 million tons of crude oil, and 25 billion cubic meters of natural gas. Primary electricity production (hydro and nuclear generation) is expected to reach some 230-280 TWh in 2000, according to the Ministry of Water Resources and Electric Power (MWREP), including small hydro plants with capacities under 500 KW. It is not possible at this time, and with available information, to form a judgment whether all these targets will be achieved. The degree of uncertainty is particularly high in the case of oil, since the target for the year 2000 will require major new discoveries. In the case of coal, the Government has recently expressed confidence that the coal production target can be achieved earlier than the year 2000. If only 1,200 million tons of coal output were to be attained in 2000, and all other targets were met, total primary commercial energy production would total just under 1,300 million TCE by 2000, resulting in a supply shortage in most of the above scenarios. Thus, the demand scenarios underline the necessity of defining a long-term strategy for both energy development (including coal development above previous targets) and energy utilization which will alleviate potential constraints on economic growth.

5/ Demand estimates for the QUADRUPLE and BALANCE macro cases presented in this section correspond to multi-sectoral macroeconomic projections which assume a coal production level of 1,200 million tons in 2000. In subsequent sections, and in the Main Report, coal production was assumed to reach 1,400 million tons in 2000 in the QUADRUPLE and BALANCE cases, and hence, macroeconomic projections and corresponding energy demand estimates vary slightly.

Industry-led Growth Scenarios

2.18 In examining the energy demand scenarios developed under the model, the QUADRUPLE-BASE scenario provides a good starting point. It combines the QUADRUPLE macro case -- which results in a quadrupling of GVIAO, in line with current targets -- and the BASE consumption case which represents a midpoint in the projected range of unit energy demand within subsectors. Primary commercial energy demand totals 1,555 million TCE -- over 250 million TCE above previous production targets. Consumption per unit real GDP falls from 2.13 kgCE/$US in 1980 to about 1.54 kgCE/$US in 2000, a decrease of 1.6% p.a. Consumption per unit GVIAO falls faster, by a total of about 35%, or 2.1% p.a.

2.19 The QUADRUPLE-BASE scenario indicates a major supply/demand gap in fuel -- which includes the sum of coal, fuel oil, natural gas, and crude oil directly consumed. Electricity demand in 2000, about 1,180 TWh, is within the production range anticipated by MWREP (1000-1200 TWh). Production at this level, however, would require major increases in the share of power investments in total domestic investment (see Chapter 6). Oil distillate demand is approximately 115 million tons, which could be met domestically if crude oil production reaches 200 million tons, assuming a refinery distillate yield similar to that in 1983 and that adequate new refining capacity has been built. If crude oil production in 2000 is significantly below targeted levels, however, substantial gaps between distillate supply and demand would exist.

2.20 Fuel demand can best be put in perspective by viewing both total and final demand, because the fuel requirements of China's energy industries (which are included in total demand but not in final demand) are particularly large. The net fuel consumption for thermal power generation currently anticipated by MWREP for the year 2000 accounts for roughly 25-30% of the total fuel component of energy production targets. If the fuel requirements of the coal and petroleum industries are also subtracted from total fuel production targets, the balance left to meet final demand will permit an increase in final fuel use during 1980-2000 of only 55-70%. The above figures also assume that refinery throughput increases to almost 200 million tons and that all resulting increases in fuel oil supplies are domestically consumed. If some fuel oil is exported, as currently hoped, fuel supplies to meet final demand would be even lower.

2.21 In the QUADRUPLE-BASE scenario, final fuel consumption is projected to increase to about 2.3 times the 1980 level by the year 2000, reaching about 875 million TCE (see Table 2.2). With the gross value of output of manufacturing industries[6/] growing at over 8% p.a. (in line with current targets), these industries account for nearly 75% of the total increase in final fuel consumption. Shifts in the structure of industrial output are expected to reduce overall fuel intensity in industry -- metallurgy, for example, is

6/ The manufacturing industrial sectors include all industry except for the energy production industries. Hence, non-energy mining is included.

projected to grow by only 6.5% p.a. Improvements in the efficiency of energy use are also projected. Fuel consumption per unit gross output value in the manufacturing sector is projected to decline to 54% of the 1980 level by the year 2000, a decrease of 3.0% p.a.[7/] Nevertheless, the sheer speed of industrial growth drives up final fuel consumption in the manufacturing industries by about 370 million TCE during the period.

Table 2.2: FUEL CONSUMPTION: QUADRUPLE-BASE SCENARIO

	Million TCE		Annual Average Growth Rate
	1980	2000	1980-2000 %
Manufacturing industry	236	604	4.8
Residential/commercial	91	173	3.3
Transportation	21	27	1.3
Agriculture /a	21	47	4.1
Other	10	25	4.7
Total Final Consumption	379	876	4.3
Power industry (net)	100	314	5.9
Other energy industries	50	93	3.2
Total Consumption	529	1,283	4.5

/a Township and village industries (formerly referred to as commune and brigade industries) outside of the agricultural processing field are included under manufacturing.

2.22 Projected demand for both oil distillates and electricity in the QUADRUPLE-BASE scenario could be met if production targets are attained, but meeting these targets represents a major challenge. The scenario shows oil distillate demand growing by about 6.1% p.a. during 1980-2000, with transportation accounting for about one-half of incremental consumption. Electricity would register a 7.1% p.a. demand growth. Despite high growth rates in power consumption in the residential and transportation sectors (13% p.a. and 14% p.a., respectively), the high rate of industrial growth implies a continued dominance of the manufacturing sector in final power consumption (see paras. 2.60-2.62). In the QUADRUPLE-BASE scenario, manufacturing accounts for 80% of the increase in final electricity use. Because thermal power generation is

---

7/ Unit consumption of all fuel and feedstock (including distillates) in manufacturing industries is projected to also decline at 3.0% p.a.

expected to continue to provide most of China's electricity output through 2000, the electricity demand growth corresponding to high industrial output growth rates increases the pressure on fuel demand.

2.23 For the QUADRUPLE case, the HIGH and LOW assumptions for unit consumption yield a range of 380 million TCE (from 1,385 million TCE to 1,765 million TCE) in primary commercial energy demand projections for 2000, as shown in Table 2.3. Different assumptions concerning unit energy demand in manufacturing account for the largest share of the difference between the two scenarios (see Table 2.18).

Table 2.3: RANGES OF AGGREGATE ENERGY DEMAND FOR THE QUADRUPLE MACRO CASE

	Total Primary Commercial Energy Demand (mil. TCE) 1980	2000	Reduction in Consumption per Unit GDP 1980-2000 (% p.a.)	Reduction in Consumption per Unit GVIAO 1980-2000 (% p.a.)
Base Consumption Case	605	1,555	1.6	2.1
Projected Range a/	605	1,385 - 1,765	1.0 - 2.2	1.5 - 2.7

	Final Energy Demand in Manufacturing Industries (mil. TCE) 1980	2000	Reduction in Consumption per Unit Gross Manufacturing Output Value 1980-2000, % p.a.
Base Consumption Case	316	945	2.3
Projected Range a/	316	835 - 1,050	1.8 - 2.9

a/ The projected range is defined by the difference between the QUADRUPLE-LOW and QUADRUPLE-HIGH scenarios.

2.24 Even with the optimistic assumptions of the QUADRUPLE-LOW scenario, however, forecasts for total energy demand exceed the production targets expressed in the past by a substantial amount. In order to provide sufficient fuel to generate the electricity demanded, the fuel required by other energy industries, and final fuel demand -- an increase in fuel supplies well above targets would be required if the quadrupling of GVIAO presented in the QUADRUPLE macro case is to be achieved.

2.25 Production of primary electricity above targeted levels could alleviate the fuel shortage by displacing some thermal power production. Current goals for hydro and nuclear generation, however, are already very ambitious (see Chapter 6), and it appears unlikely that sufficient additional primary electricity can be made available in time to have a significant impact on the total energy balance by 2000.

2.26 One option would be to increase consumption of domestic fuel oil. This would be possible if crude oil production exceeds 200 million tons in 2000 and the fuel oil yield from refineries were increased from the present output pattern. This option, however, would provide only limited relief, if feasible, and its economic merit would have to be evaluated considering the low incremental cost of coal production (see para. 2.54).

2.27 Consequently, in view of the difficulties of increasing domestic output of energy resources other than coal, China's cheapest and most abundant fuel, coal output would have to be increased. Coal production above 1,200 million tons in 2000 and the development of transportation facilities required for its distribution would be necessary to provide the quantities of additional energy required to meet demand for the QUADRUPLE case solely through domestic sources.

2.28 Although increased domestic energy demand could be met by importing fuel (i.e. coal or fuel oil), this does not appear to be an economically viable long-term option, given the low cost of exploiting China's huge coal reserves. Temporary imports of coal or fuel oil, however, should not be ruled out -- such imports could be at times well justified if they allow economic output that would otherwise be foregone due to supply shortages. In order for fuel imports to have a substantial impact on China's long-term energy balance, however, a major effort would be required for additional ocean-freight infrastructure development. The large investments for such development would be difficult to justify.

2.29 Coal production levels on the order of 1,400 million tons by the year 2000 may be possible if all the necessary steps are taken soon concerning project preparation, investment allocation and production incentives, and the provision of infrastructure and transport facilities. Coal production at this level could enable domestic energy supply to meet the lowest consumption scenario projected in the QUADRUPLE macro case (and allow exports of fuel oil of about 20 million tons). To meet the mid-range demand projections (the QUADRUPLE-BASE scenario), however, coal production would have to be almost 1,600 million tons by 2000.

2.30 In sum, the quadrupling of GVIAO from 1980 to 2000 presented in the QUADRUPLE macro case would require, on the supply side, an increase in coal production to at least 1,400 million tons and the achievement of production targets for all other types of energy. On the demand side, it would require dramatic success (the QUADRUPLE-LOW scenario) in reducing energy consumption per unit output value, particularly in industry. Without this, it will be difficult to achieve growth rates of more than 7% p.a. in GVIAO and more than 8% p.a. in manufacturing output during the 1980-2000 period. Slower growth in industrial output may or may not imply slower growth in GDP, depending upon the extent of changes in the structure of GDP.

2.31 The macro MODERATE case illustrates the effect of slower growth in GVIAO and industrial output on energy demand. In this macro case, GVIAO grows by 5.9% p.a. during 1980-2000, while manufacturing output grows by 6.8% p.a. The resulting energy demand projections compare with those for the QUADRUPLE case as shown in Table 2.4. The lower demand for energy in the MODERATE case is due primarily to the slower growth of output of the manufacturing industries.

Table 2.4: COMPARISON OF AGGREGATE ENERGY DEMAND IN THE QUADRUPLE AND MODERATE MACRO CASES a/

	Year 2000 (mil. TCE)	Growth Rates 1980-2000, % p.a.
Primary Commercial Energy Demand:		
QUADRUPLE macro case:		
Projected range	1,385 - 1,765	4.2 - 5.5
Base consumption case	1,555	4.8
MODERATE macro case:		
Projected range	1,180 - 1,500	3.4 - 4.6
Base consumption case	1,320	4.0
Final Energy Demand in Manufacturing:		
QUADRUPLE macro case:		
Projected range	835 - 1,050	5.0 - 6.2
Base consumption case	945	5.6
MODERATE macro case:		
Projected range	670 - 840	3.8 - 5.0
Base consumption case	755	4.5

a/ Projected ranges result from application of LOW and HIGH unit energy consumption cases.

Lower energy demand in these industries due to slower output growth accounts for about 80% of the decrease in total primary commercial energy demand that results from employing MODERATE rather than QUADRUPLE case assumptions.

2.32 In both QUADRUPLE and MODERATE macro cases, the share of industry and infrastructure in GDP rises from 48% in 1980 to about 57% in 2000. Hence, the slower growth of industry in the MODERATE case implies a slower growth in total net economic output. GDP per capita grows by only 4.2% p.a. during 1980-2000, compared with 5.3% p.a. in the QUADRUPLE case.

2.33 Even with this reduction in growth, however, fuel supply falls short of demand at the mid-point of the projected range (almost 60 million TCE), if fuel supplies do not exceed previous production targets.[8/] To balance fuel demand with current production targets using BASE consumption coefficients, growth in GVIAO, manufacturing output, and per capita income would be even less than projected in the MODERATE macro case. Hence, if China's economic development continues to follow a pattern in which industry's role in growth continues to increase, the failure to increase fuel production above targeted levels or the inability to achieve the most optimistic unit energy demand levels could significantly reduce the rate of economic growth. Different conclusions are revealed, however, if the commerce and service sectors assume greater prominence and industry plays less of a role in future overall growth, as illustrated in the BALANCE macro case.

The BALANCE Macro Case

2.34 If development patterns over the next 15 years break from past trends, and the commerce and service sector plays a greater role in economic growth, the GDP growth associated with the QUADRUPLE case could be achieved despite slower growth in GVIAO and manufacturing output. In 1980, the share of industry and infrastructure in China's GDP was already exceptionally high compared with that in most market economies. This situation is a fundamental reason underlying China's high energy use relative to GDP (see Chapter 1). In the QUADRUPLE case, the share of industry and infrastructure continues to rise steeply, to some extent dampening the effects of other factors serving to reduce energy intensity. In the BALANCE case, the share of industry and infrastructure in GDP rises only slightly while the share of industry alone drops. The BALANCE case, compared with the QUADRUPLE case, assumes a greater degree of improvement in the efficiency of use of capital and intermediate goods, in part due to more substantial growth in the service sector. Assumptions concerning final consumption and trade in manufactured goods differ only slightly between the QUADRUPLE and BALANCE cases. The difference between the relative roles of manufacturing versus commerce and services in GDP in the two cases has a substantial impact on the future energy intensity per unit GDP, as shown in Tables 2.5 and 2.6.

2.35 The lower energy demand levels in the BALANCE case are almost entirely due to lower final energy demand in the manufacturing sector (see Table 2.6). Final energy demand in commerce and services is substantially higher than in the QUADRUPLE case, but this only partially offsets the difference in final demand in manufacturing because unit energy intensities are higher in manufacturing than in commerce and services. Energy use in the transport sector is slightly lower in the BALANCE case, due to a minor relative decrease in the demand for heavy freight transport.

8/ The gap between total primary commercial energy demand and total production targets is only about 35 million TCE. With slower demand growth, crude oil production of 200 million tons, and a refinery distillate yield similar to that in 1983, a surplus of over 15 million tons of distillates exists which could be exported.

Table 2.5: COMPARISON OF AGGREGATE ENERGY DEMAND IN THE QUADRUPLE AND BALANCE MACRO CASES a/

Macro Case	GDP Growth 1980-2000 % p.a.	Growth in Manufacturing Gross Output Value 1980-2000 % p.a	Shares of Industry and Infrastructure in GDP (%) 1980	Shares of Industry and Infrastructure in GDP (%) 2000	Primary Commercial Energy Demand (mil. TCE) 1980	Primary Commercial Energy Demand (mil. TCE) 2000	Reduction in Energy Intensity per Unit GDP 1980-2000 % p.a.
QUADRUPLE	6.6	8.2	48	58	605	1,385-1,765	1.0 - 2.2
BALANCE	6.6	7.2	48	50	605	1,270-1,610	1.5 - 2.7

/a Projected ranges in energy demand reflect the difference between LOW and HIGH consumption cases.

Table 2.6: TOTAL FINAL COMMERCIAL ENERGY DEMAND BY SECTOR, QUADRUPLE AND BALANCE MACRO CASES /a
(million tons of coal equivalent)

		2000	
	1980	QUADRUPLE Macro case	BALANCE Macro case
Agriculture /b	45	95-100	95-100
Transportation	41	105-135	95-120
Residential/commercial	103	195-270	220-305
Manufacturing	316	835-1,050	695-870
Other	18	45-55	50-60
Total Final Consumption	523	1,275-1,610	1,155-1,455

/a Projected ranges in energy demand reflect the difference between LOW and HIGH consumption cases.
/b Township and village industries not engaged in agricultural processing are included under manufacturing.

2.36 The mid-range demand estimates for the BALANCE case (BALANCE-BASE scenario) result in a small surplus of oil distillates by the year 2000 (some 7 million tons), compared with a small deficit in the QUADRUPLE case (some 4 million tons) (See Appendix C). More important in connection with primary energy demand, however, is the difference in total fuel demand. This results both from lower levels of final fuel demand and from lower levels of total electricity demand, caused primarily by slower growth in the output of manufacturing in the BALANCE case:

Table 2.7: COMPARISON OF FUEL DEMAND IN THE QUADRUPLE AND BALANCE MACRO CASES

		2000	
	1980	QUADRUPLE-BASE Scenario	BALANCE-BASE Scenario
Final Fuel Demand (mil. TCE)	379	875	795
Total Electricity Demand (TWh)	301	1,180	1,060
Total Fuel Demand (mil. TCE)	529	1,285	1,160

2.37 In spite of the lower consumption levels projected for the BALANCE case, substantial gaps persist between energy demand and previous energy production targets. At the middle of the projected range, the gap is approximately 130 million TCE. At the lowest end of the demand range, the energy production targets would just about meet aggregate demand, but only if all energy produced were domestically consumed.9/ Compared with the QUADRUPLE case, however, supply and demand in the BALANCE case could converge through a variety of combinations of feasible reductions in unit consumption and increased energy production. If coal production reaches about 1,400 million tons by the year 2000, supply would meet demand at the mid-point of the projected range.

2.38 In conclusion, applying different assumptions concerning the structure of GDP, future coal production, and unit energy demand within major subsectors, three basic scenarios emerge in which energy supply and demand are basically balanced, and GDP per capita in 2000 reaches or slightly exceeds the target of US$800 (see Appendix C for details):

Macro Case	Consumption Case	Coal Production Year 2000 (mt) /a
(1) QUADRUPLE /b	Low	1,430
(2) BALANCE /b	Base	1,465
(3) BALANCE	Low	1,275

/a Estimates assume (somewhat arbitrarily) that 30 million tons of fuel oil (equivalent to about 60 million tons of raw coal) are exported in 2000. Greater or lesser fuel oil exports would require greater or lesser coal production levels. Calorific values of coal produced are assumed to remain constant throughout 1980-2000 at 5000 kcal/kg -- the average commonly assumed in China. If average calorific values increase significantly, coal production requirements could be substantially less.

/b Multi-sectoral model projections were adjusted to take into account a coal production in level of about 1,400 mt in 2000, as opposed to the targeted 1,200 mt.

2.39 Two of these three scenarios, however, rely on achieving the most optimistic assumptions regarding improvement in physical energy efficiencies and the extent of structural change within major subsectors represented in the

9/ This would imply that refinery distillate yields would be reduced below current levels in this scenario, and all increased fuel oil production would be consumed domestically.

LOW consumption case. Through its management of the energy allocation system and the various economic levers which affect incentives for improving energy efficiency, the government can play a pivotal role in determining the extent to which the potential for increasing technical energy efficiency will be realized. The degree to which changes in output structure within major subsectors influence energy use per unit output value -- a function of complex changes in industrial specialization, in intermediate product flows, in foreign trade, and in final consumption of commodities -- can also be influenced by policy, but policy must also consider much more than impact on energy consumption. Moreover, high levels of uncertainty should be recognized.

C. Trends and Issues Concerning Specific Types of Energy

Coal

2.40 Clean and efficient use of coal is critical for China's future. With production and consumption expected to reach some 1,200 million to 1,400 million tons (run-of-mine) by 2000, coal will continue to provide at least two-thirds of China's primary commercial energy supplies, and at least 85% of total commercial fuel consumption. To a very large extent, then, China's ability to meet economic development goals will depend on the extent to which coal use efficiency can be improved. At the same time, increased coal consumption carries serious implications regarding environmental pollution (especially in urban areas) -- and hence standards of living, health, and agriculture -- unless improved environmental protection measures are adopted. By the end of the century, China may well be the world's largest coal consumer. Improved efficiency and environmental protection must both be emphasized. These goals often run parallel and can often be achieved simultaneously. High priority should be accorded to domestic research and development and application of new technology from abroad, to use coal more cleanly and efficiently.

2.41 Because coal is expected to continue to play such a dominant role in China's commercial energy economy, both as a source of fuel for final consumption and as an energy source for power generation, the parameters defining future total fuel demand, discussed in the previous section, also basically define future demand for coal alone. (Fuel oil and natural gas might play important roles as fuel sources, particularly in densely populated urban areas, but they are expected to account for less than 15% of total fuel consumption in 2000.) Ranges for future coal demand are presented in Table 2.8.

2.42 The residential/commercial, manufacturing, and power sectors are expected to continue to account for more than 80% of total coal use. Macroeconomic factors, coupled with changes in the output structure within industrial subsectors, will play a major role in determining future demand, but the degree of improvement in technical efficiencies achieved in these three sectors is also critical. In the power sector, increasing deployment of large-scale modern thermal power generation units and greater development of cogeneration could reduce net fuel consumption per kilowatt-hour by some 20%

Table 2.8: FUTURE COAL DEMAND, QUADRUPLE AND BALANCE MACRO CASES /a
(Millions of tons of standard coal equivalent) /b

	1980	2000 QUADRUPLE case	2000 BALANCE case
Agriculture /b	22	50	50
Transportation	19	20	20
Residential/commercial	90	150-215	160-235
Manufacturing	189	425-555	335-440
Other	9	20-25	25-30
Total Final Demand	329	665-865	590-775
Power industry (net)	74	250-345	215-300
Coal industry	29	65-85/d	65-85/d
Petroleum industry	1	1	1
Total Primary Demand	433	980-1,295	870-1,160
Surplus (deficit) with coal production of 1,400 mt (1,000 MTCE), year 2000:		20-(295)	80-(190)

/a Macro cases assume a raw coal production level in the year 2000 of 1,400 million tons. All fuel oil production is assumed to be consumed domestically - exports would result in higher coal demand estimates for manufacturing and the power sector. Ranges reflect the difference between LOW and HIGH consumption cases.

/b One ton of standard coal equivalent (TCE) = 1.4 tons of run-of-mine coal, on average. Conversion factors for different sectors, however, vary (see Appendix A).

/c Township and village industries not engaged in agricultural processing are included under manufacturing.

/d Assumes a washery throughput of 350 million tons of raw coal in the year 2000. Coal consumption in the coal mining industry is also included.

between 1980 and 2000.[10] In manufacturing, technical improvements in the production of heavy industrial goods -- such as iron and steel, cement, bricks, and tiles -- could yield unit consumption savings of some 20 to 40% during the period, depending upon the industry (see paras. 2.79-2.84). Although future demand levels are particularly uncertain, the potential for improving the efficiency of coal use in the residential and commercial sector is fairly substantial. Improvements could be achieved through use of improved briquettes, boilers and stoves, greater development of district heating, coal gasification and -- possibly -- more extensive use of electric cooking. In most sectors, but particularly in the residential and commercial sector, improvements in the efficiency of coal use can also yield benefits in environmental protection (see Chapter 4 for further discussion of coal utilization issues).

Oil and Gas

2.43 The future structure of petroleum consumption and the future trade patterns of both petroleum and petrochemical products will be determined by both (1) Government decisions concerning investments in oil and gas, such as pipeline networks and refinery plants and (2) the development of utilization and marketing strategies for petroleum products and natural gas. The decisions involved are complex, often highly interrelated, and subject to uncertainty in key parameters. Consequently, detailed evaluation of all the alternatives, including economic analysis of the various options involved, is required.

2.44 In this section some of the key options for the petroleum subsector and their possible impacts are addressed. Two common elements emerge. First, expanded foreign trade can often represent an economically attractive alternative. Second, given the uncertainties of both future production and demand, attainment of maximum flexibility is essential and should be considered in formulating strategies for the subsector.

2.45 For simplicity, petroleum products are classified into two broad categories: (a) distillates -- including gasoline, diesel oil, kerosene/jet fuel, LPG and light chemical feedstocks, and lubricants -- and (b) fuel oil -- including commercial fuel oil and petroleum solids.[11] This permits differentiation between products that are primarily directly burned and can be relatively easily displaced by other fuels and those products that, because of

---

10/ Net fuel consumption excludes fuel consumed in the production of heat which is eventually supplied to consumers outside of the power industry.

11/ From a refining viewpoint, lubricants would usually be categorized with heavy fuel oil in a residual oil category. Lubricants were included under distillates, however, to provide categories based on demand characteristics. While many petroleum solids are not used as fuel (i.e., asphalt and petroleum wax), available data is insufficient to allow differentiation.

technological limitations, are more difficult to displace (except in feedstock applications).

2.46 Distillate production in 1980, as defined above, totalled approximately 38 million tons, accounting for some 54% of gross refinery output.[12/] Due to the characteristics of the crude oil currently produced in China, such yields require substantial secondary conversion -- in 1980, cracking capacities stood at approximately 28 million tons (see Chapter 5). In recent years, efforts have been made to increase distillate yields -- cracking capacities were reported to have reached 35 million tons in 1983, with distillate yields up to an estimated 58 to 60% of gross refinery output.

2.47 Several scenarios for distillate and fuel oil production in the year 2000 are presented in Table 2.9. All the scenarios assume that the practice of directly burning crude oil in industry and for power production is eliminated, and, arbitrarily, that domestic production of crude equals domestic supply (i.e., no crude oil trade is assumed). Hence the share of refinery throughput of crude oil production is shown to increase nearly to the maximum level (considering oil field losses and use, and losses in transportation). Under these assumptions -- if refinery distillate yields are about the same as in 1983 and if the goal to produce 200 million tons of crude oil by the year 2000 is achieved -- growth in distillate and fuel oil production would be approximately 5.6% p.a. and 4.2% p.a., respectively. Domestic distillate production would almost meet the mid-point in the projected wide range in distillate demand.[13/] Demand levels at the low end of the spectrum would allow substantial distillate exports, while the high end of the demand spectrum would require substantial imports.

2.48 In a more pessimistic scenario, where crude oil production reaches only 150 million tons in 2000, meeting domestic demand for distillates would be difficult without substantial imports, even if refinery distillate yields were increased. If crude oil production is substantially higher than the goal of 200 million tons, China would have a wide range of options for exports, including crude and product exports.

2.49 Demand for oil distillates is projected to grow by 5.0-7.2% p.a. from 1980 to 2000 (see Table 2.10). Since road transport is expected to grow relatively rapidly, the share of the transport sector in final distillate consumption is projected to increase from some 38% in 1980 to almost 50% in 2000,[14/] despite substantial improvements in energy efficiency. The share of industrial consumption could either fall or rise sharply, depending on the

---

12/ Gross refinery output is defined to include fuel oil consumed in refinery operations, while net refinery output excludes such fuel oil.

13/ The projected range considers both QUADRUPLE and BALANCE macro cases, and the full range between low and high unit assumption cases.

14/ When fuel oil is included in petroleum product consumption, the share of the transport sector is substantially lower -- 24.6% in 1980.

Table 2.9: SCENARIOS OF PETROLEUM PRODUCT PRODUCTION AND OIL DISTILLATE DEMAND - YEAR 2000 (millions of tons)

	1980	2000 /a			
Crude oil production	106	200		150	
Refinery throughput	75	194		146	
Gross refinery distillate yield	53.5%	60%	70%	60%	70%
Net output: Distillates /b	38	112	130	84	98
Fuel oil /c	31	70	52	53	39
Total	69	182	182	137	137
Distillate surplus (deficit)	3	20-(29)	38-(11)	(8)-(57)	6-(43)
Projected range of distillate demand	35	92-141 /d			

/a Total refinery use and losses are assumed at 6% of throughput, with 2% being refinery fuel oil use.

/b Includes gasoline, diesel oil, kerosene/jet fuel, LPG and light chemical feedstocks and lubricants.

/c Includes fuel oil and petroleum solids. Excludes refinery fuel oil consumption.

/d The projected range considers both QUADRUPLE and BALANCE macro cases (with GDP growth of about 6.6% p.a. during 1980-2000 in each case), and the full range between LOW and HIGH unit consumption cases.

Table 2.10: FUTURE DEMAND FOR PETROLEUM DISTILLATES

	Millions of tons	
	1980	2000 /a
Agriculture /b	9	18-22
Transportation	13	44-67
Residential/commercial	1	3-4
Manufacturing	7	15-32
Other /b	4	10-14
Total Final Consumption	34	90-139
Energy Industries	1	2
Total Consumption	35	92-141

/a Includes both the QUADRUPLE and BALANCE macro cases, and the full range between LOW and HIGH consumption cases for each.

/b Township and village industries not engaged in agricultural processing are included under manufacturing. Consumption by trucks for rural highway transport is included under transportation.

/c Includes all lubricants and unallocated consumption.

development of the petrochemical industry. The share held by agriculture (excluding rural truck and automobile consumption) is projected to decline from approximately 26% in 1980 to 16 to 20% in 2000, due to slower growth in field mechanization and petroleum-based agricultural processing compared with past decades (see Chapter 7).

2.50 Total distillate consumption in road transport is projected to increase by 3 to 5 times by 2000. Probably the most important factors influencing consumption are the rate of road freight growth (in terms of payload ton-km), trucking load factors, particularly for own-account trucks, and the degree of improvement in the rated energy efficiency of trucks -- which is a function of both truck size and design (see Table 2.11). The impact of these factors on consumption will be determined largely by policies dealing with road construction, regulation of own-account trucking, and development of the truck manufacturing industry (see paras. 2.91-2.97).

2.51 Total demand for petroleum distillate feedstocks in the chemical industry is projected to increase from some 4.5 million tons in 1980 to 10 to 22 million tons in 2000. Key factors influencing demand are the development of alternative feedstocks (natural gas, fuel oil, and coal) and the growth rate of domestic production of key petrochemicals. The use of petroleum distillates as feedstocks will to some extent depend upon the regional availability of natural gas and the characteristics of the gas produced. Difficult choices exist, however, not only regarding the best use of natural gas, but also regarding the extent to which the higher costs associated with the use of some feedstocks, such as fuel oil or coal, are justified. These options are linked to both the economic costs of distillate feedstock supply and decisions concerning petrochemical development in general, and to the appropriate balance between domestic production and petrochemical imports or exports.

2.52 Development of China's plastics industry may have a substantial impact on future total distillate demand (see Table 2.11). In many countries plastics have been increasingly substituted for metal products, with advantages that include lower total costs and lower total energy use. In India, Egypt, South Korea, and Brazil, per capita consumption of primary thermoplastics grew by more than 9% p.a. during 1974-80. For China, relevant factors include not only the rate of growth in thermoplastics consumption, but also decisions regarding the balance between domestic production and imports. In 1982, approximately 40% of primary thermoplastic consumption was met by imports. If per capita consumption of plastics rises by 7% p.a. from 1982 to 2000, the difference in feedstock demand corresponding to plastic import shares of 10% and 60% in 2000 may result in a difference in distillate demand of over 7 million tons.

2.53 Major choices also exist regarding fuel oil use. If China's refinery throughput increases to more than 190 million tons in 2000, and distillate yields are approximately 60% of gross refinery yields, net fuel oil production will increase from some 31 million tons in 1980 to approximately

Table 2.11: SENSITIVITY ANALYSIS OF PETROLEUM DISTILLATE DEMAND IN ROAD TRANSPORT AND THE CHEMICAL INDUSTRY /a

Key Variables	QUADRUPLE-BASE Scenario assumption	Alternative assumptions	Change in demand, Year 2000, due to alternative assumptions (mt)
Road Transport			
Road freight growth (tkm), 1980-2000	10.2% p.a.	11% p.a. 9% p.a.	+5.4 -6.6
Load factor of own-account trucks, year 2000 /c	40%	30% /b 50%	+5.3 -5.2
Reduction in consumption per capacity tkm due to modification of truck designs and sizes	-25%	-15%	+4.3

	1980	2000 QUADRUPLE-BASE scenario	2000 Projected range /d
Total Distillate Demand in Road Transport (mt)	10.4	40	31-52

Key Variables	QUADRUPLE-BASE Scenario assumption	Alternative assumptions	Change in demands Year 2000, due to alternative assumptions (mt)
Chemical Industry			
Growth in plastics consumption per capita, 1982-2000 /e	7% p.a.	9.5% p.a. 4.5% p.a.	+4.6 -3.0
Share of imports in plastics consumption, year 2000 /e	40% /f	10% 60%	+4.4 -2.9

	1980	2000 QUADRUPLE-BASE scenario	2000 Projected range /d
Total Distillate Demand in the Chemical Industry (mt)	4.5	15	10-22

/a All assumptions regarding demand are as in the QUADRUPLE macro case and BASE consumption case, except for those key variables being tested. For each key variable, the alternative assumptions are substituted for the QUADRUPLE BASE assumption, and the impact of just that change on demand in 2000 is given.

/b Approximately equal to the 1980 level.

/c Own-account trucks are assumed to continue to account for 2/3 of the payload ton-km of freight moved in 2000, as in 1980.

/d Includes both the QUADRUPLE and BALANCE macro cases, and the full range between LOW and HIGH consumption cases for each.

/e "Plastics" refers to primary thermoplastics. Oil feedstocks are assumed to be used in production at the margin (1/3 naphtha, 1/3 vacuum gas oil, 1/3 atmospheric gas oil).

/f Approximately equal to 1982 level.

70 million tons in 2000.[15/] Additional quantities of fuel oil could be cracked to yield distillates, but at high cost. Other alternatives include increasing domestic use and large-scale exports.

2.54 Over the long run, it will be more economical in most cases to increase coal production to meet fuel demand and to either export or further refine much of China's fuel oil. On a kilocalorie basis, the average economic cost of coal supply, calculated according to the long-run marginal costs (LRMC) of coal production and the economic cost of its transport, is lower, by a factor of about three, than the economic cost of fuel oil, calculated according to current export prices. Over the long run, this gap can be expected to widen further, because the LRMC of coal production in China is expected to remain fairly constant, while international fuel oil prices are expected to increase in line with anticipated crude oil price increases over the long term. Other factors, however, need to be considered: (a) The balance between exports and domestic use of fuel oil supplies represents one of the most important areas where there is flexibility to respond to temporary gaps between total fuel supply and demand that may be created by either coal production shortfalls or transportation bottlenecks. The future balance between overall fuel supply and demand is expected to be tight. If coal supplies cannot consistently meet demand, increased domestic use of fuel oil as a direct fuel could be well justified if it permits economic growth that might otherwise be lost; (b) Costs associated with converting oil-burning plants to coal-firing are high and the infrastructural development and pollution control requirements for use of coal in densely populated urban areas are considerable. These factors can undermine the economic advantage of using coal as opposed to fuel oil.

2.55 Although available supplies of natural gas in energy equivalent terms are expected to be less than fuel oil or distillate supplies, natural gas could play a significant role in China's energy future, particularly in areas such as Sichuan or Guangdong. In many feedstock and fuel applications, natural gas has a relatively high value per unit energy compared with other energy sources, because of its potential for highly efficient use. Considering the industrial process alone, natural gas offers advantages over other feedstocks (naphtha, gas oil, fuel oil, or coal) in the production of synthetic ammonia, including lower plant capital costs and more efficient use. To the extent that the content is high enough to allow economical separation -- ethane, butane, and propane also represent ideal feedstocks. Indeed, discoveries of new quantities of relatively wet natural gas could have a significant impact on petroleum distillate demand in the chemical industry. As a fuel, natural gas use has major advantages in terms of the potential efficiency of use, particularly when compared with coal, and especially in the residential/commercial sector, or in the power industry (where combined cycle technology can be employed).

2.56 Evaluation of the optimal use of natural gas is, however, highly complex, and must be pursued on a site-by-site basis, due to regional varia-

---

15/ Figures also include output of solid products.

tions in the demand for different energy applications, in the opportunity cost of different fuels, and in the costs of gas transmission and distribution corresponding to the various options for use. Because regional factors can play such an important role in determining the best strategy for natural gas use, evaluation is best pursued through location-specific assessments.

Electricity

2.57 Demand for electricity is conservatively projected to grow during the 1980 to 2000 period by roughly 6.5 to 7.5% p.a. in the QUADRUPLE macro case and by 6 to 7% p.a. in the BALANCE macro case, excluding cogeneration in industrial enterprises. In both cases, the share of electricity in total final commercial energy consumption is projected to rise substantially, from 18% in 1980 to 26 to 27% in 2000. The share of electricity in final industrial energy consumption is also forecast to rise, from 22% in 1980 to 31-32% in 2000. Nevertheless, the elasticity of growth in electricity demand relative to growth in GDP is expected to be fairly close to 1.0, which is low compared with other developing countries (see Appendix B, Table B.3) and represents a substantial reduction from the elasticity of approximately 1.7 experienced in China from 1970 to 1980.

2.58 Sectoral demand for electricity is projected to develop as shown in Table 2.13.

Table 2.12: PROJECTED ELECTRICITY DEMAND/GDP GROWTH ELASTICITIES, 1980-2000

	QUADRUPLE Macro Case	BALANCE Macro Case
GDP growth	6.6% p.a.	6.6% p.a.
Electricity demand growth	6.5 - 7.5% p.a.	5.9 - 6.9% p.a.
Elasticity	1.0 - 1.15	0.9 - 1.05

Table 2.13: PROJECTED ELECTRICITY DEMAND BY SECTOR, QUADRUPLE AND BALANCE MACRO CASES /a
(TWh)

	1980	2000	
		QUADRUPLE Case	BALANCE Case
Agriculture /b	26	55	55
Transportation	1	20	20
Residential/commercial	26	95-115	120-140
Manufacturing	170	640-805	540-680
Other	5	15	20
Total Final Consumption	228	825-1,010	735-895
Power industry	45	160-195	145-175
Other energy industries	28	75-80	75-80
Total consumption	301	1,060-1,285	955-1,150

/a Coal production is assumed to reach 1400 million tons by 2000. Ranges represent the difference between LOW and HIGH unit consumption cases.

/b Township and village industries outside of the agricultural processing field are included under manufacturing. Rural residential and commercial use is included in the residential/commercial sector.

2.59 Probably the most important single factor underlying the projected relatively low elasticity of electricity demand is the projected change in the structure of industrial output, both between and within major industrial subsectors. Electricity use in transportation and in households is expected to grow particularly fast, but in each case growth is measured against small base levels. Major uncertainties do exist, however, particularly in regard to the future long-term growth of electricity demand of enterprises engaged in commerce and services.

2.60 The Ministry of Railways foresees an increase in the share of electric locomotives in total railway haulage (freight and passengers) from 2% in 1980 to more than 40% by the year 2000. This increase in electric locomotive use, together with anticipated increases in the use of electricity in general railway operations (stations, repair shops, etc.), imply a growth in electricity use in the transport sector from less than 1 TWh in 1980 to almost 20 TWh in 2000.

2.61 Urban and rural household electricity use, measuring only about 5 TWh in 1980, is estimated to increase to some 40-60 TWh by 2000, even without substantial popularization of home refrigerators or air-conditioners and without significant use of electricity for cooking, other than in certain rural areas where small-scale hydropower resources are particularly abundant. If use of electric cooking appliances or home refrigerators were to become more widespread, household electricity use would be substantially greater, but still would probably account for less than 10% of total power consumption. Increasing residential use of electricity may, however, cause a disproportional increase in the daily peak load demand, with a corresponding need for additional generating capacity to prevent power cuts and black-outs.

2.62 Future electricity demand in the commerce and service sectors[16/] of both urban and rural areas is highly uncertain, in part due to uncertainty about the impact of system reform. In light of the rapid growth in power demand in these sectors in recent years, projections in Table 2.13, which assume long-term electricity demand growth at rates equal to growth in the output value of commerce and services, may be low.

2.63 Barring a major increase in the electricity intensity of the commerce and service sectors, the industrial sector is expected to continue to account for better than 70% of final electricity consumption. As with total energy consumption, the lower demand for electricity projected for the BALANCE case versus the QUADRUPLE case is due to slower growth in industrial output, although higher demand levels in the commerce and service sectors in the BALANCE case partially offset the difference. In the QUADRUPLE case, the share of final electricity consumption held by industry rises from approximately 75% in 1980 to 78-80% in 2000, whereas in the BALANCE case that share is 73-76% in 2000.

2.64 Consumption of purchased electricity per unit output value in industry as a whole (excluding energy industries) is estimated to remain constant, or even decrease by as much as 20% (see Table 2.14). Following trends in other countries, electricity intensities in the machine building, textile, food and related products, and miscellaneous light industries are projected to increase substantially (see paras. 2.85-2.88). The output of these industrial subsectors is also expected to grow relatively rapidly. Current electricity intensities in these industries are, however, relatively low -- in 1980, they accounted for more than 70% of manufacturing gross output value, but only 35% of manufacturing industry electricity use. The share held by the metallurgy and chemical industries in manufacturing electricity use, on the other hand, was about 58% in 1980, and electricity demand in these subsectors is expected to grow more slowly. In the case of metallurgy, the relatively slow growth in electricity demand is due to slower growth in metallurgical output relative to the output growth projected for other industries. In the case of the chemical industry, however, electricity consumption per unit output value is forecast to fall sharply. Decreasing electricity intensities in the chemical subsector represent a clear international trend. In China, however, this trend is expected to be further accentuated by both slow growth of the synthetic ammonia industry relative to the growth of the chemical industry as a whole and dramatic reductions in unit

---

16/ Commerce and service sector demand is included under residential/ commercial and "other" use in Table 2.13.

Table 2.14: GROWTH OF ELECTRICITY DEMAND IN INDUSTRY, QUADRUPLE AND BALANCE MACRO CASES /a

Subsector	Electricity intensities in 1980 (kWh/1000 Y gross output value)	Change in electricity intensities, Year 2000 (1980 = 1.0)	Growth in in gross output value, 1980-2000		Growth in electricity demand, 1980-2000	
			QUADRUPLE case	BALANCE case	QUADRUPLE case	BALANCE case
			---- (% p.a.) ----		---- (% p.a.) ----	
Metallurgy	980	0.88-0.99	6.4	4.8	5.8-6.0	4.6-4.8
Chemicals	910	0.43-0.57	8.6	7.5	4.0-5.6	3.1-4.6
Building materials	490	0.94-1.05	7.1	6.2	6.8-7.3	5.9-6.4
Machine building	190	1.00-1.27	8.4	7.2	8.4-9.7	7.2-8.5
Other	180	1.21-1.74	8.2	7.4	9.4-11.2	8.5-10.3
Total Manufacturing Industry	380	0.8-1.0	8.1	7.1	6.9-8.1	5.8-7.1

/a Coal production is assumed to reach 1,400 million tons by 2000. Ranges in demand coefficients and demand growth reflect the difference between the LOW and HIGH unit consumption cases. See also Table 2.21.

consumption of electricity in the synthetic ammonia industry (see Table 2.17). The share of the synthetic ammonia industry in total electricity consumption in the chemical industry is expected to fall from about one-third in 1980 to roughly 10% in 2000.

D. Trends and Issues in Industrial Energy Demand

2.65 Of all the economic sectors industry generates the highest demand for commercial energy and will largely determine total energy demand. Improving energy efficiency in the production of various commodities -- through both technical transformation and improvements in operational management -- could greatly reduce the energy intensity of industrial production. Future patterns of output growth for different commodities, however, may be at least as important, involving such issues as the role of manufacturing in economic growth, changes in the structure of final consumption of industrial goods and industrial trade patterns, improvements in the efficiency of use of capital and intermediate goods, and materials substitution.

2.66 A comparison of the levels of energy demand projected for the QUADRUPLE and BALANCE macro cases underlines the critical impact of different patterns of output growth among the major manufacturing subsectors on total energy demand in manufacturing (see Table 2.15). In the QUADRUPLE case, the share held by manufacturing industry in total final energy consumption would rise from 60% in 1980 to about 65% in 2000. In the BALANCE case, it would remain constant at about 60%. The slower growth in the gross output value of the manufacturing industries represented in the BALANCE case results in projected energy demand levels in 2000 which are 140-180 million TCE less than in the QUADRUPLE case, a relative reduction of some 17%.

2.67 While assumptions concerning final consumption and trade in manufactured goods are slightly different for the QUADRUPLE and BALANCE cases,[17/] the most important factors underlying the different resulting industrial growth projections are assumptions regarding the degree of improvement in efficiency of use of capital and intermediate goods (see the Main Report, Chapter 2). With less use of capital per unit of output, the supply of capital goods needed to meet a given final output can be reduced. To the extent that intermediate products, such as basic metals, can be used more efficiently, through substitution among different materials and materials savings, supply requirements for these goods can also be reduced for a given final output. Reductions in the relative supply requirements for capital and intermediate goods,

---

17/ Growth in final domestic consumption of manufactured goods is only slightly lower in the BALANCE case than in the QUADRUPLE case (household consumption of manufactured goods rises by 7.2% p.a. during 1981-2000 in the BALANCE case, and 7.6% p.a. in the QUADRUPLE case). Total manufactured imports in 2000 are about the same in the two cases, but total manufactured exports in 2000 are 15% lower in the BALANCE case, accounting for about one-tenth of a percentage point of the difference in industrial growth rates.

Table 2.15: ENERGY DEMAND IN THE MANUFACTURING INDUSTRIES, 1980 AND 2000 /a

Subsector	Growth in gross output value, 1980-2000 (% p.a.) QUADRUPLE case	BALANCE case	Final energy demand, 2000 (million TCE) 1980	QUADRUPLE case	BALANCE case
Metallurgy	6.4	4.8	81.2	160-185	125-145
Chemicals	8.6	7.5	76.0	155-205	135-175
Building materials	7.1	6.2	49.1	135-165	115-135
Machine building	8.4	7.2	28.0	95-125	75-100
Food, beverage and tobacco	8.9	8.8	13.1	55-80	55-80
Textiles	7.6	6.6	21.8	80-100	65-80
Other	8.3	6.9	25.8	100-120	75-95
Unallocated	-	-	20.8	45-60	40-50
Total	8.1	7.1	315.8	825-1,040	685-860

/a Coal production is assumed to reach 1,400 million tons in both macro cases. Ranges in demand reflect the difference between the LOW and HIGH consumption cases.

in turn, results in reductions in the amount of energy needed to produce these goods. The degree to which these "indirect" improvements in energy efficiency can be attained in future industrial development may be just as important as direct energy efficiency improvements in China's efforts to reduce energy intensities in industry.

2.68 This is illustrated by considering inputs from the metallurgy industry to the machine building sector. In 1981, metallurgy inputs to machine building accounted for approximately one-half of total metallurgy output. Following international trends, metallurgy input per unit of machine building output value is projected to decline in both the QUADRUPLE and the BALANCE cases. In the QUADRUPLE case, the rate of decline is 2.0% p.a. from 1981 to 2000; if this decline were not to occur, the corresponding increase in metallurgy output for machine-building needs would require an additional 50-60 million TCE, even with substantial energy conservation. On the other hand, if such inputs were to decline slightly faster -- at the BALANCE case assumed rate of 2.5% p.a. -- the corresponding decrease in metallurgy output in the QUADRUPLE case would entail a reduction in energy demand in the metallurgy industry of about 12 million TCE (about 7%).[18/]

2.69 Due to changes in inter-industry input-output relationships and to relatively minor changes in the structure of consumption and trade of manufactured goods, both the QUADRUPLE and BALANCE cases portray significant shifts in the structure of manufacturing output between major subsectors by 2000 (see Table 2.16). Among the three most energy-intensive manufacturing subsectors, declines in the shares of the metallurgy and building materials industries in total manufacturing output are to a large extent offset by an increase in the share of the chemical industry (see the Main Report, Chapter 2). The output share of the metallurgy industry is projected to drop substantially, due to decreasing unit material demands in other industries, substitution between metals (i.e., aluminum for steel), and substitution of plastics for steel. The share held by the building materials industry is also projected to fall, primarily due to slower growth rates in construction relative to manufacturing output (the construction industry consumed more than 80% of total building materials output in 1981). The share held by the chemical industry, on the other hand, is expected to increase, following international trends of increasing chemical inputs per unit of output in industry as a whole.

2.70 The projected impact on energy demand of changes in the structure of output among major manufacturing subsectors is significant, but not dramatic. If all major subsectors were to grow at the same rates from 1980 to 2000 (i.e., 8.1% p.a. in the QUADRUPLE case and 7.1% p.a. in the BALANCE case), total energy demand in the manufacturing sector in 2000 would be some 7% higher in the QUADRUPLE case, and approximately 9% higher in the BALANCE

18/ Estimates include consideration of major indirect effects, such as increases/decreases in metallurgy to metallurgy flows corresponding to increases/decreases in net metallurgy output.

Table 2.16: ENERGY INTENSITIES AND SHARES OF GROSS OUTPUT VALUE IN THE MANUFACTURING INDUSTRIES /a

	Energy intensities, 1980 (TCE/Y 1,000 gross output)	Share of manufacturing gross output value (%), 2000		
		1980	QUADRUPLE case	BALANCE case
Metallurgy	1.7	10.6	7.8	6.9
Chemicals	1.3	12.9	14.1	14.0
Building materials	2.1	5.2	4.3	4.4
Machine building	0.2	26.3	27.9	26.9
Food, beverages, tobacco	0.2	13.9	16.1	19.0
Textiles	0.2	20.7	19.0	18.8
Other	0.6	10.4	10.8	10.0
Total	0.7/b	100.0	100.0	100.0

/a Includes rural collective industries.

/b Includes 21 million TCE not allocated among subsectors.

case.[19] The most important difference in terms of the impact of subsector structural change on energy demand between the two macro cases is the degree of decline in the output share of the metallurgy industry.

2.71 The composition of output among major manufacturing subsectors represents only one aspect of anticipated changes in the structure of manufacturing output; changes in the structure of output within major subsectors are also expected to have an important impact on energy demand. In this analysis, the impact of such intra-subsector structural changes has been incorporated through changes in the unit energy consumption coefficients for major subsectors.[20] Important factors include increasing specialization (resulting in increasing gross output value with relatively small increases in energy demand); improvements in the efficiency of use of up-stream, semi-finished products in down-stream industries; changes in the structure of final domestic demand; and changes in trade in key, energy-intensive products.

2.72 Excluding structural changes caused by foreign trade changes, evidence from other countries suggests that the two manufacturing subsectors where intra-subsector structural change may have the greatest impact on energy demand are the chemical and machine-building industries. In China's chemical industry, the impact of structural change may be particularly marked because slow growth is anticipated in nitrogen fertilizer demand relative to demand for chemical products as a whole. While production and application of other types of chemical fertilizers may grow rapidly, nitrogen fertilizer requirements in 2000 are expected to be only about double 1980 levels (see Annex B: Agricultural Prospects to 2000). If synthetic ammonia production only doubles from 1980 to 2000, while total chemical industry output grows by 7.5 to 8.6% p.a. (projections for the BALANCE and QUADRUPLE macro cases, respectively), the effect on the energy intensity of the chemical industry will be striking: The synthetic ammonia industry accounted for approximately one-half of energy

---

19/ Estimates assume unit energy consumption in major subsectors at BASE consumption case levels. It is important to note that projected energy consumption coefficients decrease as output increases in the metallurgy, chemical and building materials industries, where unit consumption projections are further broken down among certain commodities, due to increasing shares of output from new, more energy-efficient plants. In this hypothetical case, therefore, unit energy consumption is higher in the chemical industry, and lower in the metallurgy and building materials industries, than in the actual projections.

20/ Unit energy consumption coefficients for the nonammonia chemical industry, machine building, and the light industrial sectors were estimated largely on the basis of trends in other countries. These trends reflect both changes in structure and changes in technical energy efficiencies, but it is not possible to differentiate between the impacts of each. A clearer understanding of the potential impacts of intra-subsector structural change on energy demand could, in theory, be gained by expanding the detail of input-output analysis.

consumption in the chemical industry in 1980, but less than 20% of chemical industry gross output (see Table 2.17).

2.73 While large changes in the relationship between total imports, exports, and domestic gross output for major energy-intensive manufacturing subsectors are not anticipated by 2000,[21] changes in the relationship between trade and domestic output for several key energy-intensive commodities could have a substantial impact on energy demand. In the chemical industry, changes in the share of plastics imports relative to total plastics consumption could alone result in differences in total petroleum distillate demand in the chemical industry in 2000 of some 50% (see para. 2.52). Changes in the share of steel product demand met through imports have already been shown to have a substantial impact on energy demand in China. Between 1982 and 1983, the share of steel product imports in total steel product consumption in China climbed from approximately 12% to 24% (total steel product imports increased from 3.94 million tons to 9.78 million tons). If the 5.84 million tons of increased steel product imports had been produced domestically, the energy intensity of China's entire economy (measured in terms of energy consumption per unit GVIAO) would have decreased by only some 2.0% between 1982-83, as opposed to the actual 2.7%.[22]

2.74 The relative economics of domestic production versus trade of energy-intensive products ultimately rest on many factors. And some options that have been effective in reducing industrial energy intensities in other countries, such as reductions in energy-intensive exports [23] or heavy reliance on imported scrap for steel production,[24] may not be relevant for China. Due to the quantities consumed in China, major increases in import

---

21/ In the metallurgy and chemical subsectors, net imports are projected to continue to account for less than 10% of total domestic demand. In the building materials industry, net exports are expected to remain under 3% of total domestic output. For details, see Annex D of the Main Report.

22/ Estimates based on average "comparable" unit energy consumption per ton of crude steel in China's steel plants in 1983 (1.22 TCE/ton), and the 1982 ratio between crude steel and steel product production (1:0.78). Estimates include an approximation of the additional gross output value which would be gained from an increase in steel production.

23/ In Japan, for example, decreases in the production of nitrogen fertilizers for export played a major role in reductions in the energy intensity of the chemical industry during 1970-79.

24/ In Italy, imported scrap (7.4 mt) and pig iron (0.7 mt) accounted for about 35% of total pig iron and scrap used in the steel industry in 1980, and hence, total energy consumption per ton of steel produced was among the lowest in the world. While increasing scrap or pig iron imports in China may be possible in the future, the quantities required in relation to future steel production levels to have a dramatic impact on energy consumption probably exceed availability.

Table 2.17: ENERGY CONSUMPTION INTENSITIES IN THE CHEMICAL INDUSTRY; RECENT TRENDS IN SELECTED COUNTRIES AND SCENARIOS FOR CHINA /a

A. Changes in Energy Consumption per Unit Gross Chemical Industry Output Value in Selected Countries, 1970-79
(% p.a.)

Country	Fuel & feedstock	Electricity	Total energy/b
Canada	+2.7	-3.4	+0.6
Germany, F.R.	-2.7	-1.5	-2.2
Italy	-5.2	-2.3	-4.2
Japan	-2.5	-4.6	-3.1
UK	-3.0	-2.7	-2.9

B. Scenarios of Chemical Industry Energy Consumption in China, QUADRUPLE Macro Case

	Growth in gross output value, 1980-2000 (% p.a.)	Energy consumption, millions of tons of coal equivalent: 1980			2000		
		Fuel and feed-stock	Electri-city	Total	Fuel and feed-stock	Electri-city	Total
Synthetic ammonia	3.4	31.4	7.1	38.5	39-42	6-7	45-49
Other chemicals	9.3	22.9	14.6	37.5	66-100	42-57	108-157
Total	8.6	54.3	21.7	76.0	105-142	48-64	153-206

Reduction in Energy Consumption per Unit Gross Output Value, 1980-2000
(% p.a.)

	Fuel & feedstock	Electricity	Total energy/b
Synthetic ammonia	1.8-2.2	3.7-4.3	2.1-2.5
Other chemicals	1.5-3.5	2.0-3.5	1.7-3.5
Total	3.4-4.8	2.8-4.2	3.2-4.6

/a Electricity consumption is calculated at a thermal replacement value of 2,900 kcal/kWh.

/b Changes in the structure of output in the countries concerned appear to have had a substantial impact on energy intensities. In Canada, physical production of olefins and nitrogen fertilizers grew by 10.7% p.a. and 10.0% p.a., respectively, during the period, while gross chemical industry output value grew by 5.7% p.a. in constant terms. In Italy, net imports of olefins increased from virtually zero in 1970 to about 12% of domestic consumption in 1979 - if net imports of olefins had been produced domestically in 1979, the reduction in total energy intensity in the chemical industry would have been closer to 3.8% p.a. during 1970-79, as opposed to 4.2% p.a. In Japan, production of nitrogen fertilizers fell from 2.11 million tons in 1970 (100% N) to 1.46 million tons in 1979, due to a fall in exports.

Source for A: Appendix B, Tables B.11-B.13.

shares for some commodities also pose issues concerning logistical feasibility and the impact on regional and world markets.

2.75 Subsector unit energy consumption coefficients, accounting for both intra-sectoral structural change and improvements in direct energy efficiency, are presented in Table 2.18. In both QUADRUPLE and BALANCE macro cases, total energy consumption per unit gross output value in manufacturing is projected to decline by a total of 31 to 45% from 1980 to 2000 (1.8-2.9% p.a.).25/ These projections are compared with available data on trends in other countries since the increase in oil prices in 1973 (Table 2.19). The extent and direction of projected structural changes in industrial output in China are, in some cases, considerably different from recent trends in other countries where the oil crisis and/or recession have had an impact on the structure of production. In the US, for example, total energy intensities in manufacturing fell by a total of only about 5% from 1960 to 1976 (-0.3% p.a.), before falling by 28% from 1976 to 1983 (-4.6% p.a), due largely to economic recession in the energy-intensive industries.

25/ In the metallurgy, chemical, and building materials subsectors unit consumption estimates were calculated with breakdowns for key energy-intensive products, where unit consumption estimates were calculated on a physical basis, taking into account different consumption levels for existing and new plants. In these industries, slower growth in the BALANCE case yields slightly higher coefficients than in the QUADRUPLE case, due to a decreased role of new plants. For all manufacturing, however, this effect is counter-balanced by differences regarding the extent of inter-sectoral structural change between the two macro cases, and hence aggregate total energy consumption coefficients are roughly the same.

Table 2.18: PROJECTED ENERGY CONSUMPTION COEFFICIENTS PER UNIT GROSS OUTPUT VALUE IN MANUFACTURING SUBSECTORS, YEAR 2000, QUADRUPLE MACRO CASE /a (1980 = 1.00)

	Fuel and feedstock /b			Electricity			Total energy		
	High	Base	Low	High	Base	Low	High	Base	Low
Metallurgy	0.58	0.54	0.48	0.92	0.90	0.88	0.66	0.62	0.57
Chemicals	0.50	0.43	0.37	0.57	0.51	0.43	0.52	0.45	0.39
Building materials	0.81	0.76	0.67	1.05	1.01	0.95	0.84	0.78	0.70
Machine building	0.67	0.61	0.50	1.27	1.17	1.00	0.87	0.80	0.67
Food, beverages, tobacco	0.86	0.71	0.65	2.19	1.68	1.30	1.11	0.89	0.78
Textiles	0.70	0.60	0.56	2.09	1.81	1.64	1.05	0.90	0.82
Other	0.81	0.75	0.70	1.35	1.22	1.00	0.96	0.86	0.79
Total									
QUADRUPLE Case	0.61	0.54	0.48	1.00	0.90	0.79	0.69	0.62	0.55
BALANCE Case	0.61	0.54	0.48	0.99	0.89	0.78	0.69	0.62	0.55

/a Coefficients for metallurgy, chemicals and building materials for the BALANCE case are slightly higher, due to slower output growth, and hence a decreased role of new plants in output.

/b Includes all fuel and oil distillates.

Table 2.19: RECENT CHANGES IN ENERGY CONSUMPTION PER UNIT GROSS MANUFACTURING OUTPUT VALUE IN SELECTED COUNTRIES (% p.a.).

Country	Period	Fuel and Feedstock	Electricity	Total Energy /a
Japan	1973-80	-4.2	-0.2	-2.4
France	1973-80	-3.4	0.0	-2.1
Germany, F.R.	1973-80	-4.7	-0.7	-3.2
UK	1973-80	-5.6	0.2	-3.6
Brazil	1973-78	-3.4	0.9	-2.0
India	1973-78	-3.2	-0.1	-2.5
South Korea	1973-80	-0.8	1.8	0.1
Philippines	1973-79	-1.7	-9.2	-4.3
Turkey	1973-79	-1.6	1.2	-0.1

/a Includes biomass energy use in Brazil, India and the Philippines. Electricity is converted at 2900 kcal/kWh.

Source: Appendix B, Table B.7.

2.76 Future improvements in direct energy efficiency in China hinge to a considerable extent on two important factors: the role of new plants in manufacturing output by the year 2000 and anticipated changes in average plant sizes (i.e., the role of small-scale plants in future output).

2.77 If manufacturing output grows to 4 or 5 times the 1980 level by 2000, most of China's manufacturing capacity will be new by the end of the century. Efforts to improve the energy efficiency of existing plants will be important over the short and medium terms, but over the long term today's capacity will play a relatively minor role in total manufacturing in most subsectors. The technology of new capacity will be critical in improving the energy efficiency of manufacturing plants by the end of the century. Success depends on factors such as China's ability to transfer and disseminate new technology from abroad, to improve integrated planning and project design in industrial construction, and to achieve effective and timely improvements in the efficiency and quality of capital goods domestically produced. Indeed, the formulation and implementation of policies promoting energy efficiency in connection with new plant construction during the remainder of the 1980s may have more of an impact on industrial energy demand during the 1990s than policies to improve energy efficiency in existing plants.

2.78 A preponderance of small-scale plants in many energy-intensive sectors is a major factor underlying current high energy intensities in industrial production, as discussed in Chapter 1 (para. 1.23). Reductions in the role of these plants in future output and greater emphasis on production in advanced large-scale plants may play a major role in future energy efficiency improvements. Substantial economic trade-offs exist, however, as capturing economies of scale may lead to higher transportation costs and greater capital intensity. In the building material industries, small-scale plants are expected to continue to account for high shares of output. In many other industries, deemphasizing small-scale production may often be justified, but local conditions -- including the availability of local, low-cost energy resources -- may at times enhance the viability of small plants, even if they are relatively energy inefficient.

2.79 In 1980, nearly one half of final energy consumption in industry was in the production of iron and steel (22%), ammonia (12%), cement (5%), and bricks and tiles (7%). With energy conservation in existing plants, introduction of improved technology in new plants, and appropriate shifts of varying degrees away from small-scale production, total unit energy consumption in these industries might be reduced by 2000 as shown in Table 2.20.

Table 2.20: SCENARIOS OF REDUCTIONS IN ENERGY CONSUMPTION PER TON OF PRODUCT IN FOUR ENERGY-INTENSIVE INDUSTRIES, 1980-2000 /a

Crude steel /b	25-32
Synthetic ammonia	35-40
Cement	13-20
Brick and tile	12-32

/a Estimates are critically dependent upon projections of output growth, which largely define the role of new capacity. The ranges provided depict the range between the LOW and HIGH consumption scenarios.

/b Includes only energy used in producing steel ("comparable" consumption), and not energy used in producing pig iron which is not used in steel production, mining, equipment manufacturing, etc.

2.80 In the iron and steel industry, energy consumption per ton of steel dropped from 11.2 gcal/ton in 1978 to approximately 8.5 gcal/ton in 1983, due to a reduced share of small-plant output and to technical and operational improvements. Further declines in unit energy consumption in existing plants are expected to be less dramatic, because much of the potential for relatively simple and inexpensive conservation measures has been realized. Unit consumption in new, large, and advanced steel plants, however, could be some 25 to 35% lower than the average for 1983, depending largely upon plant scale and integration, the share of scrap-based electric arc furnaces in production, and the quality of raw materials. In addition, energy conservation in areas other than steel production is critical. These areas include energy used for production of foundry pig iron, factory equipment and refractories; for mining; and for sideline activities.[26] In 1980, about one-quarter of pig iron production was in small-scale blast furnaces, largely for foundry use, with unit consumption levels apparently some 80% higher than in larger plants. While foundry pig iron needs must be met -- shortages are currently reported -- substantial energy savings could be achieved with production of pig iron in larger plants and/or increasing use of scrap in foundries.[27]

2.81 In synthetic ammonia production, major reductions in unit energy consumption can be achieved both through reliance on large-scale plants to meet new production requirements and through adoption of conservation measures in existing enterprises, particularly small-scale plants. In 1980, small plants using coke and anthracite accounted for 55% of total production, consuming 70% more energy for feedstock and fuel and 100 times as much purchased electricity per ton of ammonia as existing large plants. By the end of the century, planning authorities expect total production from small plants to be about the same as today, but they envision reductions by approximately one-third in unit feedstock/fuel and electricity use.[28] In existing large- and medium-sized plants, significant potential for energy saving also exists, and may be easier to achieve. In large plants, reductions in unit consumption of about 15% appear attainable.

2.82 New natural gas-based ammonia plants abroad consume a total of 7.2 to 7.5 gcal/ton - some 25-30% less than existing gas-based large plants in China, and about 60% less than the average in the Chinese industry as a whole in 1980. Use of natural gas in new Chinese plants in the future is, however, uncertain and subject to regional availability and assessment of the optimal uses of new gas supplies. Of four new large plants under construction, three are based on fuel oil and one on coal. Unit energy consumption in these plants may be some 15% and 20% higher than in new gas-based plants, respectively.

2.83 In contrast to the ammonia industry, planning authorities do not foresee a dramatic decline in the share held by small-scale plants in total cement production (about 68% in 1980) by the end of the century. While opportunities exist for energy savings in existing and new small-scale vertical kilns, opportunities for reducing unit energy consumption are prob-

---

26/ Such energy consumption is included in Chinese statistics for "comprehensive" unit energy consumption. In 1980, "comparable" energy consumption in the iron and steel industry accounted for about 64% of total comprehensive energy consumption in the industry.

27/ Energy consumption per unit output value in the iron and steel industry may also fall slightly faster than consumption per ton of steel, due to increases in output value per ton of steel. Such trends are accounted for in the consumption coefficient presented for the metallurgy industry in Table 2.18.

28/ In 1982, unit consumption of feedstock and fuel in small plants already dropped to about 15.2 gcal/ton, compared to 17.2 gcal/ton in 1980.

ably greatest in medium- and large-scale cement production, through gradual conversion of many existing plants to dry process technology, and use of dry processes in new plants. In 1980, plants using wet process technology accounted for about 63% of production in large- and medium-sized enterprises. While average unit fuel consumption in large- and medium-sized plants was about 1165 kcal/ton cement, unit fuel consumption in modern dry processes is some 30-40% lower.[29/] In large, medium, and small-scale plants, however, greater mechanization, particularly in grinding, may offset realization of opportunities to conserve electricity and, hence, unit consumption of electricity may remain constant or even increase slightly.[30/]

2.84 While little data are available regarding energy consumption in brick and tile production, traditional up-draft kilns operated by rural collectives are believed to account for about three-quarters of total production, consuming about 2 1/2 times as much fuel per piece produced as more modern kilns. Dramatic shifts away from the current concentration of production in rural areas are not anticipated, but reductions in unit consumption in rural areas could be substantial with dissemination of semi-modern technologies, including perhaps the Hoffman kiln, and movements to realize economies of scale, where corresponding increases in transport costs can be justified.

2.85 In all manufacturing susbsectors, but particularly in machine building and the light industries, the share of electricity in total consumption is expected to rise (Table 2.21). The projected increases in shares of electricity are due to a large extent to the far greater potential for fuel conservation than for electricity conservation. In machine building and light industry, electricity intensities are expected to increase during 1980-2000, while improvements in boiler technology, greater use of waste heat, etc., are expected to reduce fuel intensities. Resulting major increases in the shares of electricity consumption in these industries are in line with trends in other countries.

29/ Assuming a clinker content of 85%.

30/ Electricity, converted at 2900 kcal/kwh, accounted for about 22% of total energy consumption in the industry in 1980.

Table 2.21: PROJECTED SHARE OF ELECTRICITY CONSUMPTION IN TOTAL ENERGY CONSUMPTION IN MANUFACTURING /a
(%)

	1980	2000
Metallurgy	24	33-37
Chemicals	29	30-32
Building materials	10	12-13
Machine building	34	48-50
Food, beverages, tobacco	19	32-38
Textiles	25	48-50
Other	28	36-40
Total /b	22	31-32

/a Electricity is converted at 2900 kcal/kWh. Ranges include QUADRUPLE and BALANCE macro cases and all unit consumption cases.

/b Includes unallocated fuel consumption.

2.86 In the machine-building industry, the limited data available for other countries suggests that, while there is no distinctive recent trend regarding electricity intensities relative to output value, the share of electricity in consumption has tended to rise over time, with increasing mechanization, and fuel intensities have tended to drop (see Appendix B, Tables B.14-B.16). The share of electricity in total 1980 consumption in China's machine-building sector was about 34%, similar to that in the US in 1958. The share of electricity in the US rose sharply from 1958 to 1981, reaching levels typical for industrialized countries today (Table 2.22).

Table 2.22: SHARE OF ELECTRICITY IN ENERGY CONSUMPTION IN THE MACHINE BUILDING INDUSTRY IN THE US, 1958-81 /a

	Percentage Share
1958	35.7
1968	47.3
1973	49.6
1978	56.7
1981	61.2

/a Electricity is converted at 2,900 kcal/kWh.

Source: Appendix B, Table B.15.

2.87 Electricity consumption per unit gross output value in China's food, beverage, and tobacco industry rose by some 5% p.a. during 1977-82. While electricity intensities may not continue to grow as rapidly over the long term, increasing mechanization in milling, packaging, and canning and growing use of refrigeration in crop and milk storage can be expected to increase electricity intensities. In all countries surveyed, electricity intensities have increased in recent years in this industry, rising fastest in Brazil and India. In the US, electricity intensities increased by more than 5.5% p.a. from 1958 to 1973 (see Appendix B, Tables B.17-B.20).

2.88 The share of electricity in total energy consumption in China's textile industry is low compared to that in most other countries (Table 2.23).

Table 2.23: SHARE OF ELECTRICITY IN TOTAL ENERGY CONSUMPTION IN THE TEXTILE INDUSTRY, SELECTED COUNTRIES AND YEARS /a

Country	Year	Share of Electricity (%)
China	1980	24.8
US	1958	42.4
	1981	59.8
Brazil	1973	52.2
	1982	69.3
India	1973	46.9
	1982	59.6

/a See Appendix B, Table B.22 for additional data. Electricity is converted at 2,900 kcal/kWh.

In three developing countries where textile industry development was considerable during the 1970s and data are available -- South Korea, Brazil, and the Philippines -- growth in electricity intensities has been rapid (see Appendix B, Table B.21). The most important explanations appear to be greater mechanization and space cooling in new, modern plants.

E. Energy Consumption in the Transport Sector

2.89 Total energy consumption in the transportation sector reached some 40 million TCE in 1980, accounting for only approximately 8% of total final commercial energy use (Table 2.24). Coal is currently the dominant locomotive fuel, and thus petroleum products account for only a little over one-half of

Table 2.24: ENERGY CONSUMPTION IN THE TRANSPORT SECTOR, 1980
(million tons of coal equivalent)

	Petroleum products	Coal	Electricity	Total	Percentage of total
Railroads	1.7	19.0	0.6	21.3	32.5
Trucks and buses /a	15.0	-	-	15.0	36.9
Automobiles	0.2	-	-	0.2	0.5
Vessels	3.7	-	-	3.7	9.1
Civil aviation	0.4	-	-	0.4	1.0
Total	21.0/b	19.0	0.6	40.6	100.0
Share of transport sector in total final commercial energy consumption (%)/c	24.6	5.8	0.6	7.8	

/a Includes transport by own-account trucks, as well as trucks operated by state transport departments.
/b Includes 1.5 million TCE of fuel oil.
/c Total final consumption of petroleum products includes crude oil which is directly burned as fuel in industry and power generation.

Sources: SSB Statistical Yearbook of China, 1981; Ministry of Railways; Ministry of Communications; Mission estimates.

total energy consumption in the sector[31/]. Motor vehicles, mostly trucks and buses, account for more than 90% of total gasoline consumption in the country but only some 10% of the national consumption of diesel oil (agricultural equipment accounted for about 50% of diesel oil use, while vessels, railway locomotives, and industry accounted for most of the remainder). In contrast with most other countries, gasoline accounts for about 85% of the fuel consumed by trucks and buses in China. Although road transport accounted for only about 9% of freight movement in 1980, unit fuel consumption in the trucking industry is particularly high, compared with other countries (see Chapter 1, paras. 1.36-1.37).

2.90 The structure of energy consumption in China's transportation sector is expected to change substantially in the future. Key issues include the rate of growth of different transport modes, particularly road transport; the degree to which the substantial potential for energy conservation in road transportation can be realized; and fuel substitution in railway locomotives.

31/ Tractors used for highway transport are excluded.

2.91 Compared with freight transport by rail or water, road freight transport is relatively energy inefficient. Road freight transportation development, however, serves local needs which are difficult to meet with other modes of transportation and is highly competitive with other modes for short and even medium-distance hauls, offering greater convenience through quick, door-to-door service. Given current bottlenecks stemming from underdevelopment of the sector in the past and expected rapid growth in road transport demand in the future, especially to satisfy needs in rural areas, the share of road transportation in both total freight and passenger transport should continue to increase, as in recent years. An increase in the share of total freight moved by road from about 9% of domestic tkm in 1980 to 17-20% by 2000 would correspond to annual traffic growth rates of some 9-11%, depending upon total traffic growth. This would not be extraordinary considering both the low base and recent growth rates. Road freight tkm increased more than 40% between 1980 and 1983. In passenger transportation, an increase in the share of road traffic from about 32% in 1980 to 42-46% in 2000 would imply an increase in road passenger-kilometers of 10.0-10.5% p.a., assuming a total growth in passenger transport of 8.5% p.a.

2.92 On the basis of conservative projections of road transport growth, petroleum product demand in road transportation may rise by 3 to 5 times from 1980 to 2000, even with substantial energy conservation (Table 2.25). With more rapid growth in the road transport share and/or more rapid growth in total traffic, petroleum product demand could grow even faster--perhaps to 6 times the 1980 level. In addition to the future rate of growth in road transportation, China's ability to achieve energy savings in the sector will be crucial in determining petroleum product demand, as implied by the wide ranges in demand projections. Fuel consumption per payload tkm in the trucking industry (including own-account trucks) could be reduced by 20 to 50% between 1980 and 2000.

2.93 While approximately 90% of the current Chinese truck fleet consists of trucks in the 4-5 ton range, increased production of both larger and smaller trucks is anticipated in the future. Increased use of larger, diesel-fueled trucks would bring major improvements in energy efficiency, but the extent of use will depend largely upon road development - few existing roads and bridges are built to take the corresponding axle loads. Increasing use of modern 1-2 ton pick-up trucks may also improve energy efficiencies, by gradually replacing the use of farm tractors for highway transportation in rural areas.

2.94 There is substantial potential for improving energy efficiency through improvements in truck design. In 1982, improved models in the 2-5 ton range were already being introduced, with rated fuel consumption levels 20-30% lower than older models. Improvements of engine efficiencies, however, will be closely related to developments in China's petroleum refinery industry. Clearly, trucks with payload capacities of 8 tons or more will require diesel fuel. For small- or even medium-sized trucks, continued use of gasoline may be rational, as demand for gasoline outside of the trucking industry is expected to be limited, and the advantages of diesel engines in energy efficiency are increasingly counter-balanced by their weight (they are heavier than high compression gasoline engines) as truck sizes decrease. Use of efficient, high compression gasoline engines, however, will require substantial increases in the average octane content of available gasoline.

2.95 Load factors in the own-account trucking sector, which currently accounts for about two-thirds of total road tkm, are only about 30%, compared with more than 60% for trucks operated by state transport departments. Efforts to increase the load factors of own-account trucks (e.g., through centralization of truck dispatching) or to reduce the relative role of own-account trucks (e.g. through regulation, or improvement in the quality of service by state transport departments) could substantially improve energy efficiency per payload tkm. However, efforts to increase load factors could reduce the flexibility of the trucking industry, which often represents its chief economic advantage. Therefore, the total impact of any measure to save energy should be carefully evaluated before its implementation.

Table 2.25: SCENARIOS OF FUTURE ENERGY DEMAND IN TRANSPORTATION
(million tons of coal equivalent)

	1980				2000			
	Petroleum Products/a	Coal	Electricity	Total	Petroleum Products/a	Coal	Electricity	Total
Rail transport	1.7	19.0	0.6	21.3	7-8	19-21	8-9	34-38
Road transport	15.2	--	--	15.2	45-75	--	--	45-76
Other	4.1	--	--	4.1	18-19	--	--	18-19
Total	21.0	19.0	0.6	40.6	70-103	19-21	8-9	97-133

ASSUMPTIONS REGARDING TRANSPORT GROWTH AND MODAL MIX

Freight Transport

	Modal shares (%) 1980	Modal shares (%) 2000	Growth in ton-km 1980-2000 (% p.a.)
Rail	67	59	5.4- 6.0
Road	9	17	9.5-10.2
Water	18	21	6.9- 7.6
Pipeline	6	3	2.6- 3.3
Total	100	100	6.1- 6.7 /b

Passenger Transport

	Modal shares (%) 1980	Modal shares (%) 2000	Growth in passenger-km, 1980-2000 (% p.a.)
Rail	60	50	7.4
Road	32	42	10.0
Water	6	4	6.6
Air	2	4	13.0
Total	100	100	8.5/c

/a Includes fuel oil.

/b Assumes a GVIAO growth of 6.3-7.1% p.a. during 1980-2000 (BALANCE and QUADRUPLE macro cases, respectively), and an elasticity of freight transport growth relative to GVIAO growth of 0.95.

/c Assumes growth in GDP per capita of 5.3% p.a. during 1980-2000 (similar to both BALANCE and QUADRUPLE macro cases), and an elasticity of passenger transport growth relative to GDP per capita growth of 1.6.

2.96 Improved roads can allow both better traction and truck movement at optimal speeds. Fuel consumption for the same truck and load may be some 15-25% lower over a paved road than over a gravel or earth road. Expansion of the existing network of paved roads must, however, overcome a series of constraints, including a current shortage of quality asphalt. The bulk of current Chinese crude oil supply has a very low asphalt content - most of what is sold as asphalt in China is the carbonized residue of the paraffinic crudes, which has inferior properties as a bonding and sealing agent compared to true asphalt. Present demand for asphalt is 1.2 - 1.5 million tons per year, and demands will increase with any step-up in highway construction. While large deposits of heavy asphaltic crude oil are reported to exist in the Northwest, exploitation of these deposits may prove troublesome, due to extraction and transport difficulties.

2.97 Dramatic increases in passenger transportation by sedans is not expected in China by the end of the century, but bus traffic is expected to increase rapidly, particularly in rural areas. Motorcycle transportation could become a factor in petroleum consumption by the end of the century, as has been the case in several other developing countries (e.g., India and Thailand).

2.98 In railway transportation, MOR foresees dramatic changes in the structure of energy consumption by the end of the century. While coal-fired steam locomotives currently handle about 80% of traffic, their share is expected to decline to 20% by 2000. The share of diesel traction is expected to double, from about 18% to about 37%, while electric traction is to be increased very rapidly, from just 2% in 1980 to 43% in 2000. The increase in electric traction would require electrification of about 1,000 km per year between now and 2000, compared to an average pace of about 500 km per year during the Sixth Five-Year Plan.

2.99 Because of the relative energy efficiency of rail transportation in general, and the greater efficiency of diesel and electric traction compared with coal-fired steam traction, energy consumption in rail transportation according to current plans would remain fairly small in relation to national energy consumption. Even with the plans for growth, railway diesel oil consumption can be expected to be under 6 million tons in 2000, while electricity use will be only approximately 2% of total power generation. With the planned shift away from steam locomotives, total energy use per tkm would fall to about one-half the current level by 2000.

2.100 For the transportation sector as a whole, major improvements in energy efficiency in both railroad and road transportation may to a large extent offset the implications of rapid growth of road transportation, so that the share of the sector in total final commercial energy consumption may rise only slightly to probably less than 10% in 2000. The structure of energy consumption in the sector, however, is expected to change substantially, with a major shift towards greater use of petroleum products. With little or no growth expected in coal consumption, the share of petroleum product consumption would increase from about one-half of transport energy use in 1980 to some 70 to 80% by 2000. Oil distillates consumption in transportation may rise from about 38% of national distillate use in 1980 to almost 50% by 2000.

3. DEMAND MANAGEMENT AND PRICING

A. Introduction

3.01 In China the state plays an active and direct role at all stages of energy production and consumption management. Since 1979 improved energy demand management has been promoted through a variety of means. Conservation goals and investment allocations for conservation projects have been included in the national development plan. Enterprises have been encouraged through administrative and financial incentives to improve energy efficiency, while capabilities to assess energy conservation potential have been improved.

3.02 The results have been impressive, both in reducing energy consumption and in improving the efficiency of energy use. Primary commercial energy consumption per unit of gross value of industrial and agricultural output (GVIAO), which had been increasing steadily during 1970-77, has declined since 1978 (See Table 3.1). In addition, there have been substantial reductions in oil consumption, which dropped steadily during 1979-82. Although oil consumption increased by 6% in 1983, GVIAO grew by an impressive 10% during that year.

Table 3.1: CHANGE IN PRIMARY COMMERCIAL ENERGY CONSUMPTION PER UNIT GVIAO /a
(% change over previous year)

1970-75	1976	1977	1978	1979	1980	1981	1982	1983
+1.0	+2.4	+1.4	-1.3	-5.9	-8.7	-5.4	-3.1	-2.7

/a Consumption is defined as production minus net exports.

3.03 During 1979-81 the most important factor underlying these achievements was an adjustment in China's industrial structure. The share of heavy industry in relation to light industry declined, as heavy industry grew by just 1.3% p.a., while light industry grew by 14.0% p.a. Heavy industry's share of total industial output fell from 67.3% in 1978 to 48.6% in 1981.[1/] Because China's heavy industrial sector consumes 4.5 times as much energy per unit of gross output value as the light industrial sector, the result was an overall decline in energy consumption per unit of output.

3.04 In addition, during 1979-81 the share of industrial output from small-scale plants declined. Particularly in energy-intensive sectors, small-scale plants were ordered to improve energy efficiency or merge with larger-scale operations. In many instances, small-scale energy inefficent plants

---

1/ Computed in terms of constant 1980 yuan.

were closed; for example, in the iron and steel sector, some 300 small-scale enterprises were forced to close operations.

3.05 During 1982-83 the Chinese economy grew rapidly. Heavy industry grew by 11.1% p.a., while light industry grew by 7.2% p.a. In addition, small-plant output in several sectors appears to have been much higher than originally anticipated.[2/] Nevertheless, there was a further reduction in energy intensity. In 1984, economic growth accelerated further, with heavy and light industry each growing at about 14%. Preliminary figures suggest that energy consumption per unit GVIAO fell by almost 7% over the year. Hence, while slower growth in heavy relative to light industry played a major role in reducing energy intensities during 1979-81, it appears that since 1981 technical and operational energy savings, and savings resulting from changes in the structure of output within industrial subsectors have played substantial roles in reducing energy consumption relative to output -- a larger role than in previous years.

3.06 Changes in economic structure will continue to play an important role in future reductions in energy intensity, but a repetition of the achievements resulting from fundamental shifts between heavy and light industry as in 1979-81 is unlikely. Steady progress in the formulation and implementation of a comprehensive energy demand management program, including price reform, will be critical to realizing future energy efficiency improvements commensurate with the potential for energy savings.

3.07 This chapter starts with a description of the energy allocation and pricing system, followed by a brief discussion of the energy conservation program. Finally, the chapter reviews possible reform in the allocation and pricing systems.

B. The Allocation System

3.08 Despite recent economic reforms, energy in China has continued to be largely allocated administratively, with market forces playing a minor role in energy distribution. The most important mechanism for determining allocations of commercial energy has been the annual plan.

3.09 The annual plan provides for most of the energy used by state enterprises and fixes allocations for commercial departments, which make retail sales to residential and commercial consumers. Allocations are provided at various bureaucratic levels in the supply administration, resulting ultimately in the establishment of quotas for individual enterprises. The quotas can be reviewed during the year, and sometimes they are adjusted in response to

---

2/ For example, while small scale production of synthetic ammonia fell from 8.21 million tons in 1980 to 7.81 million tons in 1981, it increased to 8.38 million tons in 1982 although plans called for a further reduction in output.

requests made when production quotas increase or when energy quotas can be shown to be inadequate.

3.10 The actual energy supply quotas are, in principle, fixed through:

(a) consideration of quantity and quality of energy available;

(b) judgments regarding the priority of a given consumer sector or enterprise in the national economy;

(c) state laws and regulations concerning interfuel substitution or unit energy consumption for different processes, where applicable; and

(d) consideration of requests for average unit consumption levels for other enterprises in the same line of business -- and how these requests compare with historical quota levels -- and assessments, if any, of the potential for energy conservation.

3.11 The planned allocation system is somewhat different for each of the various energy sources. In the case of petroleum and petroleum products, planned allocations are controlled by the central government. Supplies are assigned to the various ministries or provinces. The supplies are then allocated by the ministries to the units under their control and by the provinces to the various subdivisions under local control.

3.12 Electricity is allocated by the state, at various administrative levels. The only exception is for consumers who generate their own power (i.e. some rural units). Most allocations are made by authorities at the administrative level that controls the grid (regional, provincial, county, etc.). Supply quotas set the maximum amount of power that can be drawn from the grid, and thus determine peak loads.

3.13 The planned allocation system for coal differs among the administrative levels that control the enterprises. Supply quotas for centrally controlled enterprises are set by the relevant ministries, whose allocations are in turn set by the State Material Supply Bureau in conjunction with the State Planning Commission. The quotas for local state-run enterprises are set by provincial administrations or their subdivisions.

3.14 The coal distribution system also varies with the controlling agency. Centrally distributed coal, comprising some 55% of output, consists of coal produced in centrally controlled mines and in some provincial mines, particularly those in Shanxi Province. This coal is provided both to centrally controlled enterprises and to provincial administrations, which in turn allocate the coal to subdivisions under their control. Coal distributed by local governments, comprising some 30% of output, consists of coal produced in most provincial mines, in mines controlled by prefectures and counties, and some coal purchased from collective mines. This coal is provided to local state-run enterprises not fully covered under the central distribution system. As much as 15% of all coal is distributed directly by rural townships and villages (part of it self-consumed) outside of the planned allocation system.

3.15 In addition to allocation through the planned quota system, enterprises can obtain some commercial fuel (but not electricity) outside the plan, although almost always at higher prices. Some fuel procurement outside the plan occurs in most state enterprises; in some instances it can represent more than 50% of consumption. Above-quota allocations can be obtained from state supply administrations, other enterprises, or in some cases directly from energy producers. Generally high-priority enterprises receive adequate quotas for their needs while the lower priority enterprises must rely on time-consuming and costly alternatives to supplement their quotas. Collective enterprises obtain energy from plan allocations or through purchases from a variety of sources. Some rural collectives produce their own coal or electricity.

3.16 Household and agricultural commercial fuel supplies have traditionally been allocated at an aggregate level by the central government and subdivided among local state administrations. Final allocations to agricultural units have been based on the reported horsepower of agricultural machinery inventories. Urban residential consumers purchase fuel from local commercial departments. Fuels often have been rationed during shortages.

C. Price Systems

Determination and Role of Prices

3.17 Prices in China have been predominantly determined by administrative decisions rather than by market forces. They have also been strongly influenced by such considerations as income distribution and the need to generate budgetary revenues. The resulting price structure for energy products is quite arbitrary, inasmuch as it does not bear direct relationships to opportunity or production costs. Prices do not contain information which could facilitate economically efficient decision-making. There has been inadequate concern for the relationship between the prices of the various energy sources and the effect that the relative price structure has on the mix of energy use.

3.18 Pricing decisions have generally been made by central administrative units, although decisions have also been made at the provincial or local level for some commodities. The prices of crude oil, petroleum products, and electricity are determined centrally. The prices of crude oil and electricity vary in some parts of the country. Because of differences in transport costs, petroleum product prices are not uniform countrywide. Coal prices are set by central authorities, although the prices of coal controlled by local governments have been increasingly determined at the local level. Surplus supplies or above-quota input requirements are often traded or purchased at prices that vary substantially from official prices, reflecting market forces for these small shares of the market. Natural gas prices are not uniform and do not appear to be set according to standard criteria. They seem to be determined specifically for each user, depending on the circumstances of consumers and producers; for example, gas prices are different for the various fertilizer complexes.

3.19 State-owned enterprises rarely have had authority to set their output prices. Nevertheless, they can influence pricing decisions by the relevant authorities. Since in the past, the performance of enterprises has been evaluated mainly by the quantity rather than the value of their output, prices had only a small effect on their decisions. Some collectives and rural enterprises have more autonomy for price setting and also are somewhat freer to trade their inputs and outputs. Thus, prices have greater influence on their behavior. Generally prices have had more effect on household demand, except when rationing was employed in times of scarcity.[3/]

3.20 Although in principle administered prices in China are based on costs, the very long intervals between major price adjustments -- extending to decades -- have resulted in major differences between prices and costs. In general, prices of primary products -- such as energy and raw materials -- whose production costs have risen substantially over the past two decades are now priced much below marginal costs, while prices for many manufactured goods -- whose production costs have declined with the expansion of outputs over the past two decades -- have remained at a relatively high level. Principles such as the need to maintain low prices for essential consumer goods or to provide high profits for state-owned industry in order to guarantee budgetary revenues have also interfered with cost-based pricing. In addition, the process of approving price changes is difficult and lengthy, and the Chinese system has generally excluded capital costs in establishing prices.

3.21 On several occasions there have been efforts to implement across-the-board price reforms, but they were stopped short because of concern over the potential effects of inflation on a population accustomed (since 1949) to controlled pricing. Coal prices are an example: from the early 1950s until recently they had only been changed three times and are still very low relative to cost. On the other hand, in calorific terms, coal was until recently priced higher than fuel oil and, consequently, there was little financial incentive to switch from fuel oil to coal. This ran counter to the Government's policy of promoting the switch to coal.

3.22 Producer prices have played a substantive distributive role by generating significant profits in the production of some fuels (e.g. oil) while barely covering operating costs for others (e.g. coal). Except for the non-state sectors (e.g., township-owned coal mines), however, producer prices have not greatly influenced investment decisions. Profits of energy producers in the state sector are in most cases remitted to the state budget. The central authorities (and local authorities in some cases) have played the major role in directing investment decisions and in providing financing through budgetary grants for the exploration and development of natural resources.

3/ This is true only for some prices. Prices of LPG, coal briquettes, natural gas, manufactured gas, and raw coal for urban households have been kept low.

Recent Reforms

3.23 Recent reforms in China generally have included a greater reliance on profits as an indicator of performance, more autonomy to enterprises and farmers to set prices and a more important role for market forces in the determination of prices. In particular, the enhanced role of profits has led to a greater role for prices.

3.24 The recent changes in the price system, however, have been more modest than reforms in other components of the economic system. For the most part, prices remain administered. Even administered adjustment of relative prices has been difficult. Nevertheless, the influence of prices on decision-making is increasing, and policy makers are attempting to use prices for the management of production and demand. The Government has therefore repeatedly stated its commitment to price reform as the crucial element of its overall program of system reform. Before a fundamental price reform, it has also attempted to alleviate the adverse impact of irrational prices on incentive and resource allocation.

3.25 For instance, in order to increase marginal prices for coal and crude oil while minimizing the corresponding increase in average prices, the central allocation system now distinguishes between basic quotas and above-quota supplies, and two-tier pricing has been introduced under which above quota transactions are at higher prices. The amount of energy that is being purchased outside planned allocations (and thus subject to market forces) has also been rising.

3.26 The recent reforms have been most pronounced in the coal subsector. The State Planning Commission recently approved MOCI's proposal to raise coal prices during 1985, including (i) 10-25% price increase for all coal produced in the coal deficient regions in East China; (ii) 5-9% price increases to reflect coal quality differences, and a 50% price increase for production in excess of the 1984 base quota; and (iii) an approximately 100% increase for production above the annual production quota. The above measures are expected to raise coal prices for central mines by about 10-15% in 1985. In addition because of recent price increases, the number of collective producers and their coal production have been rising.

3.27 Investment and production decisions concerning oil continue to be centrally administered. Increases in oil production have received priority in recent years and high production targets have been set. Recently higher prices have been paid for above-quota production. This has ensured financial viability for oil fields in the face of rising costs of production. Under present financial arrangements, however, all net income is taxed and returned to the Government.[4] Although production has increased in response to the recent directives and price incentives, inadequate attention has been given to optimizing output over time. Consequently, some fields may have been producing beyond their capacity at the expense of their long-term potential.

3.28 The Government has also used price and tax adjustments to encourage energy efficiency and inter-fuel substitution. Prices of diesel and kerosene have been increased. Beginning in 1982 a special tax of Y 70/ton has been levied on crude and fuel oil that is burnt as fuel. Above-quota prices for crude have been set at higher levels -- close to international prices at the official exchange rate of that time.

Overview of Energy Prices

3.29 In general, prices in China are not set according to international prices and are low in relation to economic costs, with the exception of some petroleum products and electricity for residential consumers. Table 3.2 shows Chinese average retail and international prices (where relevant) in early 1985 for the major energy sources. Comparisons of energy prices in China with international prices are extremely complex and must be interpreted with caution, particularly because it is difficult to analyze energy prices in isolation from prices of other commodities in China and because of uncertainties about the appropriate level of the exchange rate for such comparisons. The comparison in Table 3.2 nonetheless shows that the prices of coal, crude, and fuel oil are particularly low compared with international prices, while gasoline, and kerosene prices are relatively high.

3.30 Coal Prices. Coal prices in China are low relative to other prices and to production costs. Average mine-mouth coal prices in early 1984 were about Y 4.0/million kcal, at an average calorific value of 5,400 kcal/kg. Current prices are about 60% of the long-run marginal cost (LRMC) of coal production.[5] Until the recent price increases (see para. 3.26) coal prices had not been adjusted across the board since 1979, when they were increased by

---

4/ The petroleum sector is one of the major surplus sectors in China. Although some high-cost fields receive contributions from the Government, the surplus from other fields such as Daqing more than offsets those transfers. Under the two-tiered price system, the differential between the domestic and international prices for above-quota production from all the oil fields in China is pooled together by Ministry of Petroleum Industry which allocates the funds back to the various oil fields according to individual needs for investment funds, as approved by the Government. The remaining funds are paid to the Government.

5/ LRMC of coal production at Shanxi are about Y 36-44 per ton, for 6,000 kcal/kg coal. Railway charges for coal transport are about 80% of LRMC. LRMC of railroad transport are estimated at over Y 0.02 per ton/km.

Table 3.2: CHINESE RETAIL AND INTERNATIONAL ENERGY PRICES, EARLY 1985 a/

	Unit price			Price per million kilocalories		
	Chinese ave. retail price			Chinese ave. retail price		
	Yuan	US$	International price (US$)/b	Yuan	US$	International price (US$)/b
Petroleum Products (tons) /c						
Gasoline	800	286	278	76.2	27.3	26.5
Kerosene	735	263	263	71.4	25.5	25.5
Diesel oil	560	200	245	54.9	19.6	24.0
Fuel oil /d						
Directly burned	155	55	179	15.5	5.5	17.9
Other	85	30	179	8.5	3.0	17.9
Crude oil (directly burned) /d	186	65	-	17.9	6.4	-
Natural Gas ('000 cu m)						
Associated /e	100	36	-	-	-	-
Nonassociated /f	170	61	-	-	-	-
Coal (tons) /g	34	11	34	6.3	2.3	6.3
Electricity ('000 kWh) /h						
Residential	160	-	-	57.1	-	-
Commercial & small industries	81	-	-	28.9	-	-
Large industries	63	-	-	22.5	-	-
Agriculture	54	-	-	19.3	-	-
Average	66	-	-	23.6	-	-

/a Chinese prices are for allocations within the national plan. Yuan are converted to US$ at Y 2.8/US$.
/b Petroleum product prices are FOB Singapore, March 4, 1985. Coal price is for steam coal, FOB Qinhuangdao, China, late 1984, 5,400 kcal/kg equivalent.
/c Actual prices may vary with transport distances, and in some cases according to consumer category.
/d Assumes an average transport cost of Y 30/ton. Transport distances, and hence costs, are certainly lower on average for crude by comparison to fuel oil but have been calculated at the same rate to provide a better comparison between the two fuels.
/e Associated gas price for end-users varies depending on the distance from the oilfield and is assumed, on average, to include Y 20/MCM for gas treating and Y 30/MCM for gas transport.
/f Includes trunk line fee of Y 30/MCM and an additional Y 10/MCM from the trunk line to the end-users.
/g Estimate for late 1984. Actual coal prices vary substantially according to quality and type of producer supplied within the national system. Washed coal from MOCI mines may cost end-users as much as Y 70/ton, while raw coal from nearby mines may cost as little as Y 15/ton.
/h This information refers to 1982. However, to the best of our knowledge, the same tariffs prevailed in early 1985. Actual tariffs paid by consumers include a surcharge of 10-20% charged by local authorities for local infrastructural services.

Note: Calorific values are assumed as follows:

Gasoline	10,500 kcal/kg
Kerosene	10,300 kcal/kg
Diesel oil	10,200 kcal/kg
Fuel oil	10,000 kcal/kg
LPG	10,800 kcal/kg
Crude oil	10,200 kcal/kg
Natural gas	9,310 kcal/kg
Coal	5,400 kcal/kg
Electricity	2,800 kcal/kWh (thermal replacement value for 1983)

about Y 5-6 per ton. The coal industry shows lower profits than most other industries. In 1983 the MOCI roughly broke even, but many mines incurred losses.

3.31 Coal prices are fixed at the ex-mine levels by the central government for the mines under its control. Centrally allocated coal is priced almost uniformally throughout China. Exceptions are coal produced in Anhui, Jiangxi and Hunan -- which is priced with a 10% surcharge -- and in Henan -- where there is a 5% surcharge. The latest price adjustments are extending the surcharges to other coal-deficient regions. This reflects in part varying coal production costs from region to region. The average mine-mouth price in early 1984 was about Y 22 per ton, but prices for specific coals vary with a number of quality factors, including coal grade, ash, moisture, and sulphur content.

3.32 Local authorities are given some freedom to set prices for coal produced locally. In some regions local coal prices are influenced by market forces, particularly for output from collective mines, which is often sold to other provinces. Typically this causes variations in mine-mouth prices of between Y 10-60 per ton. The average for larger MOCI mines producing a greater portion of washed coal is about Y 26 per ton (for example, the list price of lump, low-ash, washed coal can be Y 50/ton).

3.33 Retail coal prices include transport costs. Rail is the predominant transport mode; rates were increased in December 1983 to an average of about Y 0.016/ton-km. Typically consumers pay about Y 10/ton in transport cost, but this can be higher than Y 30 per ton if road transport is used over long distances.

3.34 The current price structure does not adequately reflect the relative value of different coal qualities. The coal price formula takes no account of calorific value, although it does consider ash content. As a result, lignite is sometimes priced only marginally below export-quality coal. In addition, current prices do not reflect the economic cost differences for coal produced in various regions of the country.

3.35 Domestic coal prices in China are among the lowest compared with domestic coal prices in many coal-producing countries, a measure that largely reflects relative mining costs. Price quotations for other countries are shown in Table 3.3.

Table 3.3: AVERAGE MINE-MOUTH COAL PRICES FOR SELECTED COUNTRIES, 1982

Countries	Prices (In 1982 US$/million kcal)
China /a	2.0
United States	4.8
Fed. Rep. Germany	15.8
France	15.2
United Kingdom	15.5
Japan	15.2
Brazil	7.1
Colombia	3.2
Philippines	8.0
India	3.2
South Africa	2.0
Zimbabwe	2.0

/a At the official exchange rate of early 1984, Y 2.00 = US$1.00.

Source: Bank estimates.

3.36 Petroleum Prices. Ex-refinery prices of petroleum products and retail prices for crude oil (directly burned), petroleum products, and natural gas as of early 1985 are presented in Table 3.4. Ex-refinery prices for each given petroleum product are nearly uniform nationwide. Some variations exist from region to region, primarily resulting from transport costs for crude oil inputs to the refineries. Retail petroleum prices include mark-ups charged by commercial departments and taxes, which vary from product to product according to state policies. Retail prices also include transport costs, which vary significantly from region to region.

3.37 As shown in Table 3.4, the domestic structure of petroleum product prices is unlike the international structure. Kerosene and gasoline are priced relatively higher than diesel fuel (compared with international price ratios), but the differences do not appear to be substantial. Fuel oil prices, however, are extremely low, both in relation to domestic prices of other petroleum products and in relation to the international ratio between fuel oil and other product prices. There is little information on the level and structure of natural gas prices, but they appear low in relation to the international prices of competing fuels, i.e. the FOB price of fuel oil.

Table 3.4: PETROLEUM PRICES, EARLY 1985 a/

	Ex-refinery prices			Retail prices	Inter-
	Northeast China	Guangzhou	National average	national average	national prices
	----------(Y/ton)-------------			(Y/ton)	(US$/ton) /b
Gasoline					
66 octane	560	-	-	-	-
72 octane	580	-	-	-	-
Average	-	620	590	800	278
Kerosene	420	520	420	735	263
Diesel oil	240/c	280	240	560	245
Fuel oil					
Directly burned	n.a.	n.a.	n.a.	155/d	179
Other	n.a.	n.a.	n.a.	85/d	179
Average	45	91	55	132/e	179
Crude oil					
Ex-well	-	-	100/f	n.a.	205
Directly burned	n.a.	n.a.	n.a.	186/g	205

/a All Chinese prices refer to prices for allocation within planned quotas.
/b Gasoline, kerosene, diesel oil, fuel oil: FOB Singapore, March 4, 1985. Crude oil: OPEC average export price, FOB February 1985.
/c For industrial consumers.
/d Assumes an average transport cost of Y 30/ton.
/e Directly burned fuel oil is estimated at 90% of consumption (excluding refinery consumption).
/f Ex-well prices in Northwest China and the Zhongyuan field are slightly higher, at Y 130/ton.
/g Assumes an average transport cost of Y 30/ton, in order to provide a better comparison with fuel oil prices. Actual average transport costs are certainly significantly lower.

3.38 Oil producer prices are currently more than sufficient to cover current financial production costs of the oil industry as a whole. Further increases are being considered to ensure that oil fields with high and rising costs would cover their operating costs without transfers from the Government budget. As a pragmatic interim measure, a two-tier pricing system was introduced in 1981, whereby above-quota production is sold at Y 400/ton. This practice, if implemented without regard for a strategy for optimal reservoir depletion, may result in overproduction of the oil fields at the expense of overall oil recovery.

3.39 Electricity Tariffs. Average electricity tariffs are well below long-run marginal costs. Electricity tariffs as of 1982 are presented in Table 3.5. In that year the national average tariff was 6.6 fen per kWh. The standard tariff structure has generally remained unchanged since 1953, and is nearly uniform nationwide, except for the Northeast China Regional grid, where tariffs have traditionally been lower (even though this is an area where supplies are quite short). Special subsidized rates have been introduced from time to time to help new industrial and agricultural users during their initial years. These preferential rates, however, have seldom been revoked after the beneficiary firms matured. The average revenue per unit of energy has been declining owing to increased consumption by these groups.

Table 3.5: ELECTRICITY TARIFFS, 1982
(Fen /a per kWh)

Consumer category	Northeast China	Other areas	National average
Residential	8.8	15.0-20.0	16.0
Small industries/commercial	6.7	8.0-8.5	8.1
Large industries			
Demand charges (Y per month)			
On maximum demand	5.0	6.0)	
On KVA installed	3.5	4.0)	6.3 /b
Energy charge	3.5	5.8)	
Agriculture	6.0	4.4-5.7	5.4
Average	5.2	6.7-7.4	6.6

/a 100 fen = 1 Y.
/b Demand charge prorated over kWh used.

Source: Ministry of Water Resources and Electric Power (MWREP).

3.40 Agricultural consumers are charged the lowest tariff on the scale, while residential consumers are charged the highest - 16.0 fen/kWh. The relatively high tariff for residential consumers has been used to control their power use. For other users, demand is regulated through physical quotas. Tariffs for large industrial users are close to the average tariff and include a small demand charge.

3.41 In the context of Chinese accounting practices, which in the past did not include in costs any charge for fixed capital assets, the power sector as a whole has achieved satisfactory financial returns, despite the relatively low tariffs[6/]. However, this may change in the future because many major capital construction projects will now be financed through foreign and domestic loans rather than through state budgetary allocations. This is likely to result in higher financial burdens for the power sector. In addition, the unit costs for new capacity are increasing, particularly for hydroelectricity. Fuel costs have also been rising, particularly with the new tax on the direct burning of petroleum products, the higher coal prices, and increases in rail tariffs (which mostly affect coal prices).

3.42 For non-residential consumers average electricity tariffs are well below the LRMC.[7/] Marginal energy costs are closely linked to the economic cost of coal for each grid. On average this cost probably varies little from the current energy charges for large industries. Marginal capacity costs, on the other hand, are likely to be much higher than present charges for maximum demand; in the future, tariffs would have to reflect these costs and be based on peak-load pricing. In the short run, installed capacities are given and increases in demand translate into fuel or outage costs. In this case, capacity costs are equal to the economic cost of power cuts. In the long run, outage risks can be reduced and investments can be made within a least-cost program, such that an increase in demand translates into fuel and capacity costs. In this case, capacity costs are related to the investments required to meet peak demand and are expected to range from Y 15 to Y 30/kW per month (excluding low voltage distribution). In the long run China will have slack capacity at night and in the summer, when cogeneration plants used for district heating recover their full power rating. This may lead to differences in marginal cost from peak to off-peak and from summer to winter.

6/ Average power tariffs in other Asian countries in 1982 were: India, US¢4.2/kWh; Indonesia, US¢7.7/kWh; Thailand, US¢7.7/kWh; Malaysia, US¢9.5/kWh; South Korea, US¢9.6/kWh.

7/ Marginal cost of power supply is defined as the change in total cost of service resulting from small changes in demand. Its main components are: marginal energy cost, marginal capacity cost of generation and marginal capacity cost of transmission and distribution. This cost may change according to the place and time of use. Prices that are equal to marginal cost provide the correct signal to decision-makers that should result in market equilibrium at a volume of supply that optimizes economic efficiency. For every hour of system operation, the short run marginal energy cost of the system is the incremental running cost of the plant best suited to accommodate demand variations. Marginal capacity costs are defined as those expenses the power utility is ready to incur in order to maintain reliability of service, regardless of fuel costs. Usually, in a predominantly thermal system, this reliability will be required for provision of capacity (kW) during peak periods. In systems with a large hydro component, generating capacity expenditure may be required not only for purposes of ensuring kW availability at peak, but also to ensure firm energy in dry years.

D. Energy Conservation

3.43 In recent years China has given high priority to reducing growth in energy consumption and energy use per unit of output. The program for energy conservation has included a strong energy demand management program and some rationalization of the energy price structure. While the roles of prices and other financial incentives have been increased, however, administrative measures have remained the key instrument of the energy conservation strategy in the short run. In the long run, the Government hopes to increase energy efficiency through selective allocations for the construction of new infrastructure, the establishment of more energy-efficient enterprises, and major enterprise expansions or renovations. Administrative measures have included regulations for energy use, the creation of energy conservation centers, tightening supply quotas under the plan, and the provision of bonuses.8/

3.44 Enterprise incentives to increase energy efficiency have been introduced by reducing the allocation of supplies relative to production or profit targets. Unless enterprises reduce their unit energy consumption, they face possible penalties for not meeting output quotas, or they lose bonuses or additional profits for above-quota production. Moreover, new state laws and regulations concerning various unit energy consumption ceilings and interfuel substitution have been introduced.

3.45 In addition to these external pressures imposed by administrative measures, technical innovation and operational improvements to increase energy efficiency require decisions within enterprises. Hence it is crucial to improve capabilities for accurate measurement and reporting of consumption, for analysis of energy use patterns, and for implementation of energy saving actions. Although serious efforts to develop these capabilities have been made only recently, there is already evidence of improvement.

3.46 All state enterprises are mandated to install energy-consumption metering equipment by 1985. In addition, industrial enterprises that consume more than over 50,000 TCE per year must establish energy conservation units. Some 5,000 enterprise conservation units had been created as of early 1984,

---

8/ Bonuses are given for consumption below supply quota levels, as long as the production quota has been met. The bonus is a percentage of the difference between the supply quota and actual consumption. The bonus for coal is 8-15%, for fuel oil is 3-8%, for gasoline is an average of 3%, and for electricity is an average of 8%, respectively, of the cost of the energy saved. In Liaoning Province, reported figures were 13% for coal, 8% for fuel oil, and 15% for electricity. Note that when the percentage bonuses are applied to prevailing retail prices, the highest bonus per unit of energy saved is for electricity, followed by fuel oil, and finally coal. Such bonuses are distributed among enterprise workers. Additional conservation bonuses are given to workers for exceptional efforts in energy conservation work. In Liaoning Province, a first class bonus amounts to Y30 per worker, and a second class bonus amounts to Y 20 per worker.

usually with two or three full-time staff members under the supervision of a plant manager or chief engineer. The units are responsible for calculation of energy balances, implementation and evaluation of conservation measures, long-term energy planning, and training.

3.47 In order to assist enterprises, 50 energy conservation centers and 70 energy measurement stations -- usually under the auspices of local economic commissions -- have been created. At least one center exists in every major city. The role of these centers is to provide direct assistance and not to conduct research on new, more efficient technology. The centers provide a wide range of services for all types of enterprises, including auditing and meter installation, training information on new technologies, assistance to local governments, and consulting services for feasibility analysis of energy conservation projects. The conservation centers are a critical bridge between the producers of new, more energy efficient equipment and energy consumers. The staffs of conservation centers average about 20 persons. Operating funds are obtained from government allocations and/or service fees charged to enterprises. The energy measurement stations are less comprehensive, providing assistance primarily in energy auditing and the design, location, installation, and maintenance of measuring equipment.

3.48 There is little doubt that the energy conservation program has been highly successful. There are, however, a series of problems associated with using administrative measures in the absence of economic signals that accurately reflect opportunity costs (including opportunities in the world market). For example, an enterprise faced with energy supply quotas that have been tightened relative to output quotas and with no simple methods to improve energy efficiency may have to search for above-quota energy at any cost, particularly if the amount of energy required to fulfill output targets is relatively small. Since the main goal of individual enterprises is to fulfill their output quotas, obtaining small amounts of energy at exorbitant economic costs (such as driving a mid-sized truck long distances to pick up coal) may be in the interest of the enterprise, even if it is not economic for the country.[9/] Also, there are no strong incentives to use inputs efficiently if quota allocations are close to input requirements.

3.49 From an economy-wide perspective the attractiveness of energy-conservation investments should be examined in terms of the cost of energy to the overall economy. Individual enterprises will, however, evaluate the projects in terms of financial paybacks that incorporate the prices they actually pay. Given current prices, their evaluations could be different from those

---

9/ Use of own-account trucks to travel long distances to pick up small amounts of coal is apparently quite common, although very expensive. If a 4-ton Jiefang truck travels 1,000 km each way to pick up a load of coal, the gasoline costs would typically be over four times the cost of the coal purchased, at current prices. In terms of opportunity costs, the value of the gasoline consumed alone is about double the value of the coal procured. In addition, significant indirect costs are incurred in terms of staff and stock operation time.

made by the central administration. In coal conservation projects, for instance, the average investment cost per ton of raw coal saved in 300 major projects undertaken during 1981 was reported as Y 135. With an average retail price of coal supplied within the plan at about Y 30 per ton, enterprises face a payback period of some 6 years.[10/] If delays in output, for example, are considered, the payback period is even longer. The central authorities, however, face a current average LRMC for coal production and associated transportation of some Y 60 per ton, or twice the selling price, and hence may view the payback period on an investment of Y 135 per ton of coal saved as being less than one-half of that facing enterprises. Thus, these conservation projects would look much better to the central authorities than to the enterprise.

3.50 In a technical sense, improving energy efficiency may be defined as reducing energy consumption per unit of physical output or output value. Such efficiency, however, may not be desirable from the economic perspective. For example, it is not always desirable to aim for maximum energy saving, if this impairs the overall economics of production, operational reliability, or ease of plant operation. What is desirable for one plant in one location may not always be appropriate for a plant elsewhere. The economic evaluation of energy conservation investments would have to be based on a comparison of all costs and benefits associated with the energy saving investments, and not solely on the potential technical energy efficiency.

3.51 The use of administrative measures also raises problems because general criteria are applied to enterprises that operate under very different circumstances. One approach that apparently is being tried is to prepare guidelines for use by state authorities, establishing, for instance, a ceiling investment level per ton of coal equivalent saved, based on calculations of the real economic cost of energy. The consideration of economic costs and benefits in the preparation of the guidelines is a step in the right direction. However, the use of general ceilings may be problematic because the economics of energy conservation investments may vary dramatically for each case.

3.52 Although recent measures have been very effective to promote energy savings, the complexities involved in attempting to fine-tune the system to provide signals other than through prices to consumers and provide incentives for further economic improvements in energy efficiency are significant and will become increasingly difficult to overcome. One problem with the quota system is that, because historic consumption is a key factor in setting quotas, there may be no incentive for enterprises to reduce consumption because this may result in an even larger quota reduction in the future. Indeed it may be financially advantageous for the enterprises to keep quotas as large as possible: stockpiles can be saved for future production or sold or traded for other, more valuable, commodities.

10/ This figure includes a discount factor of 10% p.a. Additional costs and benefits from conservation projects are not considered in this calculation, but are often major and should also be taken into account in the investment evaluation.

3.53 Another problem resulting from the use of administrative measures is the system's inflexibility. Quick changes in energy supply, which may be necessary to respond to changes within enterprises (such as the development of new products and processes, expansion, etc.), are likely to be difficult. Because of such problems, and because other types of energy procurements may be uncertain or even impossible, many enterprises may prefer to maintain business as usual rather than incur the risks involved in changes in production. This is true even if such changes are profitable and highly desirable for the economy.

E. Price Reform

3.54 There are thus clear advantages in continuing reform toward a more flexible approach that provides more autonomy to individual entities. The system would increasingly rely on an energy price structure (including levels and relative prices) that reflects the relative scarcity of each competing fuel. This would influence consumption in the direction of the optimal or least-cost mix of energy sources required to meet future demand. Such reform would be a key component of the energy utilization and development strategy necessary to reduce the potential gap between expected supply and demand of energy by the year 2000. Two key advantages of higher energy prices as compared with administrative regulation are (a) that they get passed on in higher product prices and hence reduce consumption of energy-intensive products; and (b) that reductions in energy use occur automatically where the economic cost of reductions is least, provided that other prices are national and enterprises profit-sensitive. (Energy price reform is discussed further in Chapter 10 of the main report).

3.55 The current two-tiered pricing system for some fuels remains a troublesome compromise. In theory, given an appropriate level of quotas for producers and consumers, a movement of only above-quota prices to levels reflecting opportunity cost has the potential to achieve some of the same demand management incentives that would result from pricing all energy at opportunity cost. At the same time, the quota allocations would ensure the availability of basic supplies to all consumers and the maintenance of low prices for these allocations, which is especially important for the welfare of low-income consumers. However, inequities would undoubtedly persist regarding the average cost paid by different energy users, depending on the level of the quota allocated to them. Moreover, for the system to be effective in providing correct incentives, quotas in all enterprises would have to be consistently set at levels appropriate to allow for a sufficient margin between quota and above-quota consumption. The complexities involved in fine-tuning the quota system would probably make this approach extremely difficult.

3.56 It is important, especially to ensure optimal resource allocation (both within the energy sector and between it and the rest of the economy) and to provide incentives for conservation, that prices for each type of energy should continue to move so that they accurately reflect the incremental resource cost of supply to the national economy. This cost is the higher of

(a) the economic cost of supply [11/] and (b) the foregone opportunity cost of the resource in alternative uses (including the alternative of leaving the resource in the ground for future use).

3.57 From a purely economic point of view, for tradeables such as petroleum products, or products that substitute for tradeables, the economic cost is the opportunity cost measured by import or export price, whichever is relevant, plus or minus transportation and handling costs. For non-tradeables such as electricity, the relevant cost is the economic cost of supply measured by the expense required to meet a marginal increase in demand that is sustained into the future. This cost includes future operating and capital expenditures and excludes sunk or other costs which are incurred whether or not the additional unit is produced.

3.58 Obviously the issue of the appropriate pricing principle for potentially tradeable goods such as coal is more complex for China than for most other countries. For instance, China's domestic coal market is many times larger than the size of the international coal market. Only about 1% of the country's production is currently exported, but if in the long run China were to exploit its comparative advantage in coal, international prices may be driven down toward China's LRMC. In this case, therefore, the LRMC seems a more appropriate guide to prices than the current international prices. With respect to the coal price structure, prices in principle should reflect calorific value (and other characteristics of the coal such as ash content) more closely so that relative prices provide the proper signals to producers and consumers. In addition, prices should reflect the economic cost differences observed in various regions of the country. Mine-mouth prices in areas where coal is scarce should be higher than in low-cost regions, such as the North, where coal is in surplus. This would provide incentives to consume coal from the lower cost areas and would encourage overall production -- an especially important factor for the promotion of investments in coal by local governments and collective enterprises in coal-deficient regions. The Government's current policy is not only to gradually increase prices to the level of economic costs, but also to adjust the relative price among the various types of coal to reduce the existing distortions.

3.59 In the power sector, additional funds will have to be provided to finance higher investment costs through an increase in tariff revenues or an increase in state investment allocations, or both. An adjustment in the tariff structure as a means to pass on increasing costs to consumers, as well as to provide increased revenues for the power industry, has the potential benefit of encouraging conservation. This applies especially to the

---

11/ For depletable resources the economic cost of supply is defined as the long run marginal production cost which includes exploration, development and delivery costs plus a depletion premium which measures the value of the resource in the ground. For power it is defined as the incremental cost of all adjustments in the system expansion plan and system operations attributable to an incremental increase in demand that is sustained into the future.

industrial sector, which accounts for over 70% of power consumption. Of particular importance for large industries would be to move from uniform energy charges to rates based on the LRMC of power supply, varying according to locality, season, and time-of-day. In such schemes, most of the capacity cost will be recovered from peak users who are primarily responsible for system expansion.

3.60 More generally, a pricing system in which cost differences are reflected in power tariffs should increasingly prevail over administered rationing in order to ensure an efficient use of electricity. Restructured power tariffs would be particularly beneficial in areas that have wide cost differences and power shortages, and should precede large investments in power transmission lines and coal transportation facilities. For smaller consumers, the cost-based approach to pricing can be recommended with some simplifications and consideration of income distribution. For example, an off-peak rate for irrigation may be more important than tariffs which reflect differences between distribution costs in rural and urban areas. A reduction in connection fees and in the energy charge for consumption up to 50 kWh/month is an efficient form of subsidy and is generally sufficient to cover basic needs of low-income consumers.

4. COAL

A. Overview

4.01 China is one of the world's largest coal producers. The country has abundant reserves of good quality coal that can be mined relatively easily. The coal industry has expanded rapidly over the last three decades, with production growing from 66 million tons in 1952 to more than 770 million tons in 1984, an average growth rate of about 8% p.a. During 1980 and 1981, however, production actually declined below 1979 rates, and the industry only recently returned to close to historic rates of growth (see Appendix D.1). Although production in the short term has sometimes been achieved at the expense of long-term development potential and conservation of resources, the coal industry has shown resilience and dynamism in the face of many adversities. The industry now accounts for more than 70% of all commercial energy production.

4.02 The government target expressed during the early 1980s is to produce 1,200 million tons of coal per year by the year 2000, but coal requirements to sustain rapid economic growth may be even higher (see Chapter 2). To meet this target (not to mention surpassing it) will require further strengthening of production incentives, adequate financing, streamlining of project preparation and implementation and, perhaps most importantly, improved coordination between mining, coal transport, power generation and other large coal consumers. China has several important strategy options for the coal industry, which need to be integrated to form a balanced development program. These include issues such as regional development of coal resources, choice of the appropriate scale of mining and mining methods, improvements in project design and management, and adequate investment financing.

B. Organization of the Coal Industry

4.03 The Ministry of Coal Industry (MOCI) controls 580 of China's 20,000 mines. The MOCI mines are grouped under 84 Coal Mine Administrations (CMAs) or Coal Industry Companies (CICs). The CMAs and CICs report to Provincial Coal Boards,[1/] which in turn report to MOCI as well as to their respective provincial governments. The remaining mines are run either by the state through local governments at the provincial, county, or prefecture level, or as collective township and village (commune and brigade) enterprises.

4.04 The State Planning Commission (SPC) determines annual coal production targets together with MOCI, the Ministry of Railways (MOR), and coal user ministries. MOCI then allocates targets to each Provincial Coal Board for the volume of production, operating costs, and profits, depending on different conditions such as past overall performance, local averages, and national parameters. Arrangements for the delivery of coal quotas are made through

---

1/ Some of these Coal Boards were formerly the Coal Bureaus in the provincial governments.

direct contracts between the consuming, producing and transporting units in line with the annual production plan. There is frequent contact between MOCI or local authorities and consumers, as well as MOR representatives, to deal with problems that arise, for instance, regarding quality of coal delivered.

4.05 Most mine support activities are organized under the auspices of MOCI. These include geological exploration, project design and construction, manufacture of mining equipment, scientific research, and provisions for workers' health, education, and training. MOCI is also responsible for seeking foreign funds for joint venture coal projects through its affiliated institutions, the China National Coal Development Corporation, and the China National Coal Export and Import Corporation.

4.06 MOCI operates technical schools throughout China (see Table 4.1), and employees attend them on a work release basis. These institutions, which range from university level to vocational training, help to meet the coal industry's need for professional engineers, geologists, administrators and cadres, skilled technicians, and artisans. However, both their quantity and quality need to be improved. MOCI also sponsors selected students for overseas training.

Table 4.1: MOCI EDUCATION FACILITIES, 1983

	Number	Enrollment	Graduates/year
Universities & colleges	12	15,609 /a	3,490
Technical schools	40	16,534	5,889
Skilled worker training schools	110	31,522	14,190
Cadre schools	54	12,039	n.a.

/a In addition, about 15,000 workers are enrolled in "open" universities run by the CMAs.

Source: MOCI.

C. Coal Reserves

4.07 China's proven coal reserves of 640 billion tons are believed to be the largest in the world. Economically recoverable reserves in China are sufficient to meet projected demand for well over 100 years. China has more than 500,000 sq km of coal-bearing areas. Coal reserves are not evenly distributed: two-thirds of coal reserves are in the North, of which half are in Shanxi Province (see Appendix D.1). The distribution of economically recoverable reserves is even more skewed, the North accounting for almost 75% (and Shanxi alone 40%) of the total. The South and East, the most populous regions, are poorly endowed, with only 14% of total reserves and 10% of economically recoverable reserves.

Table 4.2: COMPARISON OF COAL RESOURCES AND RESERVES - USSR, US AND CHINA
(billion tons)

		Resources	Reserves /a
World total		13,604	2,000
of which	USSR	5,926	276
	US	3,600	438
	China	3,200	640
USSR, US & China as % of world total		80%	65%

/a Includes all deposits up to a depth of 900 m and a minimum seam thickness of 70 cm. Although broadly comparable, the definition of reserves in China differs from international standards.

Sources: China Coal Industry Yearbook, 1982 and Colliery Guardian, November 1983.

4.08 Most of China's coal reserves are hard coal, 17% of which is anthracite and 69% bituminous coal. Only 14% of reserves are lignite. Hard coal reserves are of good to medium quality. Ash content in situ is usually 10-25%,[2/] but generally sulphur is less than 1% and the calorific value is over 6,000 kcal/kg.

D. Coal Production

4.09 Central mines (tongpei meikuang, or mines from which output is distributed by the central government) have access to major coal deposits and account for just over half of coal production: 50.8% or 363 million tons in 1983 (Table 4.3). These mines provide coal principally for national rather than local requirements; approximately one-third of their production is traded interprovincially, going from coal-surplus to coal-deficit areas. The remaining production comes from locally controlled mines. Many of these are small-scale, with production of less than 600,000 tons/year. Many collective mines produce only on a part-time basis. Although total production is now rising, due to strong growth of collective mines and to a recovery of central mines, it dropped by 15 million tons per year (mtpy) in 1980, when production

2/ When mined, the ash content increases due largely to contamination with rock (dilution). The ash content of raw coal has risen from 22% in 1957 to 27% in 1981, but the increase is not due to any significant change in the in situ ash content of coal mined and only some of the increase in dilution is due to mechanization.

Table 4.3: RAW COAL PRODUCTION BY TYPE OF ADMINISTRATION, 1965-82
(million tons)

	1965		1979		1980		1981		1982		1983 /a	
	Volume	%	Volume	%	Volume	%	Volume	%	Volume	%	Volume	%
Central mines/b	164.3	70.9	357.8	56.3	344.4	55.5	335.0	53.9	349.9	52.5	363.0	50.8
Local state mines/b	57.8	24.9	171.5	29.0	162.1	26.2	160.0	25.8	170.3	25.6	182.0	25.4
Township & village mines/b	9.7	4.1	106.3	16.7	113.6	18.3	126.6	20.3	146.1	21.9	170.0	23.8
Total	231.8	100.0	635.5	100.0	620.1	100.0	621.6	100.0	666.3	100.0	715	100.0

/a Preliminary figures.
/b Central mines refer to mines from which output is distributed by the central government (tongpei meikuang), local state are mines operated by provinces, prefectures or counties, and township and village mines (formerly referred to as commune and brigade mines) are operated by rural collectives (xiangjen meikuang).

Source: MOCI.

from central and local state mines fell by more than 20 mtpy, largely as a result of neglected long-term development work during the previous period of instability.

4.10 In 1982, China produced some 140 million tons of anthracite and small amounts of lignite. The remaining 500 million tons were bituminous thermal coal, about two-thirds of which had coking properties (Appendix D.1).

Cost of Production

4.11 China is a low-cost coal producer by international standards.[3/] Chinese operating costs are typically about Y 20/ton, while mine capital costs average approximately Y 110/ton capacity (including mine-related infrastructure, such as workshops, rail lines to mine-gate, but excluding other infrastructure, such as trunk rail lines and welfare facilities). Geological and mining conditions are very favorable, and wages are low (the average wage, plus bonuses, is less than Y 100/month). The latter compensates for low labor productivity: only about 0.92 tons per manshift in MOCI mines in 1982.

4.12 Mining conditions and costs vary among regions. The North, which contributes a large part of production, enjoys the lowest costs, as reserves lie in thick, gently-dipping coal seams, usually less than 300 m deep. Average operating costs in Shanxi in 1983 varied between Y 10 per ton for small-scale mining of outcrops and about Y 18 per ton for large mechanized mines. Average investment costs (including, in the case of larger mines, related infrastructure and social services such as housing, schools and hospitals) varied between Y 60-70 per ton for small mines and Y 120-140 per ton for large mechanized underground mines.[4/] Costs in other regions are normally higher because mining conditions are less favorable.

4.13 Long-run marginal costs (LRMC) have been estimated for incremental production of about 500 mtpy, which would cover mines beginning production approximately to the year 2000. These are based on available information concerning geological and mining conditions in the country, on about 20 projects started or about to be started, and on average cost data by type of mine in several regions of the country. (The methodology used is described in Appendix D.2.) LRMC for the North were calculated to be Y 36-44 per ton for coal of about 6,000 kcal/kg. Given the abundant reserves exploitable at low cost and provided that real wage increases are largely compensated for by productivity gains, LRMC in real terms are not expected to increase significantly in the future. For Central and Northeast China, LRMC (after adjustment for quality differences with coal in North China) are believed to be almost Y 60

3/ Only South Africa, India and the western US mines are competitive with Chinese mining.

4/ The much lower cost of small mines is offset by their shorter life and other problems (see para. 4.17).

per ton. Costs in the South are almost twice as high as in the North. LRMC in these regions are expected to show a moderate upward trend (perhaps 1% per year or so), given the more limited economically exploitable reserves.

4.14 China's competitive position in the international coal market, particularly in the Pacific Rim, is strong and even likely to improve with time. In early 1984, FOB prices received by Chinese exporters were about US$40 per ton (Y 80 at the exchange rate current at that time) for thermal coal, although they averaged about US$50 per ton during the 1980-83 period. FOB prices for coking coal and anthracite are US$5-10 higher. LRMC of export-quality Chinese coal are about Y 50 per ton for the North.[5/] Because railway costs are estimated (on a LRMC basis) at just over Y 0.02 per ton-km (compared to average total railway charges for coal of about Y 0.016), coal in North China can be delivered at coastal ports for about Y 70 per ton, including a railway charge of about Y 20 per ton, which is low by international standards (Appendix D.2). Moreover, given the proximity to Japan and other regional markets, ocean freight rates for China are generally lower than those paid by other coal exporters.

E. Sector Issues and Constraints

Regional Coal Development

4.15 Chinese planners have long faced a choice between (a) concentrating coal production in the North where costs are lowest and (b) developing more costly coal resources closer to consumption centers to reduce transport costs. In the past emphasis was given to producing near consumption centers. Current plans, however, emphasize relative increases in coal production in the North (particularly in Shanxi Province), which is expected to produce some 60% of incremental production (Table 4.5).

4.16 It is difficult to establish precisely whether the planned regional distribution of coal production conforms to a least cost development program. Any such program should minimize mining plus transport costs of coal delivered to consumers. On the basis of current LRMC, there appears to be hardly any difference in cost for coal delivered to, say, the Northeast between projects located in the North and those located closer to the market. Nevertheless, when looking as far ahead as the year 2000, the proposed regional emphasis appears well placed because the comparative advantage of the North in coal production is likely to grow with time (Appendix D.2).

5/ Including a 20% adjustment to bring average coal to export specifications; this is because Chinese coal has a medium to high ash content and usually requires washing before being exported. Among major international coal producers, LRMC of production of export coal are estimated at about US$30-35 per ton in the US (for eastern mines), Australia and Canada, and about US$20-25 in South Africa. They are projected to increase by about 1% per year in the long-term.

Type of Mine Development

4.17 The Government's long-term policy is to develop both large-scale and small local mines, taking advantage of their relative strengths. Development of centrally controlled, large-scale mines has been emphasized in major coal basins, in order to provide stable and long-term coal supplies for China's major urban demand centers. Large scale mines in China can achieve greater productivity, have higher reserve recovery rates, and are safer than existing small mines. In many instances, small-scale mining of large deposits has preempted large-scale exploitation, resulting in low production rates.[6/] Additional problems connected with small-scale mine development include generally shorter mine lifetimes, less stable production, and poor safety records. Small-scale mining also entails major advantages, however, such as shorter construction times and an ability to mobilize local financial and management resources. Perhaps most important, local scattered mines are able to serve local markets with minimum transport costs.

4.18 The development of small collective mines has made a major contribution to increases in coal production during the last decade and a half, and especially in recent years, local mines in relatively coal-rich areas have begun to make significant contributions towards meeting demand in major urban centers. Several changes have been promoted recently. First, the central government has increased the resources allocated for investment in and maintenance of local mines. Second, incentives have been offered to local governments to increase production (e.g., a lower sales tax on local coal and special grants for increasing coal shipments to other provinces or for surpassing specified production quotas). Third, regulations have been introduced to allow governments in coal-deficit localities to invest in areas that have coal reserves but lack the resources to develop them. Finally, measures have been taken to improve technical levels and safety in local mines (even though this will increase costs) and to reduce the competition for reserve blocks between small and large mines.

Mining Methods

4.19 Modern mining technology co-exists with the most rudimentary methods of production in China. The choice of technology is intrinsically tied to the scale of mining, and this is in turn tied to the size, depth and mineability of coal deposits. Small-scale mining using traditional labor-intensive methods seems to make sense for small deposits (such as small outcrops) or for the peripheral areas of larger deposits lying close to the surface. Open-pit coal mining accounts for less than 5% of total production; most deposits amenable to this mining method (which by its nature is mechanized) are in remote locations in western Shanxi and Nei Monggol. Medium or large-scale mining is required for deeper deposits that require costly shaft sinking.

6/ For example, a few large deposits lying close to the surface in populated areas (also in Shanxi) have in the past been developed through numerous small mines, though they would have been suitable for low-cost, large-scale open-pit mining.

4.20 For centuries, coal production in China has relied on the small-scale development of outcrops, but future development will depend increasingly on deeper deposits. The North (including Shanxi) possesses vast reserves of high quality coal in seams that are generally too deep for small-scale or open-pit mining. However, they can still be exploited at low cost through one mechanized mine or several smaller nonmechanized mines. The former alternative offers savings on shaft sinking costs (one pair of shafts rather than several shafts would be needed) and on surface and transport facilities (given the spatial concentration of facilities). The latter offers lower equipment costs and a shorter construction time.

4.21 The issue of mechanization deserves particular attention in an economy such as China's, which has an abundant, underutilized labor force but scarce capital. The level of mechanization in China is lower than in other countries. Increased mechanization is regarded by MOCI as necessary to increase production, efficiency and resource recovery. Consequently, since 1979, MOCI has accelerated development of mechanization of mining and excavating. Nevertheless, the current low level of mechanization is frequently economically justified given the relative abundance of labor and appropriate mining conditions, though it results in low productivity. For shallow deposits (around 150 m), nonmechanized mines are cheaper to construct and operate per unit of output than larger, mechanized mines. For deeper deposits (200-400 m), mechanized mines are competitive.

4.22 Mechanization is expected to gain an economic edge with time and therefore to play an increasing role in China, as technological developments make equipment generally more efficient and as the capacity to manufacture such equipment domestically at lower cost is developed. More balanced mechanization applied to all aspects of mine development and coal extraction (including roadway drivages, coal mining, hoisting, etc.) will lead to improved productivity as those in the mining industry become more familiar with advanced technology. Finally, increased concern for safety and environmental protection is likely to emphasize the advantages of greater mechanization.

Coal Processing

4.23 Washing as a method of coal beneficiation has been slow to develop in China. A relatively small proportion of coal (approximately 18% in 1983) is washed, mainly coking coal for the steel industry. Coal washing capacity needs to be expanded, mainly for coal supplied to steel and chemical (fertilizer) plants.

4.24 Coal washing has the advantage of improving the efficiency of coal use and reducing the amount of inert material that must be transported. The lower ash content of washed coal is counterbalanced in part, however, by increases in moisture. Coal washing is, moreover, costly and often results in low run-of-mine to washed coal recovery factors. Losses in middlings and refuse can be as high as 40% (25-30% is more common), but middlings can be used if washeries are linked to power generating plants.

4.25 The potential for greater use of briquetted anthracite is also worth pursuing. Simple briquetting equipment could be particularly helpful in small mines in the colder parts of China where the shortage of domestic fuel in winter is acute, especially in rural areas. Wider use of high quality briquettes for domestic purposes, produced on an industrial scale, could decrease atmospheric pollution in cities and improve efficiency of utilization, but their manufacture for large cities would probably need to be established at a proper industrial level.

Project Design and Management

4.26 Under the current system, state-imposed design norms leave little flexibility for taking account of particular geological conditions, which can lower the cost effectiveness of some projects. There is considerable room for improvement in the design of mining projects as greater autonomy on matters such as project design is given to productive units under the system reform program.

4.27 Mine construction times are currently longer than in other countries for similar work (construction time is more than six years for central mines) and could be shortened. Coordination among the many government entities involved in project execution is sometimes poor and this results in delays. To alleviate this problem, efforts are now being made to streamline procedures and to increase the authority of CMAs over construction activities.

F. Growth to the Year 2000

4.28 The target of 1,200 million tons for the year 2000 would allow coal to maintain its share of total commercial energy production in China. Current views within the Government are that the target could even be fulfilled earlier than planned. Higher production levels, on the order of 1,400 mtpy, will probably be needed to satisfy the requirements of rapid economic growth. The production of 1,400 mtpy of coal by the year 2000 would require satisfactory resolution of the subsector issues and constraints discussed in the previous section, as well as the mobilization of resources to finance the required investments and the planning for and timely implementation of linkages between coal mining, transport and consumers. Success in all these aspects is crucial given the long lead times required to start coal production, especially in larger mines, and to put in place all the associated infrastructure.

4.29 High and low coal production scenarios by the year 2000 and possible expansion of the different types of mines over the next two decades are presented in Table 4.4.

Table 4.4: COAL PRODUCTION SCENARIOS (in million tons)

	1983 (Actual)	2000 Low	Average Growth Rate (%)	2000 High	Average Growth Rate (%)
Central mines	363	750	4.4	800	4.8
Local state mines	182	240	1.6	250	1.9
Township & village mines	170	210	1.3	350	4.3
Total	715	1200	3.1	1400	4.0

4.30 Under both scenarios the bulk of the expansion in production is concentrated in central mines (90% of all capacity increase in the low scenario). This is consistent with the Government's push for expansion of existing medium-scale mines through mechanization and construction of large mining units (both open-pit and underground) in the country's gigantic coal basins (especially in Shanxi).

4.31 Collective township and village mines can play an increasingly positive role in China as long as mining is not done in reserve blocks amenable to low-cost, large-scale exploitation. Small-scale mines make economic sense under a wide variety of circumstances and geological and mining conditions in China. Indeed, there are numerous small coal outcrops in peripheral areas of large deposits which can be economically exploited on a small scale with labor intensive mining methods. The evidence also suggests that collectives are poised for rapid increase in their coal production, partly because of the Government's recent policy to allow them to become more responsive to the market. Currently, prices for coal produced by collectives are virtually free of administrative controls and are therefore rising rapidly, as is the interest of collectives in coal mining investments.

4.32 In terms of regional emphasis, the North is expected to contribute almost 60% of incremental production under the low scenario but would need to contribute even more if the high target is to be achieved (see Table 4.5). The share of the North is larger in the high case because its geological conditions favor small-scale mining, and a very large percentage of the incremental production by collectives would be concentrated there.

Table 4.5: REGIONAL COAL PRODUCTION, 1980-2000
(in million tons)

	1980 (Actual)	2000 Low	% of Increase	2000 High	% of Increase
Northeast	99	181	14.2	185	11.0
North	205	550	59.5	715	65.4
East	105	171	11.4	175	9.0
South Central	96	131	6.0	140	5.6
Southwest	65	82	2.9	85	2.6
Northwest	50	85	6.0	100	6.4
Total	620	1,200	100.0	1400	100.0

Sources: MOCI and Mission projections.

4.33 LRMC of coal mining are expected to remain fairly stable and to be similar for both scenarios because the North, with a fairly stable LRMC, would contribute the bulk of incremental production, particularly under the high scenario. Moreover, the cost of coal delivered to consumers is not likely to change significantly because transport costs are expected to rise only slowly, if at all, over the long term. Eastward and southward traffic from the North should benefit from increasing availability of low-cost, high-throughput railway facilities such as the proposed Datong-Qinhuangdao line designated for coal transport.

4.34 Under both scenarios, most mine development is expected to be underground, but a few selected large open-pit mines should also be developed. The Government expects open-pit mining to contribute about 200 mtpy in new capacity so as to treble its share of total production to over 15% by the year 2000. Open-pit mining is an area where China requires the largest input of foreign know-how and has thus been singled out for joint ventures with international mining companies.[7/] Because direct foreign investment in coal mining could fall well short of expectations, other means of obtaining this know-how, such as contract mining arrangements, might have to be explored.

4.35 The Government plans to increase the coal washery throughput from roughly 120 mtpy in 1983 to 200 mtpy in 1990 and 300-350 mtpy in the year 2000. Considering the cost of coal washing (including the calories lost during the process) against the benefits, these targets appear reasonable. In any case, by the year 2000, almost 100 mtpy of middlings would be produced.

7/ One agreement in principle has already been signed with Occidental Petroleum (US) to develop jointly with the MOCI a large open-pit mine, partially for export.

This would require that power plants be constructed close to washing facilities to avoid large energy losses because low-calorie middlings cannot justify the cost of transporation over long distance.

Investment Requirements

4.36 Under both scenarios financing needs for coal development would be larger than in the past. In the low scenario, annual state financing requirements for central mines may amount (in 1983 prices) to Y 4.8 billion for mine development, including related mine infrastructure, and Y 1.0 million for training, research, and other MOCI activities. Mine development costs were calculated on the basis of an average investment cost per ton of mine capacity of Y 120, which allows for replacement of equipment. In the case of small mines, costs allow for a high rate of reinvestment due to their shorter life. In both cases the cost projection includes the effect of mine closures. The average yearly financing requirement in this case is only slightly larger than that available in 1983. In that year the state budget for coal capital expenditures was increased to Y 3.6 billion (from Y 2.4 billion in 1981), and collective mines must have invested several hundred million yuan to expand production by over 20 mtpy.

4.37 The average yearly financial requirements in the high scenario (also in 1983 prices) are expected to rise to about Y 6.4 billion for mine development and Y 1.2 billion for other activities. Given the Government's policy of increasing coal prices sometime within this decade, significant resources should be mobilized for investments by local government and collectives. At the same time, the resources made available to MOCI are being increased under the seventh Five-Year Plan to more than Y 6 billion a year in current terms. This would come close to meeting the MOCI financing requirements under the high scenario.

4.38 To supplement domestic funds, efforts are also being made to mobilize foreign resources in the form of foreign loans as well as direct foreign investment. However, a much deteriorated international coal market works against extensive foreign investments, because foreign investors would basically be interested in coal for export.

G. Intersectoral Coordination

4.39 Of key importance in the planning process is coordination of the activities of interacting ministries, such as MOCI, MOR, and MWREP. This affects decisions regarding location of thermal power plants, investments in infrastructure, matching of coal supply with demand and coordination with the capacity of transport modes to deliver the required amounts. However, coordination between the ministries dealing with coal, transportation, and power is presently weak, although it appears to be improving. Missed opportunities or wrong investment decisions can have significant economic costs, as discussed below.

4.40 Coordination between coal washing and power generation is also important to ensure the use of middlings. This material with a high ash content is normally mixed with coal for use by power plants. Middlings represent

15-30% of the calories contained in coal undergoing washing. They have often been wasted because there has been no market nearby and they cannot justify heavy transport costs. Thus decisions on the location of washeries (and also decisions on what coal should be washed) are closely linked to planning decisions on the location of power plants and on the type of fuel used by the power sector.

4.41 A further issue requiring coordination among various ministries and agencies involves the location of large industrial coal users such as cement and fertilizer plants at demand centers or in mining areas. In this instance, the trade-off is between the cost of transporting coal to plants located close to demand centers and the cost of delivering the output of the industrial plants from the coal-rich areas to demand centers.

4.42 Finally, another aspect of coordination and planning is to match the available coal with the demand of various industrial and other consumers (in terms of both volume and quality) in the most cost-effective manner. Production of anthracite is insufficient to meet the needs of residential, commercial, and some industrial consumers. Currently, some of the least desirable coals (e.g., coal fines with high volatile matter and high sulphur content) are often supplied to urban residential and commercial customers, unnecessarily exacerbating serious urban air pollution problems. While about 40 million tons of coking coal are consumed by domestic coke plants and a couple of million tons a year are exported, the remainder is consumed as thermal coal. Since coking coal commands a premium, an effort should be made to cut down nondiscriminating domestic use of coking coal and expand production of non-coking coal.

4.43 Coal Transport. The two major issues concerning coal transport are:

(a) The optimal balance between coal development near major consumption areas (Northeast and East) and coal development in Shanxi (including Western Nei Monggol and Northern Shaanxi). Coal in Shanxi is abundant and of good quality; therefore, both development costs and operating costs of mines are lower than elsewhere. However, transport distances to large consuming areas are in excess of 1,000 km.

(b) The trade-off between coal and electricity transport. North China has high-quality coal exploitable at low cost. The question is the trade-off between the transport of coal to industries and power plants at load centers and the transport of electricity from mine-mouth generating plants.

4.44 Major coal routes are illustrated in Map IBRD 18224 (at the end of this annex), and interregional coal transport volumes by rail are given in Table 4.6.

Table 4.6: INTERREGIONAL COAL TRANSPORT BY RAIL, 1982
(million tons)

Origins	Destinations N-E	N	E	S-C	S-W	N-W	Total
Northeast	75.4	2.0	-	-	-	-	77.4
North	22.0	109.3	21.1	15.0	0.3	1.9	169.6
East	-	0.6	67.1	1.1	-	-	68.8
South-Central	1.4	0.4	3.4	54.7	0.2	0.1	60.2
South West	-	-	-	3.4	25.5	-	28.9
Northwest	0.7	1.9	3.3	1.9	-	25.8	33.6
Total	99.5	114.2	94.9	76.1	26.0	27.8	438.5

Source: Ministry of Railways.

4.45 The inter-regional flows can be summarized as follows:

	N-E	N	E	S-C	S-W	N-W
	(million tons)					
Shipped to other regions	2.0	60.30	1.7	5.5	3.4	7.8
Received from other regions	24.1	4.90	27.8	21.4	0.5	2.0
Net flows	-22.1	55.40	-26.1	-15.9	2.9	5.8

4.46 When considering the issue of local production near consumption centers versus production in North China, it is necessary to compare the total cost of coal mining and transport to the final users. Because most rail lines out of the coal-producing areas of North China are at or near capacity, the appropriate transport cost to use in the comparison is the long-run variable cost (LRVC) based on the construction of new lines. Such cost would vary from place to place depending on local conditions, especially topography. Calculation of a rough order of magnitude indicates that LRVC of 2 to 2.5 fen/km would be adequate for the above comparison (Appendix E). This would mean that local production cost, say in Liaoning Province (approximately 1,000 km away from the Shanxi coal fields), could be about Y 20/ton higher than in Shanxi and still be competitive. Some notional costs of coal production and transport that would face coal users in the Northeast are shown below. Coal production costs vary widely, as do transport costs. A coal mine that is not on the railway can face very high transport costs. Delivery over 100 km by road in the Northeast can be as expensive as bringing the coal from Shanxi by rail. Therefore, a more valid comparison would be done on a case-by-case basis.

	Coal production cost (LRMC) /a	Transport costs to Northeast	Total
	Y/ton		
Shanxi Province	36-44	25	61-69
Northeast	60-70	5	65-75

/a Long-Run Marginal Cost (LRMC) has been calculated using the average incremental cost (AIC) method, which involves discounting (10% is used here) all incremental costs of coal production (capital and operating) and dividing this total by the discounted value of incremental outputs.

4.47 Despite reservations concerning generalization, the figures demonstrate that Shanxi coal can be competitive in coastal China despite the transport distance. Deposits in large seams are easily accessible and both investment and operating costs are lower, while the coal is generally of higher quality and calorific value than in other regions. Therefore, further development in North China appears to make good economic sense. Indeed, the region is expected to account for almost 60% of the coal production increase by the year 2000 under the "low" production scenario for the year 2000 and more than 60% under the "high" scenario.

4.48 With the greater concentration of production in the North, inter-regional flows of coal will increase greatly by the year 2000 -- leading to the second issue of whether to transport coal or to transport electricity. Much research and study are being done in China on this matter, and an analysis in Appendix E illustrates the effect of various parameters and indicates orders of magnitude. The conclusion is that for coal above 5000 kcal/kg, rail transport would be more economical than electricity transport, even if rail transportation involves the relatively expensive option of construction of a new single-track (as opposed to double-track) line. Since Shanxi coal is generally of higher calorific value (6,000 kcal/kg or more), mine-mouth power generation and long-distance transmission are likely to be justified only in the case of use of middlings, which should be increasingly available as a result of a greater washing effort.

4.49 Preliminary plans by MWREP envisage the development of 45,000-60,000 MW of thermal capacity at mine-mouth (of which 25,000-35,000 MW would be in North China, i.e., Shanxi and adjacent areas of Nei Monggol and Shaanxi), and 50,000-60,000 MW at load centers (of which 20,000-30,000 MW would be in major load centers in Northeast, East, and South China). Increased capacity at load centers would require transport of some 150-200 million tons of coal annually (calculated on the basis of 3 tons of coal per installed kW), of which the

Northeast, East and South China would account for 60 to 90 million tons, mostly from North China.

4.50 Future coal flows will generally follow the same pattern as current flows, but with large increases on the lines out of Shanxi Province and surrounding areas. While coastal shipping from northern ports to southern destinations can increase, coal will still go by rail for the first part of the journey between the mines and the ports. The Ministry of Railways (MOR) expects that the percentage of coal production transported by rail (now 66% of raw coal production) will not change greatly by the year 2000. This appears realistic; on the one hand increased mine-mouth power generation will reduce the need for transport, but on the other greatly increased reliance on Shanxi coal will increase it. Furthermore, all new generating capacity in coal-producing areas will not be exactly at the mine-mouth but will still require coal transport.

4.51 In the high production scenario of 1,400 million tons of coal by the year 2000, perhaps 715 million tons -- or more than half the total coal production -- would come from North China. This means that 450 to 500 million tons (or 4 to 5 times the planned volume in 1984) would need to be transported out of Shanxi and adjacent areas of Shaanxi and Nei Monggol. The predominant directions of flow will be east and south, since the larger deficit areas will be in East and South Central China, with smaller ones in the Northeast and Southwest.

4.52 With projects presently under construction or about to start, the rail capacity for coal transport from Shanxi should be near 300 million tons by the early 1990s. This includes the electrification of the existing double-track line between Datong and Qinhuangdao and the new double track electrified line planned in the same corridor. The latter would be suitable for heavy unit train operation and would have a capacity of over 100 million tons p.a. Construction, to start in 1985, is estimated to cost some Y 6 million/km. Other lines are also planned from South and Central Shanxi province.

4.53 To handle the 450-500 million tons, it would be necessary to (a) construct another double track electrified line for heavy unit trains similar to the new Datong-Qinhuangdao line to carry an additional 100 million tons or so p.a. (such a new line should probably go in a southeastern direction and a possible route is the Shuoxian-Shijiazhuang-Yanzhou corridor, presently under consideration); and (b) either further increase the capacity of existing lines out of the Shanxi area by double tracking and electrification or build another single track electrified line, depending on the comparative cost of such alternatives. Slurry pipelines may also contribute to relieve the pressure on railways. The major problem seems to be the availability of water in Shanxi province.

4.54 In addition to the above lines out of Shanxi for shipments to South Central China, China's north-south rail capacity must also be increased. Besides electrifying the existing lines and lengthening stations for operating larger trains, a new line may well become necessary in the 1990s. Plans are being made for such a line, running between the existing two north-south lines and sections are already under construction in Anhui province. Construction of extensions to the North may have to be accelerated at least to connect with the Lianyungang-Baoji line. For shipments to the Northeast, rail capacity must be increased north of Qinhuangdao. Some of the coal can also be shipped to Dalian and Yingkou for coastal uses in Liaoning Province.

4.55 The combined use of rail and water transport may be economical on some routes but not necessarily on all; therefore, careful analysis on a case-by-case basis should be performed before assigning the traffic to any particular route and modal combination. For example, it appears that coastal shipping from northern ports will be more attractive than the use of the Chang Jiang to deliver coal to the Shanghai area. The Government estimates that for Datong-Shanghai combined rail/water transport (through Qinhuangdao port) could be 20% cheaper than direct rail haulage. While the first two routes below can be considered for joint transport, the third is obviously not economical since rail distance to Wuhan is only 10 km shorter than to Nanjing and there are still 800 km by water remaining.

	Rail (km)	Water (km)	Total distance (km)
1. Datong to Shanghai	1,840		1,840
Datong-Qinhuangdao-Shanghai	620	1,350	1,970
2. Taiyuan to Shanghai	1,500		1,500
Taiyuan-QingDao-Shanghai	920	750	1,670
3. Taiyuan-Nanjing	1,190		1,190
Taiyuan-Wuhan-Nanjing	1,180	800	1,980

4.56 Some 100 million tons of coal could be economically transported to East and South China by a combination of rail and water transport by the year 2000. Northern ports such as Qinhuangdao, Shijiusuo, and Lianyungang are being developed for the shipment of coal, and plans are being made for a coal terminal in Qingdao. With these developments, capacity for shipping coal from the North will be around 40-45 million tons and would have to be increased by some 60 million tons by the year 2000. Development of receiving ports in southern areas seems less advanced, but the problem may not be so serious if consideration is given to simplified coal unloading facilities combined with the use of self-unloading ships. To relieve port congestion, large coal users such as steel mills and power plants on coastal locations usually develop their own terminals. The use of self-unloading ships can save costly port infrastructure such as berths for along-side mooring, shore equipment, and dredging. The only infrastructure needed to receive self-unloading ships is mooring dolphins, a coal hopper, and a conveyor belt on a simple trestle. The trestle for the conveyor belt can extend to deep water, reducing dredging cost considerably. The extra cost of a 50,000 DWT self-unloading ship compared to a regular ship is only about Y 10 to Y 12 million. This could be much less than the extra port infrastructure cost needed for conventional ships for the level of traffic that may be required by a power plant, for instance. Turn-around time in ports can also be reduced greatly with self-unloading capacities of 2,000-3,000 t/hour, thus allowing more efficient use of ships.

4.57 Besides specialized facilities for large users, the use of floating terminals should also be considered for transhipment to smaller vessels. Such floating terminals could be anchored off-shore or in river estuaries (e.g., Chang Jiang, Zhu Jiang). They could be fed by self-unloading ships from the North and could then load smaller ships and barges for final distribution through rivers and canals. The advantages of these floating terminals are the same as those mentioned above: reduced port infrastructure and reduced dredging. In addition, they can be established much more rapidly than fixed port infrastructure can be constructed. Furthermore, they can be moved should markets change over time. The combination of these solutions would greatly reduce the investments needed to develop coal receiving facilities as well as speed up their entering service.

4.58 In conclusion, the development of the necessary transport infrastructure is not an insurmountable task provided adequate planning is carried out. The new Datong-Qinhuangdao line for heavy unit trains should be available in the early 1990s, and another similar line could be available by the year 2000, along with further improvement of existing lines and the completion of a new north-south line - provided the investment level in railways is substantially increased. For coal ports in the North, the increased capacity of some 60 million tons would require 10-15 berths, which is technically feasible. Costs will vary greatly with location and may range from Y 150-200 million per berth with all related equipment. The same capacity has to be developed for receiving coal in the South, and the alternatives mentioned above may help to minimize costs.

H. Environmental Impact of Coal Use

4.59 Air pollution from burning coal, including particulate emissions in the form of fly-ash and smoke, and emissions of sulphur and nitrogen oxides, is already a very serious problem in urban China. By far the largest and most noticeable source of pollution is the burning of coal in industry and for household cooking and heating, which often leads to acute smog conditions during winter in parts of northern China. Household coal stoves and the numerous boilers used by small commercial and industrial enterprises are the greatest direct source of smoke and soot. Larger industrial plants and power stations generally have more efficient combustion systems and contribute less smoke, but generate large quantities of fly ash from the burning of pulverized fuel. Both large and small consumers contribute to the emission of sulphur dioxide, but the larger plants and power stations discharge this through relatively tall stacks, whereas smaller consumers discharge at or near ground level, with a more devastating effect on the local environment.

4.60 In northern China, coal burned has sulphur contents averaging at about 1%. Some locally produced coal in other areas may have sulphur contents as high as 5%, but on the whole, China is blessed with reserves of relatively low-sulphur coal. Nevertheless, the sheer quantities of coal consumed, and limited application of (even simple) pollution control technologies, have led to high concentrations of total suspended particulates and sulphur dioxide in many northern cities. While the national control standard for sulphur dioxide is a yearly average of 0.15 mg per cubic meter, many cities frequently exceed the standard during winter, sometimes by several tens of times. Sulphur dioxide emissions also have been increasing - in Beijing, for example, the average during winter was 0.16 mg per cubic meter in 1971, but 0.22 mg per cubic meter in 1980.

4.61 Although concentrated air pollution in urban areas represents the most immediate concern, consideration should also be given to possible long-term impacts of nationwide or regionwide coal consumption. Many scientists believe that increased levels of carbon dioxide in the atmosphere resulting from increasing coal consumption could lead to major changes in climate. Linkages may also exist between incidence of acid rain, already reported in some parts of China, and coal consumption. Nationwide emissions of major pollutants (sulphur oxides, nitrogen oxides, hydrocarbons, and photochemical oxidants) must, however, be put in proper perspective. Total sulphur dioxide emission from coal consumption in China was estimated at about 12 million tons in 1980. In the United States, with a similar land area, this level had already been surpassed in the late nineteenth or early twentieth century, and sulphur dioxide emissions reached an average of 2.4 tons/sq km in 1940, about twice the present level in China (excluding emissions from biomass combustion). In the two provinces with probably the highest density of sulphur dioxide emissions, Hebei and Liaoning, emission densities appear to be close to the current national average in the US, and 4-6 times lower than the US states with the highest sulphur dioxide emission densities (Ohio and Pennsylvania). Current densities of nitrogen oxide emissions in China due to coal are similarly low (perhaps 0.4 tons/sq km), compared with the US.[8/]

4.62 The most pressing need for altering current coal utilization practices is in the residential and commercial sector, which accounts for much of the street-level urban air pollution and uses coal particularly inefficiently. While greater use of LPG, kerosene, and natural gas may be possible in some areas in the future, available supplies of these fuels are not expected to be enough to allow a substantial shift from coal to petroleum fuels in households and commercial establishments, especially in northern China. Use of synthetic, medium-BTU gas from coal for cooking, however, may

---

8/ Total SOx emissions in the U.S. were about 20 million tons in 1940, and have increased to 24 million tons in 1980. NOx emissions totalled 6 million tons in 1940, and have increased sharply to 21 million tons in 1980. In 1980 nationwide emission densities in the US were 2.5 tons/square kilometer and 2.2 tons/square kilometer for SOx and NOx, respectively. In Ohio, densities averaged 30.5 tons/square kilometer and 11.1 tons/square kilometer, for SOx and NOx in 1980, respectively, while in Pennsylvania, densities averaged 21.4 tons/square kilometer and 8.7 tons/square kilometer (U.S. Environmental Protection Agency, National Air Pollutant Emission Estimates, 1940-80).

have potential, both as a means to reduce particulate and sulphur dioxide emissions, and as a means to improve the efficiency of coal use. Large-scale projects for production of synthetic gas from coal are already underway in several northern cities. District heating systems, which are relatively underdeveloped in China, compared with many European countries and the Soviet Union, have substantial potential as an improved method of space heating for households, offices, and commercial establishments. Both synthetic and district heating options are highly capital intensive, however, and where retrofits of existing buildings are involved costs are high. Electric cooking in most urban areas has been discouraged, because of shortages of electricity supplies. Conversion of coal to electricity for cooking, however, offers advantages of high efficiencies at end use, the potential for major improvements in environmental protection compared with direct use of coal on a small scale, and relatively inexpensive distribution, especially for existing buildings. In areas where synthetic gas production for cooking is being considered, their economic costs and benefits relative to electric cooking based on thermal power production and distribution should be evaluated.

4.63 Over the short and medium terms, it will be difficult to move away from the direct use of coal in existing buildings. In some of the East European countries which still rely heavily on the direct use of solid fuel for domestic purposes, large-scale production and distribution of high quality briquettes has brought improvements in terms of energy efficiency and the level of particulate emissions. Coal briquettes are fairly widely used in China today, but production and use can be expanded. Greater use of (low-sulphur) anthracite, improvement in briquetting technology, and design and dissemination of improved coal stoves can also yield beneficial results for this purpose.

4.64 For coal used by both large and small coal consumers, increases in the extent of coal washing can improve levels of both end-use efficiency and particulate emissions, through reduction in ash contents. In some circumstances, sulphur contents may also be reduced. However, energy losses in coal washing must be considered. In terms of kilocalories losses vary substantially (from 5-20%) depending upon the washability of different coals, the required specifications of washing plant output, washing technology, and local possibilities for using middlings. To determine the proper role of coal washing in the future, therefore, requires a comprehensive view of the economic potential for energy efficiency and of the costs and benefits of removal of pollutants before or after combustion.

4.65 In 1980, boilers used in thermal power production, industry, and space heating consumed more than one-half of China's total domestic supply of coal. With the anticipated increase in coal-fired power generation, the share of coal consumed in boilers will probably increase in the future. With rapid economic growth, most of China's boiler capacity by the end of the century will also be new. Thus, the technology of new boiler installations plays a critical role, both in China's efforts to improve the efficiency of coal use, and in efforts to check air pollution from coal consumption. In some ways, the two goals are closely related, especially when one considers that reductions in coal use due to improved efficiency also reduces the potential for air pollution, as less coal is being burned. In other ways, improved control of particulate and sulphur emissions requires specific design modifications and/or additional equipment, which will add to investment and operating costs. Additional costs, however, are dramatically lower when environmental protection control is incorporated in new, total system designs, instead of retrofitted in existing plants. With increasing concern for environmental protection in the industrialized countries, new strides have been made in the development of coal-fired boiler installations which are highly efficient and relatively clean.

4.66 The highest priority should be given to improved control of particulate emissions from industrial boilers and thermal power plants. Particulate emissions can be controlled using a wide range of equipment, including mechanical cyclones, electrostatic precipitators, bag filters and wet scrubbers. Substantial improvements in particulate control technologies have been made in industrialized countries. Sulphur dioxide removal (i.e., through flue gas desulphurization), however, may not be required in most cases, if low-sulphur coal is used although local conditions must be considered.

4.67 Fluidized bed combustion (FBC) technology represents one of the more important emerging coal technologies because it can burn any kind of fuel and, at the same time, control the emission of sulphur oxides without the use of flue-gas scrubbing units. Because of the low operating temperatures in FBC units, nitrogen oxide emissions are also low. FBC may be particularly well suited for medium-scale applications, such as industrial boilers and combustion of low-quality fuels, such as combustion of coal washery tailings in mine-mouth power plants.

4.68 The costs of different environmental protection measures vary dramatically, and assessment of what levels of additional cost are justified in a given area is always difficult. In most countries, however, the environmental and health costs of air pollution have been evaluated and a system of best practice control measures identified through emission limits and/or atmospheric standards. These standards are applied to all new installations, and may be phased in over a period of time to allow older plants to be brought into compliance. Judging from the experience of other countries, however, enterprises are rarely willing to make any substantial investment in pollution control without direct government administrative measures or financial incentives, which may be provided by a system of enforced penalties for exceeding specific, industry-by-industry standards. In China, the importance of developing adequate pollution regulations and provisions to enforce penalties can be expected to increase with reforms stressing the financial independence of state enterprises, as has recently been the case in Hungary. In addition, experience in other countries suggests that lack of attention to pollution control in the installation of new plants now could ultimately result in higher costs in the future - if the costs of air pollution are judged to be too high at a later date, the investments required to rectify the situation will be far higher than if adequate measures were taken at the time of original plant construction.

5. PETROLEUM

5.01 This chapter is divided in two sections. Section A considers issues regarding oil and gas production. It first reviews the Government's oil and gas program. An overview of oil reserves and production and of natural gas production and potential, together with the requirements of a strategy for natural gas use, follows. Sector constraints and issues are considered: the adequacy of exploration activities, the adequacy of exploration and production practices, the low operational efficiency, the adequacy of sectoral organization, and the role of transport infrastructure. Finally, the Government's future strategy for oil and gas production is examined.

5.02 Section B provides a brief overview of China's petroleum refinery industry, including the current organization and status of the industry, and a summary of the outlook for refining.

A. Production of Oil and Gas

Overview

5.03 The petroleum industry in China had substantial success between 1950 and 1980. Production increased more than tenfold, to over 100 million tons of oil and 12 bcm of gas p.a. These three decades were characterized largely by self-reliance, but also by the use of rather simple equipment and unsophisticated practices. Training for hundreds of thousands of technicians and economists, at home and in the USSR, started in the 1950s and picked up momentum in the 1960s. Huge oil-bearing structures were identified at relatively shallow depths, leading to the discovery of both giant and super-giant oilfields. Recent exploration efforts have been concentrated mainly close to existing fields in oil-bearing basins and many of the sedimentary basins and offshore tracts remain largely unexplored.

5.04 The industry now faces new and greater challenges if its production targets for the end of the century are to be met. These targets are about double recent levels. Oil production is to increase from almost 115 million tons in 1984 to 200 million tons in the year 2000. The targets for gas are to increase production from 12.4 bcm in 1984 to 25 bcm in 2000. Chinese experts estimate that with offshore production, the total output could be 20-30% above these targets. Since China's largest oil fields have already passed their point of peak productivity, China's success in meeting its goals for production in 2000 will be largely determined by the extent of new discoveries and the speed with which they can be developed. In view of the uncertainties associated with hydrocarbon exploration and production, until more drilling is done, there is no way to know exactly how much oil and gas there is in China and how much capital will be required. Future strategies for petroleum production and use will have to take into account this uncertainty.

5.05 To find the quantities of hydrocarbons necessary to reach its production goals, China must develop a long-term strategy for exploration, which could determine the most promising areas for immediate exploration, establish priorities for future exploration activities, and formulate policies on the use of foreign technology and capital. Such a strategy also could focus on the constraints that will inevitably need to be overcome if the output target for the year 2000 is to be achieved. Although exploration, development and production practices have been improved considerably in recent years, China's techniques and practices are in a number of respects substantially below international standards. The efficiency of China's own exploration activities in onshore areas will need to be improved by additional investments in appropriate modern equipment and technology, especially given the likelihood that new discoveries will probably be in deeper, more complex geological structures, and in remote locations. To be effective, these efforts will need to be accompanied by improvements in management practices. In addition, investments will be needed for infrastructure support such as transport and handling facilities.

5.06 Long-term planning is needed for China's petroleum sector, to integrate well-defined strategies for exploration, production, and transport of oil and gas. This plan should be flexible enough to accommodate future uncertainties, and it should consider several alternative scenarios. Modern planning techniques and, in particular, system analysis are necessary for the evaluation and interpretation of the many parameters considered. More generally it will be necessary for the Ministry of Petroleum Industry (MOPI) and the planning agencies concerned to shift from the short term focus of annual planning to strategic, longer-term planning for the sector.

5.07 The natural decline of the old fields could be reduced from the expected 10 mtpy (10% p.a.) to 3-5 mtpy through technical improvements. Total amounts recovered would depend on how much oil was originally bypassed. Over the short term, additional amounts can be recovered only with infill drilling and remedial work. MOPI estimates that infill drilling could yield about 4-5 mtpy starting in 1983 and tapering off to an insignificant level after 1990. The possible impact of enhanced oil recovery processes (EOR) on improving the ultimate oil recovery has long been recognized in China. The contribution of EOR applications, particularly thermal processes, to China's oil production could be as high as 10 million tons by the year 2000.[1/]

5.08 In order to reach the official oil production targets, MOPI is planning to intensify its exploration efforts and their effectiveness and to continue the development of existing fields, applying measures such as infill drilling and making technical improvements. Infill drilling will be particularly effective in fields where wells are widely spaced and there is evidence of oil being bypassed by water. Technical improvements cover general improvements in equipment, technology, and sound exploration and development practices, as well as specific remedial measures for existing wells (such as workovers, recompletions in new horizons, and installation of large capacity pumps).

1/ Transportation and refining of heavy oil could pose a problem, but this oil could yield badly needed asphalt and high grade lubricating oil.

Investment Requirements

5.09 The projected cost of finding oil in China is very difficult to assess. Data from recent experience provides an incomplete basis for analysis. On the basis of knowledge of some Chinese fields and using some international yardsticks, however, the minimum investment required to discover and develop the additional reserves required to meet China's production targets can be estimated at Y 30 billion and Y 70 billion, respectively, for exploration and development over the next 12-15 years. Given the risks and uncertainties associated with petroleum investment, this estimate only provides a preliminary benchmark. Major adjustments in investments targetted for the sector may be required as risk assessment and estimates of development needs change.

5.10 Petroleum sector investment targeted under the Sixth Five-Year Plan amounts to Y 15.5 billion (or an annual average of Y 3.1 billion), 70% of which was for petroleum development and 30% for exploration. Thus the future annual average investment figure of Y 6-8 billion represents some 2-3 times the recent level of expenditure. The importation of sophisticated tools, material, and equipment and the proposed involvement of foreign contractors might require foreign exchange of the order of $15-20 billion.

Oil Reserves and Production

5.11 Estimates of possible oil reserves are highly speculative, particularly for lightly explored areas (such as the western onshore basins) and for the almost virgin areas offshore. China's recoverable reserves of oil onshore have been estimated at 5.5 billion tons (approximately 40 billion barrels) by international experts and rather higher, at 8-15 billion tons, by Chinese experts. China has more than 300 sedimentary basins onshore, which cover 4 million sq km. Ten large petroliferous basins have been identified, two of which account for over 90% of oil production. China's continental shelf covers 1,300,000 sq km offshore, of which 650,000 sq km are thought to be hydrocarbon prospective areas. The China National Offshore Oil Corporation (CNOOC) estimates the offshore reserves at 2.7-10.0 billion tons of oil.[2/]

5.12 Additions to reserves recorded in recent years have been substantial. They offset the production decline in old fields and contributed to the net production increases in 1983 and 1984. In 1983, the volume of new reserves added to China's oil inventory was reported to be approximately 500 million tons of oil in place. Much of this increase is believed to come from probable and possible reserves of already known accumulations rather than from new fields. There are, however, recent official reports of new discoveries in the Songliao and in North China basins, with very prolific reservoirs and/or wells with very high initial rates.

2/ This compares with North Sea recoverable oil reserves of 2.2 billion tons from an area of 560,000 sq km.

5.13 Production in 1983 was 106 million tons of oil, which equalled previous production peaks achieved in 1979 and 1980. Production from the Daqing group of oil fields, which provided about half of China's oil production in 1983, and the Shengli and Renqiu fields, which provided about 20% and 10% respectively (see Table 5.1), has peaked. In 1984 oil production climbed further to 114.5 million tons.

Table 5.1: CRUDE OIL PRODUCTION BY REGION AND MAJOR FIELD
(Million tons)

	1970	1975	1977	1979	1980	1981	1982	1983
Northeast	22.37	50.68	54.87	57.36	58.59	58.63	59.19	60.24
Daqing	21.18	46.24	50.31	50.75	51.50	51.75	51.94	52.35
Liaohe and Others	1.19	4.42	4.56	6.61	7.09	6.88	7.25	7.89
North	1.02	4.68	15.55	20.40	19.11	15.26	14.33	13.58
Renqiu	-	-	12.30	17.33	16.03	12.22	11.31	10.55
Dagang	1.02	4.68	3.15	2.90	2.91	2.88	2.80	3.03
Others	-	-	0.10	0.17	0.17	0.16	0.16	-
East	4.67	16.72	17.66	19.21	17.92	16.41	16.70	18.72
Shengli	4.67	16.72	17.52	18.88	17.59	16.11	16.35	18.37
Others	-	-	0.14	0.33	0.33	0.30	0.35	0.35
Central South	0.27	0.87	1.26	3.39	4.16	4.80	5.6	6.42
Northwest	2.29	4.02	4.21	5.69	6.06	5.99	6.2	6.59
Southwest	0.03	0.09	1.09	0.10	0.10	0.09	0.1	0.1
Total	30.65	77.06	93.64	106.15	105.94	101.18	102.12	105.65

Source: MOPI.

5.14 The Government has recently initiated an extensive campaign of infill drilling, remedial repairing of oil producing and water injection wells, and well completion in new or poorly drained reservoirs. These measures contributed to the production gains in 1983 and 1984. If left without remedial work and infill drilling, production from these fields (presently cutting water at 60-75%) would have declined at an estimated annual rate of 10% (equivalent to some 10 million tons of oil per year). However, additional recovery from infill drilling and remedial work is for the most part short-lived.

5.15 Offshore exploration and development are being undertaken by CNOOC in cooperation with foreign oil companies. Invitations to bid for offshore acreage previously covered by seismic surveys were issued in early 1982. Since then, some 23 agreements for oil exploration and development have been signed, involving 29 corporations from 9 countries and covering 90,000 sq km.[3/] Oil discoveries made in the offshore Bohai basin so far are modest (peak production estimated at 5 mtpy), and some foreign companies are cutting back on their exploration efforts. On the other hand, the gas discoveries off of Hainan Island have been sizeable. It is still too early to evaluate offshore prospects or how long it would take for discoveries to be made and developed.

5.16 In view of the huge reserves of heavy oil in China (approximately one billion tons in Karamay alone), the Chinese petroleum industry has sought international cooperation (with the World Bank in Karamay and with international companies in Liaohe) in the design and supervision of pilot projects. A preliminary feasibility study indicates that, given the proper technology and suitable reservoir conditions, as much as 35% net oil recovery could be attained.

Natural Gas Production and Potential

5.17 Gas production reached 12.4 bcm in 1984, which is a slight increase over the 1982 and 1983 levels but about 15% lower than the 1979 peak (Table 5.2). Roughly half the gas produced is nonassociated, mostly from the Sichuan basin. Gas production from Sichuan declined by about 20% between 1979 and 1982. Since such a decline endangers the production of many petrochemical plants, technicians at the Sichuan fields have been under pressure to maintain the supply of gas, but this has meant producing above the fields' optimum capacity, which will reduce the total amount ultimately recovered from the reservoirs.

3/ Earlier agreements covering small areas in the Gulf of Bohai and off Hainan Island were signed with Japan Oil Company, ELF, and ARCO.

Table 5.2: NATURAL GAS PRODUCTION
(bcm)

	1978	1979	1980	1981	1982	1983
Northeast	5.00	5.17	5.27	4.30	4.13	4.14
Daqing	3.20	3.31	3.39	2.80	2.78	2.80
Others	1.80	1.86	1.88	1.50	1.35	1.34
North	0.82	0.93	0.80	0.70	0.78	0.71
Renqiu	-	-	-	-	0.15	0.12
Dagang	0.82	0.93	0.80	0.70	0.63	0.59
Others	-	-	-	-	-	-
East	1.44	1.55	1.44	1.20	0.99	1.06
Shengli	1.44	1.55	1.42	1.18	0.97	1.05
Others	-	-	0.02	0.02	0.02	0.01
Central South	0.02	0.02	0.05	0.05	0.30	0.36
Northwest	0.30	0.33	0.38	0.45	0.46	0.48
Sichuan	6.15	6.51	6.33	5.80	5.25	5.28
Total	13.73	14.51	14.27	12.50	11.91	12.03
Associated	5.95	6.53	7.23	6.20	5.96	n.a.
Nonassociated	7.78	7.98	7.04	6.30	5.95	n.a.

Source: MOPI

5.18 The Sichuan basin is an area of 180,000 sq km with a sedimentary rock thickness of up to 12,000 m. Gas is found throughout the basin at varying depths and in formations of different ages.[4/] Many experts believe that the potential for gas production is quite high. Gas zones in many of the producing fields remain untapped. The main difficulty is that the reservoirs are very tight, and production can be achieved only through the fracture system. Gas reserves have also been proven in several large structures in the

---

4/ About 60 small and medium-sized fields produce gas from 14 different producing horizons at an average depth of 3,000-4,000 m. At present, 21 seismic crews (15 of which have modern equipment) and 100 rigs are operating in Sichuan.

east and south of the basin, but they have not yet been fully tested. The target is to increase the Sichuan gas production from its present level of 5.3 bcm to 7 and 10 bcm by the years 1990 and 2000, respectively. The Sichuan Petroleum Administration Bureau's strategy for reaching these levels of production involves: (a) developing multiple gas layers within each producing field, (b) drilling deeper to tap new gas horizons, and (c) stepping up drilling activities from the present 350,000 meters to 450,000 meters p.a.

5.19 The success ratio for all wells drilled in Sichuan (exploration and development) averaged approximately 50%, which is rather low. This is mainly due to the uneven distribution of the fracture system and the extreme tightness of the matrix of the producing formation. Productivity has been held back (to 200-300 line-km per seismic crew year and one well per rig year) by several problems, which arise because the wells are not properly completed, making it difficult to apply the more sophisticated stimulation techniques which would increase the productivity of the wells. A thorough study of completion practices is required to develop methods which will facilitate later stimulation.

5.20 A gas discovery in the eastern part of Zhongyuan has been announced recently. Although it is too early to estimate the reserves, they may be as high as 100 bcm in place. ARCO has made a gas discovery off Hainan Island, which may be in excess of 280 bcm (which could result in production of about 6 bcm per year). If the projections are correct, this could be China's largest gas field.

5.21 Considering the prospectivity of Sichuan and the recent discoveries onshore and offshore, it is highly probable that non-associated gas production in the year 2000 could be as much as four times the present level. In addition, if the oil production target is achieved, total gas production (non-associated and associated) could amount to 35-40 bcm per year by the year 2000, compared to the current target of 25 bcm. If exploration efforts are stepped up, production could be even higher.

Sector Constraints and Issues

5.22 Exploration Activities. The exploration effort in China has been relatively limited. China's oil-bearing areas are extensive and almost equal the area of land basins in the US. However, most of China's land basins and offshore tracts have not yet been explored fully, if at all. Exploration is being undertaken in only 10 of the large basins, mostly where oil has been discovered. Even within these basins, exploration activities are not evenly spread but tend to be concentrated close to existing fields.

5.23 MOPI is planning to intensify its exploration efforts onshore. This would involve (a) continuing exploration around the present fields and within the basins proven to be highly prolific and (b) stepping up exploration efforts in western China, particularly around the Karamay oil belt.

5.24 Exploration Practices. The exploration methods used in China are standard preliminary surveying techniques (gravity, magnetic, electric) followed by seismic surveys. Seismic records are now made using digital systems and are of good quality. Processing of these records is done at various computer centers. Additional equipment and more powerful computers are being acquired to improve the capability of these local centers.

5.25 In several areas, Chinese techniques and practices are less efficient than international standards. The output of China's 300 local seismic crews and 13 foreign crews has averaged 50,000-70,000 line-kilometers over the past few years.[5/] (In 1983 it was somewhat above the average at 80,000 line-kilometers). However, some of the servicing equipment is outdated, and logistical support is lacking. Because of shortages of spares, indifference to time spent on standby, short working season, and lack of mobility for the crews, the output of local crews (200-400 km/crew year) is one-quarter that of foreign crews.

5.26 Operational inefficiency also results from inappropriate drilling equipment. Most of the 700 rigs used in China are light to medium rigs with a capacity to drill to depths of 3,000 m. There are few rigs rated to drill to 6,000 m. The rigs are usually overrated and do not have the necessary horsepower or pulling and pump capacity. Chinese crews usually spend one year drilling a 5,000 m well. In addition, the light rigs assigned to drill shallow wells have inadequate mobility, and much time is spent moving and installing drilling equipment. Again, indifference to time spent on standby reduces the effective drilling time (rotating bit time) to 30-35% of the total rig time, which is about half the international drilling standard. On average, 800-1,000 exploration wells (40% purely exploratory wells, 60% appraisal and delineation wells) have been drilled annually over the last few years,[6/] with a success ratio of approximately 50%. Standards of maintenance and cleanliness of drilling equipment and other mobile oil field equipment are poor, leading to low productivity and increased wear. Well completion practices are also suboptimal and may lead to reservoir formation damage. The lack of proper coring, testing, logging and cementing tools, equipment and techniques, and poor housekeeping on and around the drilling rigs further aggravate operational inefficiency.

5.27 Proper, consistent, and continuous reservoir management programs are lacking. The techniques used for separation and metering of well streams (oil, gas and water) are quite outdated and give unreliable basic reservoir data. Some technicians have indicated that modern practices and equipment (including multiple completion, differential plugging, radioactive tracers, water injection profile tools, casing logging equipment and carbon-oxygen tools) are being used, but their use may be restricted to a few pilot

---

5/ Sixty percent of the local seismic crews are engaged in exploration in the three main eastern basins and forty percent in the central and western basins. The 13 foreign crews have been contracted to work in difficult areas.

6/ The cost of drilling in China (between Y 400/m for shallow wells and Y 1,000/m for deep, high-pressure wells) is about half that in the US and one-third that in developing countries.

operations. Some reservoir computer models have been built, but they suffer from unreliable data base and poor operational feedback. There is insufficient contact between the staff engineers who design exploration programs in the oil field offices and the field staff who implement them, in part due to inadequate transport. Greater interaction between field and office staff, and improved supervision, would result in increased efficiency and better implementation of projects.

5.28 The amount of data acquired in both reservoir engineering and exploration is considerable and should be handled more systematically. In order to facilitate planning and development of a sound exploration strategy, a data bank should be built up for each basin, field and reservoir. This will contribute to improvements in reservoir management.

5.29 MOPI is planning to improve the effectiveness of its exploration activities. To this end, several measures will be taken to increase the output of seismic crews to 100,000 line-kilometers by the year 2000: (a) changing from analog to digital recording; (b) mobilizing more crews; and (c) increasing crew productivity by providing more mobile equipment and more spares and by lengthening the working season through the winter months. In addition, to increase the number of successful exploration wells drilled, the number of rigs will be increased, and heavier rigs for deep drilling as well as more mobile rigs for workover operations and for drilling in remote areas and in difficult terrain will be acquired.

5.30 Production Practices. The most prominent feature of China's production practices is the almost universal use of water injection. This appears to be explained by the success of water flooding in the largest field at Daqing. Water flooding of hydrocarbon reservoirs is initiated even when natural water drive is evident, and it has helped to sustain production from certain pools for some time. Although in some cases this method can be as effective as EOR, in some areas water flooding could lead to a severe reduction in the ultimate recovery rate, particularly where well spacing is wide and the reservoir lithology heterogeneous. In some cases, its use may not be economically justified when the loss of incremental hydrocarbons blocked in place by the water is taken into account. In each case a detailed study of reservoir characteristics and well production history is required before the appropriate secondary recovery method can be selected.

5.31 Another technique commonly used to increase the capacity of water injection and oil wells is hydraulic fracturing of the reservoir rocks. If this technique is not properly designed and is implemented indiscriminately, it may connect fractures to high permeability water bearing zones instead of opening up the low permeability hydrocarbon zones. As a result, more hydrocarbons are bypassed, and the ultimate recovery rate is reduced.[7/]

7/ Injecting at a pressure high enough to equal or exceed the overburden pressure can also create uncontrolled fractures within the reservoir sand shale system.

5.32 Sectoral Organization. The present organization of MOPI, with its central entities and field administration bureaus, has been effective in managing the petroleum production increases over the last few decades. Nonetheless the issue is whether this organization can carry the future load and achieve the Government's production targets, especially in light of the changes being introduced in the economic management system and the need to expand the planning horizon. Another issue is whether Chinese institutions are adequately prepared to respond to the demands which may arise from offshore development.

5.33 A review of the strengths and weaknesses of the present organization is needed, with a view to identifying reforms for implementing the enlarged exploration and production strategies. In line with recent reforms, greater autonomy for regional companies in field management may need to be considered, including increased flexibility for exploration, development and production activities, and for contracting of domestic and foreign services. Greater interaction between field and office staff, and better supervision, would improve the efficiency and implementation of projects. The role of MOPI in training, education, and research, and coordinating its activities with those of other entities, should also be reviewed. In addition, while maintaining the role of MOPI in exploration, the Ministry of Geology (MOG) should be given more support, particularly in certain remote areas and offshore.

5.34 The Role of Transport Infrastructure. Most of the crude oil is transported by pipeline, except for crude oil from Xinjiang which is carried to Lanzhou by rail. Products, however, go mostly by rail. The reported intention to build product pipelines should be actively pursued to relieve the railways in congested corridors such as Shenyang to Dalian, Beijing to Shijiazhuang, and other points in the South.

5.35 Transportation of crude oil, petroleum products, and natural gas does not appear to face major bottlenecks at present. Apart from the need to rehabilitate and increase capacity of some pipelines and remove bottlenecks on some networks, the transportation system seems to be functioning effectively. The options and costs of transport systems to handle increased oil supplies, however, should be analyzed and the appropriate investments must be undertaken in time to avoid bottlenecks and costly delays. This is particularly important for the development of natural gas, which requires that treatment, storage, and transport facilities be planned well in advance.

5.36 Transportation costs are an important element in deciding whether to develop hydrocarbon reserves that could be discovered in the western basins. The major transport options under study are rail or pipeline transport from the far West, should major discoveries be made in the Karamay area. The capacity of the railway line (single-track) is limited by the difficult topography restricting train weight. Shipping distances are great and development costs of either the rail or pipeline alternative will be large. The first step is likely to be to increase rail capacity in critical bottleneck sections. To justify the cost of a pipeline from Xinjiang to Lanzhou would require the discovery of large oil fields.

Future Strategy

5.37 China's petroleum industry is in a period of transition. Through its policy of opening up to international economy, China is acquiring more sophisticated technology and equipment for petroleum production. This, coupled with improvements in management and planning, could do much to solve the existing problems of the industry in areas such as the development and execution of a sound exploration strategy, improvement of operational efficiency, and optimum exploitation of oil and gas reserves. China has also attracted foreign risk capital to explore in offshore areas and is considering some involvement of international oil companies (IOCs) in onshore areas south of the Chang Jiang through joint venture contracts. Legislation for this purpose is currently being considered. The involvement of foreign companies would provide a source of investment capital, would divide some of the risks of exploration and development with the Government, and may facilitate the transfer of technology.

5.38 China will need to raise the level of sophistication of the equipment and technology used at all stages of exploration and development. Present organization, equipment and production practices lead to operational inefficiency. Technical improvements will need to be complemented by changes in management practices. This will involve, for instance, improved production planning for individual fields, with the decisions of central planners based largely on input from field managers.

5.39 Serious, but by no means insurmountable, challenges face China in fulfilling its petroleum targets. Many logistical and technical problems will need to be resolved. Future discoveries of the magnitude envisaged could be achieved by drilling in the deeper, more complex geological structures to find subtle traps and by drilling in remote locations where access is difficult, but the possibility of finding large oil fields is good. More sophisticated seismic equipment and data processing techniques will have to be employed. Heavier and more powerful drilling rigs will be needed to drill deeper with high efficiency and acceptable cost. Drilling and production practices have to be optimized.

5.40 More important, though, is the need for proper management of the oil and gas reservoirs with a view to maximizing ultimate recovery rates. Laboratories and other supporting services should be designed for applied research as well as basic scientific research. The value of research institutes attached to the various fields should be judged by their contribution towards maximizing returns and reducing costs. The use of sophisticated equipment alone is no panacea for the problems of the petroleum industry. Rather, their solution requires identifying specific operating problems and developing or importing appropriate technology to deal with them.

5.41 Better training programs at the working level are also required, particularly for drillers, welders, drivers of heavy specialized oilfield vehicles, and operators of well cementing, logging and perforating equipment. Efficient implementation of field programs depends largely on their competence.

5.42 With respect to technology transfer and international exchange, heavy emphasis has been placed on importation or joint venture manufacturing of equipment but not on technology imports. More intensive personnel training is needed, both on the job (through service contracts) and abroad (in accredited institutions and with operating companies). To expedite exploration of deep structures and in remote areas such as the West, hiring foreign drilling contractors with appropriate equipment and expertise and more involvement of foreign seismic crews may be desirable. Technical consultancy in this field will not solve the many logistical problems and will fall short of effectively transferring technology. An additional option would be to invite major IOCs with operating experience in difficult environments, to participate in exploring the northern and western basins.

5.43 Natural Gas Strategy. China has a long history of limited gas use, but there has been no systematic countrywide study to assess reserves and market potential. There are a number of questions such as reserve sizes, timing and location of gas output, production and distribution costs, and size, location and composition of the market that have to be resolved before the efficient development of natural gas can proceed. The Government has a major role to play in resolving these issues and eliminating constraints to gas use. Provision of suitable equipment and application of appropriate technology and sound practices in the field of exploration, development, and production are important prerequisites for achieving the future production targets.

5.44 In many feedstock and fuel applications, natural gas would have a relatively high value per unit of energy compared with other energy sources. Evaluating its optimal use, however, is highly complex and will need to be pursued on a site-by-site basis, due to regional variations in demand, in the opportunity cost of alternative fuels or feedstocks, and in the costs of gas transmission and distribution, which should correspond to the various uses selected. Given the characteristics of natural gas, it is necessary to make a comprehensive plan that includes requirements for the exploration and development of new gas but also allows for its transport and use, and the requirements to build a network to achieve its lowest cost distribution. To accommodate uncertainties in gas reserves, production rates and the size of the market, this plan should be flexible, with staged construction to permit continuous revisions as new information becomes available. Because regional factors can play such an important role in determining the best strategy for natural gas use, such plans entail location-specific assessments.[8/]

8/ A preliminary gas utilization study is being undertaken by CNOOC and will focus on the potential gas market in South China.

B. PETROLEUM REFINING

Overview

5.45 At the end of 1983, China had a refining capacity of about 100 mtpy made up of some 40 or 50 industrial-scale refineries, of which 33 were reported to have a capacity of more than 2.5 mtpy. Most others have capacities of only 0.5 mtpy. In addition, an unspecified number of "back-yard" refineries have been built by county and even commune (township) authorities, to meet local demand. The large number of small refineries is arguably the result of the differentials between crude and ex-refinery prices which provide substantial financial incentives for small refiners. Transport costs may also contribute, to a smaller extent, to the proliferation of small refineries.

5.46 The China Petrochemical Corporation (SINOPEC) was created in 1983 and is responsible for most petroleum refining (95%) and petrochemical production based on liquid petroleum feedstocks. SINOPEC has a labor force of 470,000 and annual sales of Y 25 billion. In 1983, it paid Y 9.5 billion in profits and taxes to the Government. The Ministry of Chemical Industry has 2.5 mtpy of petroleum refining capacity, which in 1983 processed 1.5 million tons of crude oil, as well as responsibility for petrochemical plants that use natural gas and coal as feedstocks.

Refinery Input and Output

5.47 Crude Oil Feedstock and Product Output. Petroleum refining in China faces several technical problems stemming from the characteristics of the crude oil produced in China relative to the pattern of demand for refined products. The bulk of the crude is heavy, and very waxy, and it gives a relatively poor yield of light products by primary distillation (Table 5.3).

5.48 Total refinery throughput was about 75 million tons of crude oil in 1980, and about 80 million tons in 1983. Product output is obtained through simple distillation and secondary refining (cracking) processes. Output of major refined products in recent years is shown in Table 5.4. As a result of recent increases in cracking capacity and efforts to rationalize the use of existing capacity, gross fuel oil yields have decreased from 41.7% of throughput in 1980 to 34.0% of throughput in 1983. Middle distillate yields have remained roughly constant, while yields of light products (gasoline, LPG, and light chemical feedstocks) have increased.

Table 5.3: CRUDE OIL PRODUCTION AND REFINING CHARACTERISTICS /a

Crude oil type	1982 production (mtpy)	Specific gravity	Primary distillation analysis (%) Light /b products	Residual fuel oil	Wax	Sulphur
Daqing	51.94	0.862	28.8	71.2	25.8	0.12
Shengli	16.35	0.90	25.1	74.9	14.6	0.8
Renqiu	11.31	0.884	26.0	74.0	22.8	0.03
Dagang	2.80	0.883	34.9	65.1	10.0	0.12
Karamay light	4.0	0.84	37.0	63.0	8.33	NA
Karamay heavy	-	0.96	3.2	96.76	1.56	0.31

/a Crude from the fields shown accounts for 84% of 1982 oil production in China. Production from other fields has, in general, the same characteristics.

/b Gasoline, kerosene and diesel.

Table 5.4: OUTPUT OF MAJOR REFINED PRODUCTS, 1980-83
(thousand tons per year)

Product	1980	1981	1982	1983
Gasoline	10,790	10,010	11,001	12,345
Kerosene	3,980	3,640	3,810	4,066
Diesel	18,280	17,530	17,113	18,852
Lubricants	1,970	1,500	1,399	1,342
Fuel oil /a	31,420	28,180	26,096	27,068
Other /b	5,160	7,090	9,301	12,017
Throughput	75,380	71,460	72,060	79,680

a/ Includes refinery use, estimated at 2.6 and 2.1 million tons in 1980 and 1983, respectively.

/b Estimates, based on reported throughputs and refinery losses. Figures include LPG, naphtha and other light chemical feedstocks, solvents and petroleum solids.

Sources: MOPI, SINOPEC, Almanacs of the Chinese Economy.

5.49 Cracking Plant. In 1983 three types of cracking plant were used in China: fluid catalytic cracking (FCC) with capacity of 24 mtpy, thermal cracking (including delayed coking) with capacity of 10 mtpy, and hydro-cracking with capacity of 1 mtpy. The preferred cracker feedstock is a vacuum distillate oil obtained from the residual oil resulting from atmospheric distillation of the crude feedstock. The residue from the vacuum distillation plant is also designated as fuel oil but is of lower quality than that obtained from the atmospheric distillation process.

5.50 Quality of Refined Products. Because Chinese crudes are waxy, the residual fuel oil has a very high viscosity and poses considerable difficulties in transport and handling, especially for exports. On the other hand, it is low in undesirable components such as sulphur and metals.

5.51 The wax content of the crude oil also causes problems with diesel oil and lubricants, which have a high pour point and become viscous when cold. Gasoline currently produced for domestic use in China has an octane rating of about 70 (motor octane number) which is suitable for the current truck fleet but low by international standards. Since China has few automobiles in use, the octane rating of the gasoline they need can be raised, by adding tetra-ethyl lead, to about 80 octane. Attempts to increase the fuel efficiency of China's vehicle fleet will require a corresponding improvement in the quality of refined products, particularly gasoline and lubricants.

5.52 Chinese crudes are generally deficient in asphalt, which is at present obtained in relatively small quantities from Karamay and Liaohe crude and some of the Shengli crudes. Most of the asphalt sold in China is the carbonized residue of the paraffinic crudes, which has inferior properties as a bonding and sealing agent compared to true asphalt. Present demand for asphalt is 1.2-1.5 mtpy for highways alone. The supply would need to be increased to accommodate any major highway construction program in China or a marked increase in truck traffic.

5.53 There are general complaints from Chinese consumers about the wide variations in quality and characteristics of fuels and lubricants supplied on the local market. This probably reflects a lack of adequate quality control, both at the national level and in individual refineries.

Refinery Construction and Operation

5.54 Basic refining installations and most auxiliary equipment are manufactured in China. Many of the larger refining centers have their own design, manufacturing, and construction facilities. Most cracking and petro-chemical processes and equipment, with the possible exception of catalytic crackers, appear to be imported from the US, Japan, or Western Europe, possibly because these processes have higher operating requirements (in terms of temperature and pressure) than simple distillation processes, and Chinese manufacturers cannot produce this type of equipment.

5.55 Energy losses in refinery operations, including internal consumption of fuel, are reported to have fallen from about 8.5% in 1980 to 7.6% in 1983. The measurement of both crude oil input and refined product output does not appear to be very closely monitored in all of China's refineries.

Outlook for the Future

5.56 The present trend is for refining to be concentrated in a few large, more sophisticated refineries. These refineries can produce a wide range of products more efficiently, with closer quality control and with better administrative control of the production and distribution of refined products. Large refineries offer economies of scale, a more sophisticated system of processing, and the wider range of products likely to be needed as China's industrial system becomes more complex.

5.57 During the next fifteen years, a major effort should be made to improve the quantity and quality of measurement in the refining sector. Even in the more modern refineries, many of the instruments are inoperative and quantitative measurements of total input and output do not seem very precise. The standards of firefighting and safety equipment need to be upgraded, particularly as production is concentrated in fewer and larger units, where the loss of one unit by fire would seriously affect output in a region.

5.58 A concentration of refining capacity in fewer and larger units will require additional investment in transport equipment, storage, and distribution facilities. Additional changes in transport infrastructure, as well as in refining and cracking plants, should be considered in light of anticipated oil discoveries offshore and in Northwest China. Large refineries can also be fully integrated with petrochemical plants, which may allow optimal utilization of feedstocks.

5.59 With refinery distillate yields about the same as in 1983, a throughput of over 190 million tons of crude in the year 2000 would result in enough distillate output to nearly meet the mid-point of projected demand. Higher or lower future demand would imply, respectively, imports or exports of distillate products. In any event, primary distillation capacity requirements would be almost double current reported capacity and the related costs of conversion capacity are quite high. If future crude characteristics are similar to the current ones, the additional cracking capacity to maintain the 1983 yields with a throughput of over 190 million tons would approach 60 mtpy with a cost of about US$15 billion.[9/]

5.60 There are several options for increasing the availability of distillates in China, including investment in secondary conversion and increased reliance on trade. Similarly, there are various alternatives for fuel oil use, including higher domestic use, exports, or further refinery processing to yield more distillates. In both instances the optimal choice will have to be made on the basis of careful evaluation of all the alternatives, considering the investment costs of secondary conversion capacity and forecasts of international crude, petroleum product, and coal prices and domestic demand for distillate and fuel oil.

9/ Estimates assume that cracker composition and yields are similar to those today. Possible changes in crude oil characteristics are uncertain.

6. POWER

A. Overview

6.01 Power development in China has registered high rates of growth over the past three decades. Installed capacity has grown at an average of 11.6% p.a. since 1949, reaching 76,000 MW by the end of 1983 (see Appendix F.1 and F.2). Generation grew at 13.8% p.a. over the same period, though growth has slowed somewhat in recent years.[1/] Generation reached 374,600 GWh in 1984 (up from 4,300 GWh in 1949). The sector has been doing well in the Sixth Five-Year Plan period (1981-85) and the original 1985 target of 362,000 GWh was fulfilled in 1984.

6.02 Despite these high growth rates, the power sector is unable to meet all the demands of the economy, particularly those from China's major industrial load centers. In order to catch up with current demand in all customer classes, as well as meet the requirements for China's ambitious growth targets, as much as a four-fold increase in generation will be necessary between 1980 and the year 2000. With increasing unit costs in the sector, major increases in investments for new capacity transmission and distribution will be necessary.

6.03 This chapter presents an overview of China's long-term plans for power production and transmission, and discusses some of the major issues raised. Future scenarios for electricity demand and corresponding issues are discussed in Chapter 2. Rural power supply and demand is discussed in Chapter 7.

B. Production and Distribution

6.04 In 1983, 24,000 MW of generating capacity (31.3% of the total) was hydro and 52,600 MW (68.7%) was thermal (see Appendix F.1). Cogenerating capacity (5,000 MW) accounted for roughly 10% of thermal power capacity. No nuclear power plants have yet been commissioned.

6.05 The largest hydro stations are at Liujiaxia on the Huanghe in Gansu (1,225 MW capacity) and at Gezhouba on the Changjiang (965 MW in operation). Eleven large hydro projects (i.e., over 400 MW capacity) are under construction, for total additional capacity of 10,275 MW (see Appendix F.5). The largest hydro unit in operation (300 MW) is at Liujiaxia. China has, moreover, more than 85,000 small hydro stations totalling 8,400 MW. Almost all of these (95%) are smaller than 500 kW, with an average size of about 100 kW.

6.06 The largest thermal station is Qinghe (1,100 MW) in Liaoning. Seven new thermal power stations, with additional capacity totalling 6,900 MW, are under construction and five existing plants are being expanded to add 3,600 MW

1/ In 1981, growth was only 2.9% due to economic readjustment, but has risen to 6.0% in 1982, 7.2% in 1983, and 6.6% in 1984, giving an average growth rate of 8.7% from 1970 to 1984.

of capacity (see Appendix F.5). The largest thermal unit (350 MW) is at the Baoshan thermal station, for which two such units were imported from Japan.

6.07 In 1983, there were 32 power grids with capacities of more than 100 MW each. Thirteen of these grids (including six regional and seven major provincial grids, as detailed in Table 6.1) had capacities exceeding 1,000 MW. Their combined installed capacity of 62,512 MW accounted for over 80% of the national total. By 1983 the following lengths of transmission lines were in operation: 36,716 km of 220 kV; 1,088 km of 330 kV; and 1,092 km of 500 kV. In addition, three single circuit 500 kV lines, totalling 1,375 km, are now under construction.[2]

2/ Datong-Beijing, 402 km; Yuanbaoshan-Jinzhou-Liaoyang-Haicheng, 656 km; Huainan-Pingyao, 317 km; Xuzhou-Shanghai, 680 km.

Table 6.1: MAJOR GRIDS, 1983

Grid	Area covered	Installed capacity (MW)	Energy generated (GWh)
Regional Grids			
Northeast China	Liaoning, the major part of Heilongjiang and Jilin, and part of Nei Mongol	10,136	53,650
North China	Beijing, Tianjin, Shanxi, Hebei, and part of Nei Mongol	9,840	54,830
East China	Jiangsu, Anhui, Zhejiang and and Shanghai	10,858	58,030
Northwest China	Shaanxi, Gansu, Ningxia and the major part of Qinghai	4,544	21,230
Central China	Henan, Hubei, Hunan, Jiangxi, and part of Sichuan	8,536	40,550
Southwest China	Parts of Sichuan, Guizhou, and Yunnan	4,860	21,230
Subtotal		48,774	249,520
Seven Major Provincial Grids		13,738	66,930
Total		62,512	316,450
% of National Total		81.6	90.0

Efficiency

6.08 Total fuel consumption in thermal power stations in 1980 was 112.5 million TCE, of which 69.5% was coal, 25.2% oil, and 5.3% natural gas. Gross unit fuel consumption averaged about 3,250 kcal/kWh, implying a thermal conversion efficiency of 26.5%. In China, however, thermal power conversion efficiency statistics are usually reported on a net fuel consumption basis, i.e., fuel consumed in the production of heat supplied to consumers outside the power industry is subtracted from gross consumption. Net fuel consumption in thermal power production has steadily declined in recent years, from 3,241 kcal/kWh in 1970, to 2,891 kcal/kWh in 1980, and about 2,800 kcal/kWh in 1983. System losses (through generation, transmission and distribution) amount to 15.5%.

C. Development Strategy and Prospects

6.09 While no official long-term development program has yet been prepared for the power sector, the Ministry of Water Resources and Electric Power (MWREP) has prepared the preliminary production profiles for 1985-2000 as a step towards the preparation of such a plan (Appendix F.3). The profiles are based on two broad power demand scenarios, with growth in generation rising to 500,000-520,000 GWh by 1990 and 1,000,000-1,200,000 GWh by the year 2000.[3/] These increases assume an average growth rate in total generation of 6.5-7.4% p.a. during the 1980-2000 period. These scenarios imply electricity demand growth coefficients of roughly 0.9-1.0 in relation to growth of the gross value of industrial and agricultural output (GVIAO), which is assumed to quadruple by the year 2000. (Sectoral analysis and further scenarios are presented in Chapter 2.)

6.10 The present mix of generating capacity is not expected to change much over the next two decades. Due to the long lead time for nuclear and large-scale hydro projects, the role of these forms of generation will not alter substantially before the end of the century. At that time, nuclear power might supply some 4% of total generation and hydropower 18-19% (or 22-23% if small plants are included). Thermal power will account for the balance. Current plans envision use of coal in virtually all new thermal power plants, and barring a dramatic increase in natural gas production, most existing oil- and gas-fired power plants are planned to be gradually phased out over the next two decades.

6.11 The bulk of additional hydropower is expected to come from four long-term, large-scale development schemes, with the capacities indicated below:

Scheme	Total capacity	Capacity to be commissioned by the year 2000
Upper Huanghe	12,600 WM	4,000-6,000 MW
Hongshui	10,400 MW	5,000-6,000 MW
Middle and Upper Changjiang	40,000 MW	15,000-22,000 MW
Middle and Lower Lancang River	6,000 MW	2,000-3,000 MW

Several of the 34 major hydro projects under construction (with a total installed capacity of 17,000 MW) are part of these development schemes.

3/ Excluding generation from small thermal and hydro plants. Small hydro plants are defined as those with a capacity of under 500 kW. Small thermal plants are defined as having capacities of 6 MW or less. Figures are early 1984 estimates.

6.12 The total capacity of thermal projects now under construction is about 20,000 MW. The ongoing thermal power program is based mainly on the use of 200-300 MW units. Large coal-fired thermal stations with 300-600 MW units, and perhaps even 800-1,000 MW units, are planned near major new coal bases during the next two decades. Other thermal stations will be located near suitable port areas and load centers (see Appendix F.5 for further details of major hydro and thermal power development plans).

6.13 China has developed a step-by-step approach to grid expansion and integration, with the ultimate establishment of a national integrated power grid foreseen by the end of the century. The existing regional grids will first be strengthened with 500 kV networks (or, in the case of the Northwest Regional grid, 330 kV networks). Many of the major grids will then be interconnected as surplus power becomes available in a given grid. The first interconnection will be a ±500 kV d.c. line linking the Central and East China Regional grids. With the completion of the planned power bases during the 1990s (particularly the Hongshui River and Huanghe hydro projects, and the Shanxi and Nei Monggol coal-and-power bases) an overlay of long-distance, ultra high voltage lines is anticipated, culminating in the establishment of a national grid. However, the timing of grid expansion and integration plans in the 1990s appears vague.

D. Investment Requirements

6.14 Preliminary estimates have been made of the levels of investment required to meet different scenarios of capacity and grid expansion to the year 2000 (see Appendix F.3). These estimates exclude small hydro and thermal generating plants and development of rural distribution by local units. Given the increasing unit costs in the sector, the estimates show the need for a dramatic increase in average annual investments, if capacity is to be expanded sufficiently to relieve current supply constraints and provide additional power for rapid economic growth. Under the Sixth Five-Year Plan, the average annual investment for the sector was about Y 4.15 billion. Average annual investment requirements are estimated to increase to Y 13-15 billion during 1986-90 and Y 22-29 billion during 1991-2000. These investment levels would imply a major increase in the share of power sector investment in total domestic investment -- the share of power investment in GDP would rise from 1% in 1980 to approximately 2% during 1986-2000.

6.15 The share of investment allocated to the power sector has in the past been lower in China than in many other developing and industrialized countries. The increased share estimated for the future is not unreasonable. The World Bank estimates that power sector investment requirements in all developing countries will represent about 2% of aggregate GDP during 1982-92.[4/] This is also broadly comparable with the recent shares in four major developing countries for which recent data are available (see Appendix F.4).

4/ The World Bank, The Energy Transition in Developing Countries, 1983.

E. Major Issues and Options

Hydropower

6.16 China's exploitable hydroelectric power resources, estimated at 380,000 MW, are among the largest in the world, and only about 6% of this potential has been developed. Nevertheless, the share of hydroelectric power generation in total generation is not anticipated by MWREP to change much before the year 2000. An increase in the share of hydropower could bring major benefits, one of the most important being greater reliance on a renewable energy source, and hence lower fuel requirements by the power sector and a reduction in the pressure such fuel requirements place on China's overall energy balance. Other major benefits include the potential for improved water control and the lack of air pollution problems as a result of hydro development.

6.17 Many of the most favorable sites for hydropower projects (i.e., those relatively close to major load centers) have already been developed. The bulk of China's undeveloped hydropower potential is in the Southwest and Northwest, where large-scale hydropower development would require transmission of the power over distances of 1,200-1,500 km to China's major industrial load centers. Gestation periods for large-scale projects are relatively long: even at sites with fairly ideal construction conditions, lead time of 8-10 years is expected from the time of project approval.[5/] In recent years, the gestation periods of several large projects have been further prolonged, due to unexpected geo-technical problems, shortages of funds, and other unforeseen circumstances.[6/]

6.18 Other factors are also increasing the total economic costs of hydro projects. The unit capital costs of these projects are increasing. Potential sites for large projects generally involve more complex geo-technical factors than in the past, and locations are more remote, causing higher infrastructure costs. Costs due to inundation are also rising.[7/] Indeed, except for projects on the upper Huanghe and Hongshui River, the costs resulting from inundation necessary for base load operation generally cannot be afforded.

5/ The potential for small-scale hydro development is discussed in Chapter 7, paras. 7.64-7.70.

6/ An extreme case is the 2,700 MW Gezhouba project on the Changjiang, for which the total gestation period is now expected to be 15-16 years.

7/ For the Three Gorges project, for example, compensation for inundation is expected to account for as much as one-fourth of total capital costs.

Nuclear Power

6.19 Nuclear power is just beginning to be developed but has potential to play a greater role in electricity supply over the long term.[8/] Currently, a Chinese-designed 300-MW PWR power plant is under construction at Qinshan in Zhejiang, and a 2 x 900 MW PWR plant at Shenzhen in Guangdong is well along in the planning stages. Additional reactors may be constructed in eastern and northeastern China. Currently verified uranium reserves in China are sufficient to sustain operation of 15,000 MW of pressurized water reactors for 30 years. Much of China also remains to be surveyed for uranium, and abundant thorium resources are known to exist.

6.20 The key advantage of nuclear power development is that a base load power source can be established near load centers. Development of nuclear power can, moreover, help relieve the pressure that thermal power development places on coal supplies and transportation facilities. Unit capital costs for generation, however, are on average far higher than for hydro or coal-fired options.

6.21 In the late 1970s, economic comparisons generally favored nuclear over coal-based power generation. But today, in view of the high capital costs and uneven performance of nuclear power plants in some countries, together with lower than expected international coal prices, the economic advantage of nuclear power for base load generation is uncertain. Such issues underscore the importance of evaluating the parameters that determine the economics of nuclear generation in relation to the costs of other alternatives. Nuclear generation could achieve cost parity with steam coal-fired plants, for instance, if coal prices increased (to say US$70/ton) and the cost of nuclear power capacity dropped (to say US$1,200/kW), but neither of these changes is likely to occur over the next decade.

6.22 The commissioning of a few nuclear units in China could be justified in certain circumstances, for example, in locations far from low-cost coal mines and harbor sites. In the long term, possible limitations on coal use - its price and availability, and environmental pollution - may make the nuclear alternative more attractive. The competitiveness of large-scale nuclear power development can be greatly enhanced by careful planning - foreign experience shows that a well designed and well paced program could reduce capital costs by 20-30%. Nuclear plant commissioning over the medium term should be primarily tailored to facilitate the acquisition of technology necessary for a larger scale development of nuclear power at a later stage, as well as to strengthen manpower skills.

6.23 Nuclear power requires a major long-run commitment in terms of manpower and infrastructure development. It involves technically complex

---

8/ China has taken a series of important steps for nuclear safety. China now adheres to the regulatory framework of the International Atomic Energy Agency in Vienna, and is strictly separating plant construction and operation from the licensing and safety monitoring responsibilities.

plants, severe economic consequences in case of operational failures and strict safety requirements, all of which are unique to this type of power. Major investments of effort, time and resources are needed to develop the technology and standards for equipment manufacturing in the early stages of the program as well as the autonomous safety and regulatory institutions to provide essential oversight functions. Particularly important over the long term is that plants be based on a unified standard design, which has been carefully selected and developed.

6.24 Another key aspect of program planning is the development of competent manpower. Experience shows that the existence of highly qualified and experienced engineers, technicians and plant operators is critical for maintaining safe and efficient operations, though in many developing countries this need is underestimated. For example, surveys undertaken by the International Atomic Energy Agency (IAEA) indicate a requirement for doctorate and master-level engineers and physicists ranging from a hundred or so at the pre-project stage, to several thousand during pre-construction and operation. A large scale program may require 20,000 professionals and skilled craftmen, excluding manufacturing. Although these numbers are not large in the Chinese context, they do represent a significant demand on a category of staff which may be in critically short supply, especially when it is considered that indigenous training opportunities may not exist for the needed skills. The long lead time required for the necessary manpower development must thus be taken into account in program planning.

6.25 Careful and long-term planning of specific projects is also critical, particularly in regard to plant grid interactions. Experience in other countries suggests that project-oriented studies should be initiated 12-13 years before a nuclear power plant is expected to begin commercial operation and that a minimum of 6-7 years be allowed for construction (assuming there are no bottlenecks in infrastructural development). In considering plant/grid interactions, special attention must be given to the adequacy of reserve margins, given the large unit sizes of nuclear plants.

Role of Coal

6.26 The future role of conventional thermal power generation is basically determined by the shortfall between primary electricity generation and total requirements. The major issue for thermal power development concerns plant location, particularly the appropriate split between development at coal-and-power bases and development at load centers and port areas. Currently, MWREP anticipates a split in installed capacity of 40-60% for each. Such decisions will obviously depend on the regional distribution of coal resources, regional differences in coal development costs, the relative costs of coal transportation and power transmission, and capabilities to expand transportation facilities (see Appendix E).

6.27 Several problems still require further study, however. With the increase in inland thermal power generation implied by current coal-and-power based development plans, problems of cooling water supply may become acute in some areas of northern China. Hence water availability in these areas over the long-term, and possible use of air cooling towers, need to be carefully assessed. Furthermore, since annual coal consumption in thermal power plants at load centers and port areas is expected to increase by 200-300 million tons by the year 2000,[9] the impact on air pollution, and additional investments required to control such pollution, needs to be considered. Evaluation of factors such as these should play an important role in determining plant locations and the time at which nuclear power generation could assume a major role in system expansion.

Size of Nuclear and Coal-fired Units

6.28 Pressurized water reactor technology in the US, Europe and Japan is based mainly on 950 MW (gross) reactor size. New units in the 1,200 MW range are now being commissioned but the economies of scale gained in that range are rather small and could be offset by a lower reliability. Another problem is that large size units make it difficult to match the demand closely and have tight control of the reserve margins.

6.29 Larger size units are better justified when they make full use of a limited number of available sites. Finally, some of China's regional networks would be much more vulnerable to outages as big as 1,200 MW than the much larger power pools of Western Europe or the US. Even if 1,200 MW units had the same average availability as 900 MW ones, a largely untested assumption, reserve margins would probably still need to be 15% higher.

6.30 For much the same reasons as with nuclear plants, rapid deployment of coal-fired units as large as 600 MW should be approached with caution, especially in small regional power grids. Most economies of scale are already obtained before the 600 MW stage and the advantages of standardization in terms of costs and availability can only be reaped if long series of units of the same size are installed and grid integration is sufficiently advanced. Given experience in other countries, any possible role for unit sizes above 600 MW should be carefully scrutinized.

Grid Expansion and Integration

6.31 In all of China's major grids, power demand exceeds supply and is expected to do so over the next five years. Many of the major grids are already quite large. Interconnection of most regional grids would require transmission lines over 1,000 km in length. Over such distances, the cost of interconnection is not justified by reductions in reserve requirements and load diversification alone.

6.32 As generating capacity is expanded, however, greater interconnection will become more compelling and eventually imperative because, by the end of the century, large amounts of power will have to be transmitted from west to east. Long-distance lines for bulk power transmission are a necessary component of many of the plans to construct major power bases, i.e., the hydropower projects in the southwest. In addition, integration will allow wider use of

9/ Assuming an average calorific value of 4,400 kcal/kg, as in 1980.

modern, large-scale generating equipment with improved technical and economic results.

6.33 A single synchronous national grid may not yet be necessary, however. Most of the advantages of a large-scale system can be obtained by a partial interconnection into two power pools or more (as is done for instance in India, Europe and the US). Direct current links could be used not only for transmitting energy from remote hydroelectric sites but also for providing a small backup from the fringe of one grid to others. There are many options and interconnections must be planned on the basis of long-term supply and demand targets in order to have a clear perspective of the best architecture of future grids. The technological options, timing and extent of grid integration will have to be carefully evaluated.

System Planning

6.34 Major planning and investment decisions taken now will affect the situation in the last few years of this century and beyond. All economic factors must be taken into account. In dealing with projects that have different gestation periods, accounting for the time value of money is critical. Externalities should also be considered, especially environmental pollution and the various benefits that may come from multipurpose hydro projects. A balance must be found between integration of planning at a strategic level and decentralization of program and project management.

6.35 At a time when broad strategic decisions must be made about the generating plant mix and grid architecture, the adoption of modern sophisticated system planning techniques is a key to validating these decisions and ensuring their implementation in ways that minimize cost. The sheer magnitude of the problem and its increasing complexity due to grid interaction makes such methods indispensable. Modern computer models enable planners to look beyond the per unit cost of energy in determining least cost sequences that match load forecasts; they take into account such factors as demand patterns, variations in hydrology, and random outages of generation and transmission facilities. However, the models are not without limitations and hence the importance of off-model analysis and scenario-based planning must be fully recognized; and this imposes special training requirements.

7. RURAL ENERGY SUPPLY AND DEMAND

7.01 Energy consumption in agricultural production and processing, rural households and village public facilities totaled about 300 million TCE in 1980, or about 40% of the country's total final energy consumption.[1/] Agricultural production and processing consumed about 45 million TCE of commercial energy. Rural households consumed over 250 million TCE, of which more than 85% was biomass, mostly collected and used according to age-old traditions.

7.02 China's rural sector also includes many township and village industries (formerly referred to as commune and brigade industries) not involved in agricultural processing. These industries rely primarily on coal and electric power to meet energy requirements. In terms of total energy consumption, the building materials industry is undoubtedly the most important single sector -- in 1980, commune and brigade enterprises produced 110 billion bricks, consuming over 25 million tons of coal. These collective industries have been included under industry as a whole for analytical purposes (see Chapters 1 and 2).

7.03 The household sector dominates total energy consumption in the rural sector, and current supply and consumption patterns are of serious concern. First, current energy supplies are considered inadequate to meet the current cooking and heating needs of the rural population, let alone allow for an improvement in rural living standards. According to Chinese estimates, current supplies of useful energy fall short of minimum requirements by an average of 20-25%.[2/] Second, with the rapid growth of China's rural population, the increased use of biomass fuels can no longer be sustained by the agricultural system and local ecology through traditional means without serious adverse consequences. While production of crop by-products has probably doubled since the first half of this century, the proportion of crop by-products used as fuel has nonetheless increased from about 50% during the

---

1/ Final energy consumption includes energy in the form and quantities supplied to final consumers, and is different from "end-use" energy consumption, where conversion losses in the use of energy by consumers is deducted. All figures exclude energy use by township and village industries outside of the agricultural processing field, which is different from the common Chinese practice.

2/ Proceedings of the Workshop on Rural Energy Planning in the Developing Countries of Asia (FAO, 1983); Lu Yingzhong, "The Prospects of Rural Energy in the PRC" (Fifth Annual International Conference of the IAEE, 1984).

early 1930s to 60-80% today,[3/] inhibiting use of crop by-products as animal fodder, as an organic input for soil improvement, and as a construction material. Increasing pressure on local nonagricultural land as a source of biomass fuel has exacerbated long-standing water and soil conservation problems, as traditional fuel collection methods have often gone unchecked and immediate fuel needs have impeded efforts to reforest local areas. Hence, major challenges exist to increase rural household energy supplies, to rationalize biomass energy supply within the context of the local agricultural and ecological systems, and to increase the efficiency of energy use.

7.04 Particularly since 1970, China has promoted programs to develop local energy sources, in line with a policy emphasis on energy self-reliance in rural areas. These programs include the promotion of forestry projects to provide fuelwood, biogas generation, small-scale hydroelectric stations, small-scale rural coal mines, and, to a lesser extent, improved rural stoves, technology to use solar energy directly, and wind power generation systems. China has had considerable success in the popularization of biogas production, small-scale hydro generation, and small-scale coal mining. The Chinese leadership strongly endorses continued promotion of all the above programs. However, development policies and priorities have changed significantly since the 1970s, largely as a result of serious evaluation of past efforts and changes in rural economic policies.

7.05 During most of the 1970s, rural energy development programs were characterized by a strong emphasis on rapid popularization of least-cost technology, with reliance on local materials and equipment, and local technical abilities and innovation. These programs often paid insufficient attention to effective long-term results, quality rather than quantity, careful planning, and technical details. Current efforts to correct past deficiencies include, particularly, promotion of quality standards and greater standardization of technology, and strengthening the institutional structure for management and technology diffusion. Greater attention is also being paid to individual incentives, particularly in the forestry sector, and clarifying the roles of the state, collective and private sectors. Far greater emphasis is being placed on the construction of fuelwood lots and the promotion of improved rural stoves than in the past. The fundamental policy of promoting local energy development as opposed to increasing energy supplies from other areas through the state remains, however.

7.06 In the following pages, three sections deal with the rural sector as a whole, including current consumption patterns, regional dimensions in household fuel supply and demand, and rural energy planning. These are followed by a brief discussion of further, more specific issues in rural energy development: fuelwood supply, biogas production, the improved stove program, direct solar energy and wind utilization, petroleum product consumption in agriculture, and rural electrification.

3/ John L. Buck, Land Utilization in China (1937); Wu Wen, et al. "Our Views on the Resolution of China's Rural Energy Requirements" (1982), Nengyuan guanli (Energy Management) (1982).

A. Current Rural Energy Consumption

7.07 Based on surveys conducted in 1979, current annual energy consumption by rural households is estimated at slightly over 250 million TCE (see Table 7.1).[4] Crop by-products, consisting primarily of corn cobs and stalks, sorghum stalks, and rice, wheat and millet straw, account for 46% of total consumption. Fuelwood, mainly low-quality fuels such as small branches, brush, grass and leaves,[5] accounts for 38%. The Chinese estimate that the current fuelwood supply is provided half through "legitimate" collection[6] (which can be sustained with minimal environmental damage) and half through random collection on local nonagricultural land.

7.08 Coal currently accounts for about 13% of rural household energy consumption. Dried dung is not widely used as direct fuel in China, except in a few areas. Dung is, however, an important input for the production of biogas, which is currently used by about 3% of China's rural households.

7.09 Almost 90% of China's rural townships have some access to electricity. Although official statistics are not available, the Ministry of Water Resources and Electric Power (MWREP) estimates that about half of China's rural households use electricity, implying a level of rural household electrification that exceeds levels in most developing nations. Absolute consumption levels are low, however - total consumption by rural households and public facilities was about 7 TWh in 1980, of which perhaps one-third was used by households. Families that do not have electricity use flashlights or kerosene lanterns or traditional methods, such as candles or vegetable oil lamps, for lighting.

7.10 Average total per capita energy consumption in rural households is currently about 0.32 TCE per year. In Northern India, per capita household energy consumption in rural areas is only slightly less, at 0.25 TCE per year, despite the fact that heating requirements in China are more significant, on average. In southern China, some form of heating is usually necessary during the winter, at least intermittently, except for the lowland areas in the extreme south. In the northwest, north and northeast of China, heating requirements are most substantial, with total household energy requirements generally 50% higher than in the south. One common device for heating is the <u>kang</u>, a large bed built with bricks, but hollow inside. A <u>kang</u> is heated by a

---

4/ Chinese estimates, even those based on the same original data, often vary widely, in part due to the use of different energy conversion factors. Conversion factors used for this estimate are given in the notes to Table 7.1.

5/ Charcoal is also consumed in China, and may be included in statistics for fuelwood.

6/ Includes organized pruning and thinning of timber and protective forests, and harvesting of trees and brush grown specifically for fuel.

Table 7.1: RURAL ENERGY CONSUMPTION, 1980

	Million tons	Million tons of standard coal equivalent
Households		
Crop by-products	235	117.5
Fuelwood	180	96.4
Coal	45	32.1
Dung /a	10.4	5.2
Kerosene	1.0	1.5
Electricity /b	7.2 bln kWh	3.0
Total		255.7
Agriculture and Agricultural Processing /c		
Coal	30	21.5
Diesel oil	8.2	11.9
Gasoline	0.8	1.2
Electricity	26.1 bln kWh	10.8
Total		45.4

/a Includes dung used in biogas production.
/b Includes rural commercial and public consumption.
/c Excludes village industries not engaged in agricultural processing.

Sources and notes: Data in physical quantities are based on a survey of rural energy use conducted in 30 counties by the Energy Research Institute in 1979, as presented in Nengyuan guanli (Energy Management), Energy Publishing House, 1982; Wu Wen and Chen Enjian, Guangzhou Institute of Energy Conversion, "Our Views to the Resolution of China's Rural Energy Requirements" (paper prepared for the Joint CAS-NAS Science Policy Conference, August 1982); data on exhibit at the All-China Exhibition on Rural Energy, Beijing, September 1982. Electricity consumption estimates refer to 1980, and include consideration of MWREP data for 1982.

Conversion factors are as follows (air-dried):

Coal equivalent:	7,000 kcal/kg
Crop by-products:	3,500 kcal/kg
Fuelwood:	3,750 kcal/kg
Dung:	3,550 kcal/kg
Kerosene:	10,300 kcal/kg
Diesel oil:	10,200 kcal/kg
Gasoline:	10,500 kcal/kg
Electricity:	2,890 kcal/kWh

small stove at its base, or with waste heat from the kitchen stove - the chimney flue from the stove is constructed to pass horizontally under the kang before rising through the roof.

7.11 Although the household sector accounts for a far higher share of total energy consumption, agricultural production and processing account for a higher share of commercial energy use. Consumption includes about 27 TWh of electricity, of which about 65% is used in irrigation and drainage, and 35% in agricultural processing. About 9 million tons of petroleum products were consumed in 1980 by mobile farm machinery, pumping facilities, and processing equipment. Although allocations have increased recently, petroleum product supplies for agriculture fall short of demand. Between 1978 and 1981, state allocations actually dropped while the total horsepower of farm machinery inventories increased by 33%.

B. Regional Dimensions in Household Fuel Supply and Demand

7.12 Government policy stresses maximum reliance on local energy development to meet rural energy needs, particularly in the household sector.[7] In many areas there is substantial potential to both increase local energy production and improve the rationality of supply patterns, but the degree of development potential and the mix of options involved vary dramatically between localities. Major opportunities also exist for improving the efficiency of energy use, but the potential and options also vary. In some areas, achieving a balance between local supply and household demand that is environmentally sustainable may be fairly straightforward and easy. In other areas, it may be continually difficult, requiring careful planning of production and use, and in some cases, increasing use of supplementary energy supplies from other areas.

7.13 Rural population densities help illustrate the density of fuel demand relative to land. The availability of land, together with land utilization patterns and growing conditions, provide the key parameters for biomass supply potential. Broadly speaking, the areas of China with the highest rural population densities are the North China Plain,[8] the Sichuan Basin, the Zhu Jiang (Pearl River) delta, and pockets along the southeastern coast. Densities often exceed 600 rural persons per square kilometer over large areas. In these areas, together with parts of the Loess Plateau where biomass yields are low and coal is relatively scarce, meeting household fuel demand from local supplies is most difficult.

7/ Current policy is summarized by the 16-character slogan, "Develop according to local conditions; emphasize use of many types of energy, supplementing each other; stress comprehensive use; and emphasize results."

8/ Includes Jiangsu, northern Anhui, central and eastern Henan, western Shandong, and southern Hebei.

7.14 Crop by-products provide by far the largest energy source for rural household consumption in the North China Plain and Sichuan Basin. In Jiangsu and Shandong, it is estimated that available fuelwood supplies can meet household fuel demand for an average of less than one month per year. Farther west in the North China Plain, and in the Sichuan Basin, available fuelwood supplies are slightly higher, but still can meet only one to four months of demand. In the Loess Plateau, fuelwood supplies can meet less than one month of household demand per year, and while coal is an important energy source in some areas, crop by-products also play a key role.[9/]

7.15 Estimates of the total supply of crop by-products per rural person by province are presented in Appendix G.1. In 1981, the national average was about 450 kg per rural person. Averages are highest in the northeastern provinces (700-850 kg per person), and lowest in the southern provinces of Guangdong and Guangxi, the southwestern provinces of Guizhou and Yunnan, and the northwestern provinces of Shanxi, Gansu, and Qinghai (generally 300-350 kg per person). In the North China Plain and Sichuan Basin, supplies are close to the national average, except for Jiangsu Province (about 560 kg per person).

7.16 However, crop by-products have several high value uses, e.g., as an organic input for soil conditioning, as a construction or industrial material, and as a source of fodder. While some areas burn as much as 80% of the available crop by-products as fuel, opportunity costs can be very high, especially if other goods must be procured to meet demand that could be met by the by-products. In many areas, reducing the share of available crop by-products directly burned as fuel is considered one of the most important goals of rural energy development.

7.17 During the last three decades, crop by-products have provided the bulk of the increase in primary energy supplies for rural households in the nation as a whole, and in the North China Plain and Sichuan Basin in particular. In the future, however, anticipated increases in non-fuel by-product demand will make further increases in per capita by-product fuel consumption difficult to achieve in many areas - and often undesirable, even if possible. Increasing by-product production can no longer be counted on to alleviate rural fuel problems - the future calls for active development of alternatives.

7.18 Increased production of fuelwood in private or collective plantations has a great potential as a rational means of increasing total household energy supplies. The potential production of fuelwood plantations is basically a function of the availability of suitable land and unit yields. In most regions south of the Chang Jiang, uncultivated hilly land comprises over two-thirds of the land area. Yields may often enable allocations of less than five mu (one-third ha) per family to have a dramatic effect on fuel supply, both in terms of alleviating shortages and improving,

---

9/ Estimates of fuelwood availability are from the All-China Exhibition on Rural Energy, Beijing, 1982.

from an environmental viewpoint, current fuelwood procurement practices. In parts of northeastern and northern China, suitable land is also available, but potential yields are far lower - perhaps one-tenth of yields in the extreme south. In the densely populated lowlands of the North China Plain and Sichuan Basin, land availability often poses a binding constraint. While some regions may have the potential for increasing charcoal supplies from fuelwood plantations in neighboring areas, local fuelwood supply is limited to what can be produced from small plots of marginal land and "four-around" plantations (plantings along roads, along rivers and canals, around houses, and around villages).

7.19 In some areas, other renewable energy technologies can and have been developed as alternatives to the use of solid fuels. Annual average solar insolation rates range between 150 and 220 kcal/sq cm in most of western China, and between 130 and 150 kcal/sq cm in most of northern China and along the southern coast. Use of solar cookers and hot water heaters has progressed in a few of these areas in recent years. In addition, in many relatively mountainous areas, where conditions for small-scale hydropower development are particularly auspicious, use of electricity for cooking is beginning to be promoted. By the end of 1984 about 370,000 rural households used electricity for cooking.

7.20 Coal constitutes the third most important rural household fuel source, but data on regional variations in rural household consumption are not available.[10/] Increased use of local coal resources for household fuel represents a strong option in many areas, particularly northern China and parts of Henan and Anhui, where deposits are substantial and household fuel demand particularly high. Between 1979 and 1983, annual coal output from small-scale collective mines grew from 106 million tons to about 170 million tons, and substantial potential exists for continued production increases (Chapter 4). Strong competition exists, however, between local use in rural industry and households, and between local use and sale to the state. In areas such as Jiangsu, where total coal consumption already far exceeds local production and reserves are limited, significant increases in rural household coal consumption will further increase coal shipment requirements from other provinces.

7.21 Among the options to improve the efficiency of household energy use, conversion of biomass to biogas is considered attractive in some areas, as a technology that enables biomass to be used more efficiently as a fuel than direct combustion, and as a fertilizer, in some ways more effectively than by direct application. Key natural parameters defining the technical potential for biogas generation are the availability of resources for fermentation and temperature. In most areas, pig manure is the primary fermentation resource. Usually the manure from two mature pigs, and hence total holdings of 4-5 pigs,

---

10/ In terms of coal production, only nine provinces produced less than 10 million tons in 1981: Zhejiang and Fujian along the eastern coast; Hubei in central China; Guangdong and Guangxi in southern China; Xizang (Tibet); and Gansu, Qinghai, and Ningxia in northwest China.

is required to meet the cooking and lighting energy needs of a 5-person family. Sichuan has the highest number of pigs per rural person of any province, with an average of about three pigs per rural household, and has achieved the greatest success in biogas popularization (see Appendix G.2). Other areas with high pig populations relative to rural population are Liaoning, Yunnan, Zhejiang, Hunan and Guangdong as well as Beijing and Shanghai. Per capita pig holdings are below the national average of 0.37 in the North China Plain (except in Jiangsu).

7.22 When ambient temperature falls below freezing,11/ it is difficult to produce biogas using simple Chinese methods. The Sichuan Basin, Fujian, Guangdong, Guangxi and southern Yunnan average less than five freezing days per year. In eastern and central China, freezing days average 10 to 75 per year, while north of the Huanghe, averages exceed 100. While popularization of biogas has been significant in central and eastern China, and even further north, digestor operation becomes more and more seasonal as latitudes increase. In most of the North China Plain, family biogas units are commonly used for only 5-7 months per year (see Appendix G.2).

7.23 Significant potential also exists in most areas for increasing the efficiency of the direct use of fuel through improvements in stove technology. While current biomass stove heat efficiencies average at about 10%, the heat efficiencies of improved stoves currently being popularized average at 22-25%, with varying costs and implications for cooking convenience. Current cooking efficiencies vary substantially between regions - where household fuel supply has been a longstanding problem, more efficient cooking methods have developed traditionally, due to necessity. In one survey, the efficiency of fuelwood use in relatively mountainous areas was found to be just 5%, while the efficiency of crop by-product stoves in lowland areas averaged 12-13%. In areas where coal is used as a rural household fuel, significant improvements in end-use efficiencies can be achieved through greater use of briquettes and improvements in their quality, as well as through stove improvements.

7.24 In the future, it will probably be most difficult to substantially increase rural household energy supplies through local development in the densely populated areas of the Sichuan Basin and parts of the North China Plain where coal deposits are minimal, especially Jiangsu. These areas already have difficulties in meeting demand. Substantial potential may exist in most of these areas, however, to increase the efficiency of energy use, with two options being biogas generation and/or stove improvement. In reviewing options for the future, nevertheless, differences between technical and economic potential must be carefully considered, and the option of increasing the supply of energy from other areas must also be carefully weighed.

11/ Temperatures inside digestors must be at least 10°C to produce significant quantities of gas, but with underground construction, use of simple insulation techniques, and adjustments in the fermentation mixture, temperatures within digestors are commonly higher than ambient temperature during cooler seasons.

C. Rural Energy Planning

7.25 Realization of rural energy development potential requires, among other things, sound technology, developed in accordance with actual local conditions; the appropriate mix of policies to encourage development; good organization; and effective means of disseminating new ideas and training local people. Moreover, as most areas have a variety of options but limited capabilities, the selection of an optimal mix of options from a long-term point of view is critical. As mentioned previously, the technical potential for different types of development varies greatly between localities. In addition, the relationship between technical potential and what is optimal from a practical and economic standpoint also varies greatly. To select the best local development paths, as well as to mobilize resources, the strength of planning, particularly at local levels, will be crucial for the future.

7.26 Past experience in China has shown some of the costs of weaknesses in rural energy planning. Experience has also shown the critical importance of taking into account varying local conditions, and the complexities involved in choosing the optimal paths for different localities. Substantial progress has been made in recent years in strengthening the institutional infrastructure for rural energy development at national, regional and local levels. Local rural energy offices have been established in some areas, and play an active role in the provision of technical expertise, mobilization of resources, the training of local people, and, sometimes, the mapping out of long-term plans based on assessment of local conditions. These efforts need to be continually strengthened and reinforced.

7.27 Comprehensive evaluation of various rural energy development options represents a major challenge, due to the complexities involved. The attractiveness of household biogas generation, for example, may hinge on factors as diverse as local trends in pig slaughtering rates and recent incidence of schistosomiasis. The relative attractiveness of different options also varies dramatically between areas, so that application of general guidelines is inadvisable. The economics of biogas generation strongly depend on how it fits in with local agricultural systems, which may vary substantially even between neighboring villages. The cost of small-scale hydroelectric power generation is highly site-specific, and the relative attractiveness of development is further complicated by differences regarding externalities, local land use patterns, and local grid characteristics, if a grid exists.

7.28 Both financial and economic analysis are needed to evaluate options. While financial analysis considers profitability in monetary terms, cash flow, and financial payback periods from the point of view of a given unit, economic analysis considers the total benefits and costs to society as a whole. Hence, economic analysis considers social costs and benefits (rather than costs and benefits determined strictly by current prices) and various externalities, the costs and benefits of which may not be realized by a local unit.

7.29 One good example of the importance of considering both financial and economic aspects of a given development option concerns the linkage of small hydro units to larger power grids. Particularly under past policies, such linkages were highly attractive from the financial viewpoint of units operating small hydro plants, due to prevailing prices for sale to the grid during the wet seasons and for purchase from the grid during dry seasons. From an economic viewpoint, however, such linkages were sometimes highly costly, as the actual costs far outweighed the benefits from the point of view of the grid - particularly when the cost of additional capacity required to meet local dry season demand is included - and could represent an economic loss to the grid that is greater than the economic gain for the local area.

7.30 Economic benefits and costs for rural energy development options are often difficult to quantify, and in practice, evaluation often involves judgment about the balance between qualitative factors. Most important is to include all relevant benefits and costs in the evaluation, and to consider all of the options available. In addition, many of the relevant economic benefits and costs of different alternatives involve society outside of a locality, as in the example cited above, or in a case where afforestation for fuelwood supply affects water conservation. In such cases, state policies play the key role in encouraging optimal local decisions.

D. Issues in Rural Energy Development

Afforestation and Fuelwood Supply

7.31 Currently, only 12.7% of China's total land area is classified as forestland. Moreover, forestland is concentrated primarily in the less populated parts of the northeast and southwest. China's leadership has placed strong emphasis on afforestation since the 1950s, including the planting of protective forests for water and soil conservation, and the planting of productive forests. Afforestation work has been pursued primarily by rural collectives in mass afforestation drives. Despite the tremendous efforts made, however, results have been mixed. Official figures show that China's forested land area has increased by 20-25% during the last three decades, but statistics on forest stocks (i.e., cubic meters of wood) are revealing: while man-made forests account for 23% of the land area classified as forestland, they account for only 2% of total forest stocks.[12/] Difficulty in achieving results through mass afforestation efforts can in part be attributed to difficult conditions and lack of technical expertise at local levels, but a lack of attention to incentives for quality planting and especially aftercare appears to have been critical. Incentives pose an obvious problem in afforestation work, as benefits tend to accrue over the long term, and often indirectly. In China, however, difficulties have often been compounded by confusion about who owns and should benefit from trees that have been planted.

7.32 During the 1980s, reforms have been designed to improve results in afforestation work. Three key measures include: (a) a movement to clarify land use and tree ownership rights, particularly in areas of past dispute; (b) adoption of responsibility systems in afforestation work, whereby

---

12/ 1976 General Forestry Survey.

collective afforestation work is contracted out to specialized individual households or groups of households, and the income of these households is essentially determined by the results of their work; and (c) allocation of private plots to individual households for growing trees. The latter measure in particular may have a dramatic impact on future fuelwood supply.

7.33 As mentioned previously, about 90 million tons, or one-half of annual rural fuelwood consumption, is estimated as "legitimately" collected fuelwood. Only about one-quarter of this is currently supplied from collective fuelwood lots, while the balance is provided from pruning and thinning of forests earmarked primarily for protective or other productive uses.

7.34 In addition, an estimated 90 million tons of fuelwood is collected at random from uncultivated land, and it is this type of fuelwood collection that China's leaders would like to reduce through development of more rational supply methods. In 1980, directives were issued calling for the allocation of land for private woodlots, primarily for fuel, and subsequent directives and laws have reinforced this policy. While the government has set basic guidelines, most of the details of implementation have been left to local governments.

7.35 In areas where suitable barren land exists for afforestation -- only nonforested land may be distributed -- 1-10 mu may be allocated for each household (1 mu equals one-fifteenth of a hectare). Households are not given ownership of the land, which still belongs to rural collectives, but certificates are issued to households guaranteeing them ownership of the trees they plant on the land, with the right of family inheritance. Households are allowed to plant only trees on their plots; trees must be planted by a specific deadline for families to retain use of the land. Families may use, sell, or give away the wood they grow.

7.36 On the plains, where no large uncultivated areas are available, small strips of marginal land along rivers and roads may be distributed for private planting, but most fuelwood planting probably will occur as part of the usual collective "four-around" afforestation work.

7.37 About 70 million rural households had been allocated land for private woodlots by the end of 1984, representing some 45% of China's rural households. Land allotments totalled 26 million hectares - seven times the fuelwood lot area reported in the mid-1970s (see Table 7.2).

7.38 No state subsidies are available for the private woodlot program, but provisions have apparently been made to supply seedlings on credit. Seedlings are supplied by state forestry farms, by collective nurseries, and sometimes by households specializing in forestry work. Technical assistance is sometimes provided by county forestry offices or collective forestry units. Adequate provisions for both seedling supply and technical assistance will be critical for the success of the program.

Table 7.2: FORESTED LAND AREA IN CHINA, CIRCA 1976

Forest classification	Area (mln ha)	% of total
Timber	98.00	80.5
Economic /a	8.52	7.0
Protective	7.85	6.4
Fuelwood	3.67	3.0
Bamboo	3.15	2.6
Special /b	0.67	0.5
Total	121.86	100.0

/a Forests that provide fruits, nuts, edible oils and other cash crops.
/b Forests used for aesthetic or experimental purposes.

Source: 1976 General Forestry Survey data, issued by the National Forestry Bureau, in Zhongguo Nongye Dili Zonglun (A General Treatise on the Agricultural Geography of China), 1980.

Biogas Production

7.39 In China, the production of biogas has been viewed as a particularly appropriate technology, because it not only provides a clean fuel that can be used more efficiently than traditional solid fuel, but also provides high quality organic fertilizer and helps to improve rural sanitation. Two important factors conducive to the popularization of the technology in China are a strong tradition in the collection and fermentation of organic wastes for use as fertilizer, and a well-developed hog industry, operated by households and collectives, yielding ideal organic inputs for biogas production, which can be easily collected.

7.40 During the 1970s, about 7 million family-sized digestors, 800 biogas stations for motive power and about 1,000 very small electricity generating units using biogas were constructed.[13/] While the speed of popularization was remarkable, recent frank evaluations of the program during the 1970s have underlined serious problems, many of which stem from an overemphasis on rapid popularization, and lack of emphasis on achievement of effective results. Several Chinese estimates conclude that the actual number of family-sized digestors in operation is only 3-4.5 million. In Sichuan, where construction of some 5 million digestors was reported in the late 1970s, only 1.2 million digestors were reportedly in operation in early 1984. The chief problems have been poor construction, resulting in leakage problems; a lack of understanding regarding management techniques at local levels; and, in some cases, a lack of adequate supplies of inputs for fermentation. Poor construction has been due to both inadequate expertise at local levels and overemphasis on the use of low quality, particularly cheap, construction materials. With the use of low quality construction materials, the actual lifetime of many digestors was only 3-5 years.

7.41 These mixed results have by no means led to an abandonment of the biogas program, but policies have been redirected to place greater emphasis on improved quality and management, as opposed to speed in popularization. The importance of institutional development has been well recognized, and organizations at the various collective and state levels concerned with basic and applied research, training, and management have been strengthened. Digestor construction is now pursued primarily by specialized teams, sometimes organized into biogas companies. In many areas, digestors are being constructed under contracts, which provide for technical inspection and guarantee operation for at least three years. Use of low quality construction materials, such as "triple concrete" [14/] is being de-emphasized, and most digestors are now built with commercial cement. Local teams for digestor management have been organized in many villages. While new digestor construction appears to be slower than during the middle and late 1970s, results appear to have

---

13/ Most motive power and electricity generation systems are based on dual-fuel, converted diesel engines, where biogas provides 70-90% of the fuel.

14/ Triple concrete is a traditional Chinese building material made from lime, sand, and clay, mixed in special proportions with water.

improved substantially -- some areas report that over 90% of the digestors built since 1979 are currently in operation. Digestor lifetimes of 10-20 years are now anticipated.

7.42 The availability of funds to cover the capital cost of digestor construction and a sufficient supply of inputs for fermentation are the two most important constraints facing the household biogas program. Largely due to the new emphasis on use of quality materials, material costs for new family-sized digestors have increased from Y 20-50 during the 1970s to an average of about Y 100 today. Labor costs for construction are generally Y 50-80, while the cost of accessories (pipes, stoves, lanterns, etc.) add about Y 20-30. Hence, total construction and installation costs can be on the order of Y 200. Subsidies are usually available to households, most often from the collective, but the amount varies dramatically. In Sichuan, collectives may provide nothing or up to Y 100 per digestor.

7.43 The relationship between the costs and direct and indirect benefits of biogas production varies to such an extent that judgments on economic viability must take account of specific local conditions. One critical variable is the utilization factor of units -- the number of days per year a digestor is used. This is largely a function of both climate and the availability of fermentation inputs.

7.44 In most Chinese family-sized systems, some night soil and crop by-products are used in conjunction with pig excreta inputs, but pig manure provides most of the fermentation material. Manure supplies are only adequate for family-sized operations where families have pig holdings well above the average (see para 7.21). Currently, considerable research is being conducted on means of increasing the share of crop by-product inputs, which could both alleviate input supply constraints and improve the value of crop by-products as an organic fertilizer.

7.45 Large-scale, community-size biogas digestors to supply gas for motive power, electricity generation, and household needs are receiving increasing emphasis. Some systems are based upon inputs from liquor or beer manufacturing enterprises, while others are pursued in conjunction with large livestock-rearing operations (e.g., 100 pigs), managed by specialized households. As of early 1985, some 20,000 rural households were supplied with gas from community-sized biogas systems, and such systems are expected to play an increasingly important role in the future.

Improved Rural Stoves

7.46 China has only recently begun a major program to develop and disseminate more efficient rural cooking stoves. The program appears to stem mainly from recent appraisals of the seriousness of current rural energy problems, and from an assessment of the potential a stoves program has to reduce fuel requirements and increase useful energy supplies at a relatively low cost. Goals have been ambitious: in the Sixth Five-Year Plan, dissemination of 25 million improved stoves was targeted for 1985, implying use of new stoves in about 15% of China's rural households. By the end of 1984, more than 18 million improved stoves were reported to have been disseminated.

7.47 Most rural families currently cook on large, brick stoves, built in a square, with round holes at the top to hold cooking bowls and an opening at the base for fuel input. Often, no chimmey is used, and the smoke is vented in the house. Heat efficiencies tend to average about 10%.

7.48 Currently, many improved stoves are being developed, using metal, clay or brick and catering to different types of needs. While higher efficiencies have been attained using laboratory designs, the heat efficiencies of the stoves being disseminated are typically 20-25%, and costs per unit are typically Y 40-60. Much of the popularization effort is focused on field demonstrations and displays, usually organized by local rural energy offices. While state support is provided for research and development and the popularization effort in the national plan, state subsidies have not been made available for stove purchases.

7.49 As in other countries that have promoted use of improved stoves, one of the constraints on popularization may be a degree of inconvenience compared with traditional stoves. The improved stoves in China typically have smaller input openings and combustion chambers, which helps improve efficiencies, but requires greater preparation of fuel and more frequent feeding. In addition, because rural stoves often represent a key source of household heating, successful promotion of improved stoves often must take heating requirements into account, in addition to efficiency. Hence, major challenges exist not only in popularization work, but also in design work, in order to adequately meet efficiency, convenience and heating requirements, while keeping costs low.

Direct Solar and Wind Energy Utilization

7.50 Development of a wide variety of technologies for direct solar energy utilization has begun in China, including hot water heaters, cookers, photovoltaics, crop driers, de-salinization systems, greenhouses, and new passive solar housing designs.

7.51 Over 100,000 square meters of solar collectors for hot water supply have been installed to date, many of which are in Beijing or its suburbs. About 30 factories currently produce flat plate collectors, with costs ranging from Y 70-160 per square meter. Simple hot water heating systems have been developed in some areas for rural use - in the rural areas of Beijing Municipality, small, simple systems have been installed by some households, at a cost of about Y 40 per unit.

7.52 Solar cookers have been increasingly promoted in recent years, with about 100,000 units reportedly in use. Parabolic reflector cookers are most common. Some 100 manufacturers currently produce cookers, which cost Y 70-100 each.

7.53 Photovoltaic cells were first developed in China about 25 years ago for aerospace applications. Single wafer silicon cells with conversion efficiencies of 15% have been developed in the laboratory, but several factories use monocrystalline silicon rejected from other industrial processes, producing cells with conversion efficiencies as low as 5%. Cadmium sulfide cells also have been developed, with efficiencies ranging between 5% and 8%, and research on gallium arsemide cells has begun. Solar cells have been used on land primarily as a source of electricity for railway signals, remote communications equipment, and electric livestock fences.

7.54 Solar greenhouses are rare, but simple crop-growing greenhouses are common, particularly in the suburbs of northern cities. Most greenhouses are constructed with cheap plastics, which must be replaced every year.

7.55 Utilization of solar energy can and should be expanded substantially in the future, in both urban and rural areas. Simple hot water heaters have become increasingly cost competitive in many other countries; in parts of China, substantial potential for development remains largely untapped. Development of improved plastics for solar collectors and greenhouses could significantly improve results. Use of state-of-the-art technology for production of silicon cells could expand potential applications. Although costs of silicon cell arrays produced in China have dropped significantly in recent years, they are still about Y 80 per peak watt, compared with US$7-10 in Japan and the US. With further improvements in manufacturing technology and mass production, costs of photovoltaic power generation in other countries also are expected to continue to fall substantially below current levels during the next decade. In housing construction, some aspects of passive solar design have been traditionally employed in China, but substantial potential nevertheless exists for greater use of simple, low or no-cost passive solar features in new houses.

7.56 Wind energy has been used in China since ancient times for water pumping and threshing in some rural areas, but the development of wind-powered electricity generation systems has begun only recently. Along the coast of Zhejiang, Fujian, and Shandong, and in Nei Monggol and parts of the northeast, wind speeds of over 6 meters per second for 2,500 or more hours per year are reportedly common. In Nei Monggol, portable wind generators in the 100-250 watt range have been popularized in some areas, often for household use. In other areas, a few larger generators have been built, in the 20-40 KW range.

7.57 Substantial potential exists for expanding the development and popularization of wind generators of different sizes, including large systems. In other countries, development has focused on systems for isolated, remote areas and for existing electricity grids. Large systems, in the 1 MW range, have been developed, with capital costs as low as US$1,000/KW, excluding any storage. One major advantage is the relatively short lead time for construction - even large systems can be put into operation in 1-1/2 years.

Petroleum Product Consumption in Agriculture

7.58 During the middle and late 1960s and the 1970s, promotion of agricultural mechanization was a cornerstone in Chinese agricultural development strategy. Since 1979, however, rural reforms have resulted in an emphasis on smaller scale production by individual households, which has slowed, or in some cases rolled-back, the development of mechanized field operations. While statistics on the total area plowed by tractors show an increase from about 16 million hectares in 1965 to about 42 million hectares in 1979, the reported tractor-plowed area has declined every year since then, reaching about 34 million hectares in 1983. Following increases averaging over 8% p.a. during 1965-79, the land area irrigated with power equipment has remained about constant during 1979-83, accounting for 56-57% of the total irrigated area.[15]

7.59 At the same time, however, reported inventories of tractors and trucks for agricultural use have increased rapidly during 1979-83 (Table 7.3). The growth in tractor inventories, especially for walking tractors, can to a large extent be explained by recent rapid growth in rural transport demand. With shortages of trucks in general, and of small, pick-up trucks in particular, tractors have been increasingly used for short-distance road transportation. In assessing the future petroleum consumption in the agricultural sector, the distinction between demands for transport fuel and for fuel for field operations and agricultural processing is important.

Table 7.3: REPORTED INVENTORIES OF TRACTORS AND TRUCKS FOR AGRICULTURAL USE, 1965-83
('000 units)

	Large and mid-sized tractors/a	Small-sized and walking tractors	Trucks for agricultural use
1965	73	4	11
1979	667	1671	97
1983	841	2750	275

/a Tractors of 20 HP or over.

7.60 Rural road transportation, currently a major bottleneck in development of the rural sector, is expected to grow rapidly in the future. Substantial opportunities exist for improving the efficiency of petroleum use. One- to two-ton pick-up trucks, for example, use about one-half of the energy per capacity ton-kilometer as existing walking tractors. Despite such opportunities, however, petroleum consumption for rural road transportation is expected to rise sharply, both over the short and long terms.

7.61 In the future, petroleum product consumption for mechanized field operations and agricultural processing will in many ways be determined by government policy, as in the past. Judging from recent trends, however, the deployment of mobile farm machinery for field operations may grow far more

15/ The total horsepower of power irrigation and drainage equipment, however, increased by a total of about 10% during 1979-83.

slowly over the next decade and a half than during the 1970s. In addition, while energy use in irrigation and drainage, and particularly in agricultural processing, may grow at substantial rates in the future, increasing availability of electricity is expected to allow a continuation of recent trends toward greater use of electricity (as opposed to petroleum) in these applications. Therefore, if small-sized trucks increasingly displace use of tractors for rural transport, petroleum consumption by agricultural machinery may grow relatively slowly over the long term, resulting in a decrease in the intensity of petroleum consumption relative to agricultural output. If the gross value of agricultural output grows by 4.6% p.a. during 1980-2000 [16/] petroleum consumption could develop as indicated in Table 7.4.

Table 7.4 PETROLEUM PRODUCT CONSUMPTION IN AGRICULTURE

Intensity of consumption Relative to GVAO	Millions of tons	
	1980	2000
1.0	9	22
0.9	9	20
0.8	9	18

Rural Electrification

7.62 China's program to expand rural power supply during the last 15 years represents probably the most massive rural electrification effort ever attempted in the developing world. Rural power supplies have increased roughly tenfold since 1965, rising to about 49 billion kWh in 1982, excluding supplies to county-level industrial enterprises.[17/] Pumping and irrigation accounted for 37% of rural power consumption, collective industries 22%, agricultural processing 20%, residential and commercial uses 17%, and other uses 4%. Consumption by collective industries and residential and commercial consumers has registered the most rapid growth in recent years.

16/ Multi-sectoral model, QUADRUPLE and BALANCE cases. See the Main Report, Chapter 2.

17/ If county-level industrial enterprises (state-owned) are included, rural power supplies totalled about 85 billion kWh. Official figures on rural power supplies vary, depending on what is included. The figures quoted here are from MWREP. They include electricity consumed by agriculture and agricultural processing in collective and state units; by collective industries; and by households, government institutions and commercial enterprises in rural villages and towns.

7.63 By 1982, 89% of China's 54,000 townships (communes) and 70.6% of its 710,000 villages (brigades) had access to electricity (see Appendix G.3). MWREP estimates that about half of China's rural households use electricity.

7.64 Large grids, based on medium-sized and large plants, provide most of the power for areas with high loads and high population densities (such as the Zhu Jiang delta and the North China Plain), but small plants (especially hydro plants) are also important in supplying rural consumers. In 1982, over 80,000 small hydro plants [18/] were in operation, with a total installed capacity of 8,080 MW (about 35% of total hydro capacity). Total generation by these plants reached 16.3 billion kWh, accounting for slightly less than 20% of total rural consumption, including consumption by county-level industries.

7.65 The role of small hydro plants is far more significant, however, when extension of service is considered. In 1982, 40% of China's rural townships relied on these plants for their electricity supply, and small hydro plants were the main source of electricity in over one-third of China's counties. Although small hydro plants have been constructed in all regions, most are in the East, South Central and Southwest Regions. Initially, the plants tended to be very small (i.e., 10-50 kW) and were constructed using relatively crude technology, such as wooden rotor turbines. With steady development of local and national capabilities and local electricity demand, however, the plants have become larger and more sophisticated. Moreover, small hydro plants have increasingly been linked together to form local grids, and even connected with large regional grids. Indeed, in southern China, the program of small hydro development has brought about a pattern of rural electrification that is fundamentally different from that in most developing countries: electrification has not come through extension of the large grid systems, but rather through the development and gradual interlinking of many small, but growing, local grids.

7.66 Small-scale thermal power plants also provide a decentralized source of rural power. Small thermal plants with a total capacity of about 2,000 MW are in operation; some are likely to be in urban areas. Most small thermal plants are coal-fired, with only a few diesel-fired plants in operation.

7.67 Recently, 100 counties where small hydro resources are particularly abundant were selected for completion of full electrification based on small hydro plants by the late 1980s. Development will include electrification of over 90% of the households, including use of electricity for cooking if appropriate. Greater quantities of electricity will also be provided for agriculture and rural industry, and in some areas efforts will be made to establish new, electricity-intensive industries. It is hoped that this program can later be expanded to cover many additional counties. A review of the location of small hydro resources and the current extent of electrification by region can provide a rough indication of the potential role of small hydro plants in

---

18/ Defined as stations with single generating units rated at less than 6 MW, or total station capacities (including several generating units) of less than 12 MW.

extending electricity service (see Table 7.5). Development may be particularly important in the southwest, where much of the population without electricity service is in remote mountainous regions, and small hydro resources are huge by any standard.[19/]

Table 7.5: DISTRIBUTION AND DEVELOPMENT OF SMALL-SCALE HYDROPOWER RESOURCES

Region	Wild potential reserves (MW)	Exploitable resources/a (MW)	Installed capacity, 1982 (MW)	Percentage of exploitable resources developed, 1982	Proportion of non-electrified villages, 1982 (%)
Northeast	3,000	1,960	185	9.4	0.8
North	4,600	1,640	228	13.9	7.7
Northwest	28,100	9,360	476	5.1	13.4
East	14,400	9,420	1,953	20.7	30.0
Central-south	31,500	15,540	3,417	22.0	24.5
Southwest	68,600	33,380	1,821	5.5	23.6
All Regions	150,200	71,300	8,080	11.3	100.0

/a Undefined in original source.

Source: Appendix G.3; Shuili Shuidian Jishu (Water Resources and Hydropower Engineering), No. 6, 1983.

7.68 The economics of small hydro generation relative to other alternatives for rural electrification are extremely site specific, and vary dramatically. Capital costs for small hydro projects, including labor charges, can range from Y 500/kW to over Y 2,000/kW. Plant utilization factors also vary dramatically, depending on the type of small hydro plant, characteristics of local grid networks, if any, and seasonal water flows, as well as local load characteristics. At an aggregate level, small hydro plants have operated an average of 2,000 hours per year or less, although average utilization has recently improved to some 2,500 hours per year. The seasonality of generation, due to water flow variations and the difficulty of improving regulation, has represented perhaps the most important disadvantage of development. Additional important parameters include relative transmission and distribution costs, and possible external benefits in terms of water control.

19/ The installed capacity of small plants in the southwest has also been increasing rapidly in recent years, rising by over 30%, or 400 MW, during 1980-82.

7.69 MWREP anticipates that the rapid expansion of rural power supplies will continue, achieving at least a fourfold increase by the end of the century. Rural power supply would reach 200 billion kWh, excluding consumption by county-level industries, which is about twice the total amount of power generated in India in 1980. Electricity use for irrigation and drainage is expected to grow slowly, compared with the past, but big increases are anticipated in electricity use in collective industries and the rural residential/commercial sector. It is hoped that the level of rural household electrification can be increased to about 90% by the year 2000. To achieve these ambitious goals, China plans to pursue the strategy of "walking on two legs" relied on in the past. While large grids are expected to continue supplying the bulk of rural power, emphasis will also be placed on the development of local, decentralized sources of power supply, primarily small-scale hydro plants. The government expects up to a threefold increase in the total installed capacity of small hydro plants by the end of the century, for a total of 20,000-25,000 MW. Small hydro plants will play a critical role in extending service to new areas and in increasing electricity supplies to already electrified areas where local energy resources are particularly abundant.

7.70 Under current policy, local units pay for the bulk of small hydro development costs, often with revenues provided from previous power projects. In recent years, state subsidies have been available for projects pursued by collectives, usually covering about 30% of total investment. In 1985, however, direct subsidies will be removed. This approach reduces the investment burden on the state and introduces a "willingness to pay" criterion into development decisions. State policy does influence local perceptions of costs and benefits in other ways, including establishment of the rules governing the connection of small hydro units to large grids, and the setting of tariffs for power supplied through grid extensions. In the past, state policies have in some ways promoted uneconomic behavior, and while moves have been made to correct past mistakes, policy assessment should be an ongoing process. Efforts should be made to provide better signals regarding the actual cost of electricity supply through main grids (including the cost of marginal capacity expansion), particularly when alternatives such as local power development and grid extension exist.

7.71 There is a general need to improve long-term local power planning, rather than relying on adoption of short-term, incremental measures. Efforts should be made to consider long-term load trends in a given area, and then to devise a long-term, least-cost generation and distribution development program. If eventual interconnection with other grids is feasible, early consideration of this possibility can minimize future difficulties and costs. Where the extension of a large grid is the most appropriate option for rural electrification, the costs and benefits should be carefully calculated, given the anticipated shortages in available investment funds. Experience in other developing countries shows that the high costs usually associated with grid extension are best justified where potential loads, and hence benefits, exist in a series of activities (such as rural household use, agricultural production, and rural industries).

ENERGY CONSUMPTION STATISTICS

1. A complete commercial energy balance for China, including energy use by type and by industrial subsector, has not been published. Based on a large amount of data concerning energy consumption in different subsectors, however, a detailed and internally consistent energy balance was prepared for use in drawing cross-country comparisons and projecting energy demand. The most important sources of data included the 1981 and 1983 Statistical Yearbooks of China, the 1980, 1981 and 1982 Almanacs of China's Economy, the 1982 Coal Yearbook of China, Nengyuan (the Journal of Energy), and the Ministry of Water Resources and Electric Power and other government sources. In many cases, data was only available for the year 1980, and hence, construction of a detailed energy balance was attempted for this year only. In cases where sources conflicted concerning data for specific entries, internal consistencies were checked, data were compared with similar data for other countries, and the data regarded as most accurate were used.

2. The energy balance for 1980 (Table A.1) is believed to provide a reasonably reliable picture of the energy flows in the Chinese economy. Nonetheless further improvements in measurement, reporting, and data compilation in China will hopefully provide a more fine-tuned and accurate picture in the future. In particular, greater attention needs to be given to the collection and compilation of data on energy consumption according to end use, as opposed to data on the allocation of energy to different institutional categories. Where statistics are based on energy allocations (i.e., allocations to various ministries) they may not reflect actual consumption in a specific sector, and may lump together consumption for different end uses (i.e., energy use in transportation, machine building, or workers' residences) which need to be analyzed separately.

3. Probably the greatest uncertainties regarding current commercial energy use involve the use of coal, particularly in rural areas, where coal is produced and consumed by a large number of different entities. Data on household use of coal, in both urban and rural areas, is especially uncertain. Wide differences in the calorific values of coal produced also pose major problems for accurate analysis of energy consumption. In the energy balance constructed for 1980, different average calorific values were assumed for coal consumed in several key subsectors, based largely on available Chinese data. The national average calorific value for all coal produced was taken to be 5,000 kcal/kg, in line with the current Chinese practice. The national average calorific value used for coal, however, should be reviewed - recent and more detailed surveys in China suggest that an average closer to 5,400 kcal/kg may be more accurate for coal currently produced. If detailed analysis shows that average calorific values for coal are well above 5,000 kcal/kg, statistics should be revised, as current energy consumption in China would be significantly understated.

4. Major progress has been made in recent years in improving measurement and reporting systems, and in the compilation of aggregate energy consumption statistics. Further improvements will be necessary, however, to provide the raw materials required for detailed and accurate analytical inputs for policy decisions on the energy sector.

Table A.1: CHINA: COMMERCIAL ENERGY CONSUMPTION BY SECTOR, 1980
(Millions of tons of coal equivalent)

	Oil	Coal	Gas	Electricity	Total
Primary Supply					
Production	154.3	443.0	19.0	24.0	640.3
Exports	25.5/a	5.9	-	-	31.4
Stock changes	-	4.3	-	-	4.3
Domestic supply	128.8	432.8	19.0	24.0	604.6
Energy Industry Conversion, Losses and Use					
Petroleum industry					
Field use	2.5	N	N	1.7	N
Field losses	3.5	-	N	-	N
Refineries					
Throughput	109.8	-	-	-	109.8
Losses	5.5	-	-	-	5.5
Use	3.8	N	N	1.2	N
Net output	(100.5)	-	-	-	(100.5)
Other/unallocated	3.8/b	0.4	2.1	0.7	7.0
Subtotal	19.1	0.4	2.1	3.6	25.2
Power industry					
Thermal power production	28.3	78.2	6.0	(100.1)/c	12.4/c
Heat supply credit /c	(4.7)	(3.9)	(3.3)	-	(11.9)
Station losses	-	-	-	8.0	8.0
T&D losses	-	-	-	10.4	10.4
Subtotal	23.6	74.3	2.7	(81.7)	18.9
Coal industry					
Beneficiation losses	-	12.6	-	-	12.6
Other	0.7	16.4	-	7.9	25.0
Subtotal	0.7	29.0	-	7.9	37.6

Table A.1: (cont'd)

	Oil /d Distillates	Oil /d Fuel	Oil /d Total	Coal	Gas	Elec-tricity	Total
Final Consumption	50.0	35.4	85.4	329.1	14.2	94.2	522.9
Transportation							
Railroads	1.7	-	1.7	19.0	-	0.6	21.3
Trucks and buses /e	15.0	-	15.0	-	-	-	15.0
Automobiles	0.2	-	0.2	-	-	-	0.2
Vessels	2.2	1.5	3.7	-	-	-	3.7
Civil aviation	0.4	-	0.4	-	-	-	0.4
Subtotal	19.5	1.5	21.0	19.0	-	0.6	40.6
Residential/Commercial /f							
Urban	0.4	-	0.4	57.9	0.3	6.9	65.5
Rural	1.5	-	1.5	32.3	-	3.7	37.5
Subtotal	1.9	-	1.9	90.2	0.3	10.6	103.0
Agriculture /g	13.1	-	13.1	21.5	-	10.8	45.4
Industry /h							
Metallurgy							
Iron and steel	N	N	6.0	50.3	1.3	13.3	70.9
Primary aluminum	N	N	N	N	-	2.6	N
Other	N	N	N	N	-	3.2	N
Subtotal	0.4	6.2	6.6	54.2	1.3	19.1	81.2
Chemicals							
Synthetic ammonia	1.7	1.0	2.7	24.6	4.1	7.1	38.5
Other	4.8	4.9	9.7	9.7	3.5	14.6	37.5
Subtotal	6.5	5.9	12.4	34.3	7.6	21.7	76.0
Building materials							
Cement	-	0.5	0.5	11.0	-	3.3	14.8
Brick and tile	-	-	-	22.8	-	N	22.8
Plate glass	-	1.2	1.2	-	N	0.1	1.3
Other/unallocated	-	0.3	0.3	8.5	0.1	1.3	10.2
Subtotal	-	2.0	2.0	42.3	0.1	4.7	49.1
Machine building	0.7	2.8	3.5	14.4	0.7	9.4	28.0
Food, beverages & tobacco	0.2	0.4	0.6	9.7	0.3	2.5	13.1
Textiles	0.2	5.8	6.0	10.0	0.4	5.4	21.8
Pulp and paper	-	0.6	0.6	5.4	0.1	2.3	8.4
Other light mfg. /i	0.4	2.6	3.0	9.3	0.1	5.0	17.4
Unallocated /j	1.6	6.1	7.7	9.8	3.3	-	20.8
Total Industry	10.0	32.4	42.4	189.4	13.9	70.1	315.8
Other /k	5.5	1.5	7.0	9.0	-	2.1	18.1

"N" denotes that data are not available; "-" denotes negligible consumption.

Table A.1: (cont'd)

/a Includes 19.4 million TCE (13.3 million tons) of crude oil and 6.1 million TCE (4.2 million tons) of petroleum products.
/b Unallocated consumption may include unreported refinery throughput (or losses), and/or losses in transportation.
/c Electricity is converted to TCE at a thermal replacement value net of fuel which is consumed in the production of heat which is eventually supplied to consumers outside of the power industry (listed as the heat supply credit), according to Chinese practice. Nevertheless, a statistical discrepancy exists as the standard thermal replacement value used for electricity in China for 1980 (and here also) does not quite match the reported net energy consumption in thermal power production.
/d Fuel includes any crude oil directly burned, fuel oil, feedstock and petroleum solids. Distillates are defined to include all other products, contrary to commom practice, including LPG and lubricants (see Chapter 2, para. 2.45).
/e Includes own-account trucks, but excludes tractors used for highway transport.
/f Defined according to the Chinese term, minyong, or "use by the people." It includes consumption by households, commercial enterprises (shops, restaurants, etc.), government offices and some municipal services such as recreation facilities and street lighting.
/g Agriculture includes agricultural production and agricultural processing only. Consumption by rural households, commercial enterprises, public service entities and rural industries not engaged in agricultural processing is excluded.
/h Includes township and village industries outside of the agricultural processing field.
/i Forestry industry, clothing, leather and cultural articles (including printing).
/j Includes most of the power heat supply credit and any other consumption not specified for other industrial subsectors.
/k Includes construction and other nonspecified sectors.

Note: Energy conversion factors:

Standard coal equivalent	7,000 kcal/kg
Crude oil and petroleum products	10,200 kcal/kg
Natural gas	9,310 kcal/m^3
Electricity	2,890 kcal/kWh
Coal	
Exports	6,500 kcal/kg
Beneficiation losses	3,500 kcal/kg
Power	4,375 kcal/kg
Iron and steel	5,700 kcal/kg
Railroads	5,600 kcal/kg
Chemicals	6,000 kcal/kg
Other	5,025 kcal/kg
National average	5,000 kcal/kg

Table A.2: CHINA: PRIMARY COMMERCIAL ENERGY PRODUCTION AND CONSUMPTION
(Original units)

	1965	1970	1975	1976	1977	1978	1979	1980	1981	1982	1983	1984
Oil (mln tons)												
Production	11.3	30.7	77.1	87.2	93.6	104.1	106.2	105.9	101.2	102.1	106.1	114.5
Crude exports	0.2	0.2	9.9	8.5	9.1	11.3	13.4	13.3	13.8	15.2	15.2	n.a.
Product exports	0.1	0.2	2.1	1.9	2.0	2.2	3.0	4.2	4.6	5.3	5.1	n.a.
Consumption	11.0	30.3	65.1	76.8	82.5	90.6	89.8	88.4	82.8	81.6	85.8	n.a.
Coal (mln tons)												
Production	231.8	354.0	482.2	483.5	550.7	617.9	635.5	620.2	621.6	666.0	715.0	772.0
Exports /a	3.5	2.5	3.4	2.5	2.8	3.4	4.9	6.6	6.8	6.8	6.9	n.a.
Consumption /b	228.3	351.5	478.8	481.0	547.9	614.5	630.6	613.6	614.6	659.2	708.1	n.a.
Natural Gas (bln cu m)												
Production and consumption	1.1	2.9	8.9	10.1	12.1	13.7	14.5	14.3	12.7	11.9	12.2	12.4
Primary Electricity (bln kWh)												
Production and consumption	10.4	20.5	47.6	45.6	47.6	44.6	50.1	58.2	65.5	74.4	86.4	85.5
Memo Item												
Total electricity production (bln kWh)	67.6	115.9	195.8	203.1	223.4	256.6	282.0	300.6	309.3	327.7	351.4	374.6

/a Includes coke exports which have averaged at 250,000-450,000 tons per year, but excludes small quantities of coal imports.

/b Defined as production minus exports, and hence, stock changes are included.

Sources: 1965-83: State Statistical Bureau, Statistical Yearbooks of China, 1981, 1983, 1984.
1984: State Statistical Bureau, Communique on the Fulfillment of China's 1984 Plan.

APPENDIX B

INTERNATIONAL COMPARISONS

OF ENERGY CONSUMPTION

Table B.1: SHARE OF ELECTRICITY IN TOTAL AND INDUSTRIAL FINAL CONSUMPTION OF ENERGY IN SELECTED COUNTRIES /a
(Percentages)

	(A) 1971 Commercial energy		(B) 1980 Commercial energy		(C) 1980 Total energy /b	
	Total	Industry	Total	Industry	Total	Industry
Developing Countries						
China	n.a.	n.a.	18.0	22.0	12.7	22.0
Argentina	21.0	29.3	28.7	43.6	25.7	37.4
Brazil	31.4	41.6	39.1	47.8	28.2	38.1
Mexico	21.2	29.9	24.3	32.6	21.7	29.0
India	25.2	33.7	29.8	33.0	16.2	32.2
S. Korea	14.2	22.0	22.9	36.4	21.7	36.4
Developed Countries						
US	27.0	32.3	33.3	37.6	33.3	37.6
Canada	36.9	50.1	39.5	45.2	39.5	45.2
Japan	35.5	40.9	42.0	48.9	42.0	48.9
France	25.0	32.1	32.9	42.3	32.9	42.3
Germany, F.R.	27.8	34.4	34.9	42.4	34.9	42.4
Italy	27.5	35.3	33.1	43.0	33.1	43.0
UK	32.0	29.7	36.5	40.5	36.5	40.5

/a Electricity converted at a thermal replacement value of 2,900 kcal/kWh.

/b Includes biomass.

Source: OECD (1984a) Energy Balances of OECD Countries 1970-82 and OECD (1984b) Energy Balances of Developing Countries 1971-82. Biomass consumption figures for South Korea were revised, using World Bank sources. Note that nonenergy use for nonenergy production is excluded from industrial use and included in "other sectors."

Table B.2: PER CAPITA FINAL CONSUMPTION OF COMMERCIAL AND TOTAL ENERGY IN THE RESIDENTIAL/COMMERCIAL/PUBLIC SECTORS IN SELECTED COUNTRIES, 1980

	Population, mid-1980 (millions)	Final energy consumption	
		Commercial (kgce/capita) (A)	Total incl. biomass (kgce/capita) (B)
Developing			
China	980	105	329
Argentina	28	397	493
Brazil	118	213	379
Mexico	69	265	265
India	675	25	175
South Korea	38	644	738
Developed			
US	228	4,007	4,007
Canada	24	4,745	4,745
Japan	117	1,169	1,169
France	54	1,640	1,640
Germany, F.R.	62	2,331	2,331
Italy	56	1,097	1,097
UK	56	2,074	2,074

Sources: Population figures from World Tables, 1983 edition, except for China. Energy consumption data from OECD sources.

Table B.3: GROWTH RATES OF ELECTRICITY GENERATION AND REAL GDP IN SELECTED COUNTRIES AND TIME PERIODS /a

	1960-70			1970-80		
	Electricity	GDP	Ratio	Electricity	GDP	Ratio
Developing						
Argentina	7.6	4.4	1.73	6.2	2.4	2.58
Brazil	7.1	6.1	1.16	11.9	8.6	1.38
Mexico	10.3	7.6	1.36	8.8	6.6	1.33
India	11.8	4.0	2.95	6.9	3.2	2.16
South Korea	18.5	8.4	2.20	15.3	8.2	1.87
Philippines	12.2	5.2	2.35	7.6	6.2	1.23

	1960-73			1973-79			1979-82	
	Electricity	GDP	Ratio	Electricity	GDP	Ratio	Electricity	GDP
Developed								
US	6.4	4.0	1.60	2.8	2.6	1.08	0.8	-0.1
Canada	6.6	5.6	1.18	5.1	3.3	1.55	2.8	-0.2
Japan	11.4	9.9	1.15	3.8	3.6	1.06	-0.5	4.1
France	7.1	5.6	1.27	4.8	3.1	1.55	2.6	0.6
Germany, F.R.	7.3	4.5	1.62	3.7	2.4	1.54	-0.5	0.3
Italy	7.6	5.3	1.43	3.7	2.6	1.42	0.6	1.1
UK	5.6	3.1	1.81	1.0	1.3	0.77	-3.2	-0.4

/a Growth rates based on end-point data. The 1979-82 period has been unusual for the industrialized countries, so ratios have not been calculated for that period.

Sources: (1) Electricity data for industrialized countries is from OECD (1984a) Energy Balances of OECD Countries, 1970-82. Data for developing countries is from the UN, (1984), Energy Statistics Yearbook, 1982 edition.

(2) GDP data is from World Tables, 1983 edition, and from other World Bank sources.

TABLE B.4: INTERNATIONAL COMPARISON OF THE RELATIVE IMPORTANCE OF PRINCIPAL MODES OF FREIGHT TRANSPORT
(Percentage shares of total)

	Payload tons				Payload ton-kilometers			
	Rail	Road	Water /a	Pipeline	Rail	Road	Water /a	Pipeline
US								
1940	--	--	--	--	43.6	7.1	42.5	6.8
1950	--	--	--	--	46.0	13.3	30.7	10.0
1960	--	--	--	--	36.9	18.2	30.3	14.6
1970	--	--	--	--	35.0	18.6	26.9	19.5
1980	--	--	--	--	31.1	18.5	30.8	19.6
Japan								
1955	--	--	--	--	50.8	11.2	38.0	----
1960	--	--	--	--	39.2	15.0	45.8	----
1965	--	--	--	--	30.8	26.0	43.2	----
1970	--	--	--	--	18.1	38.8	43.1	----
1975	--	--	--	--	13.1	36.0	50.9	----
1980	--	--	-	--	8.6	40.8	50.6	----
France								
1963	18.9	72.9	5.7	2.5	55.7	31.3	9.6	3.4
1970	12.9	77.7	5.5	3.9	39.8	36.9	7.8	15.5
1979	12.9	75.9	5.1	6.1	33.4	44.0	5.5	17.1
USSR								
1963	17.9	78.5	2.0	1.6	84.3	5.8	5.5	4.4
1970	15.9	80.2	2.0	1.9	78.6	7.0	5.5	8.9
1980 /b	13.1	82.8	1.9	2.2	65.3	8.0	4.5	22.2
Czechoslovakia								
1963	28.8	70.1	0.6	0.7	82.5	10.9	3.4	3.2
1970	24.7	73.4	0.5	1.4	76.4	12.6	3.0	8.0
1980	18.4	79.7	0.7	1.2	67.8	19.9	3.2	9.1
Yugoslavia								
1963	27.7	68.1	4.2	-	69.1	16.9	14.0	-
1970	9.4	87.8	2.8	-	41.6	46.1	12.3	-
Brazil								
1960	--	--	--	--	18.7	59.9	21.4	--
1970	--	--	--	-	22.0	60.3	16.2	1.5
1980	--	--	--	--	24.2	58.9	13.5	3.4
Hungary								
1970	21.8	76.5	0.5	1.2	71.0	20.9	5.7	2.4
1980	17.6	79.8	0.5	2.1	59.2	27.7	4.6	8.5
South Korea								
1961	47.9	47.6	4.5	--	88.3	8.2	3.5	--
1966	46.9	47.8	5.3	--	81.6	8.4	10.0	--
1971	25.1	66.1	8.8	--	48.9	22.1	29.0	--
1976	17.8	76.6	5.6	--	44.6	30.0	25.4	--
1981	12.1	82.4	5.5	--	37.5	35.0	27.5	--

Table B.4: (cont'd)

	Payload tons				Payload ton-kilometers			
	Rail	Road	Water /a	Pipeline	Rail	Road	Water /a	Pipeline
Colombia								
1975	1.3	96.0	2.7	--	6.1	75.6	18.3	--
1979	0.9	97.7	1.4	--	4.8	84.2	11.0	--
India								
1950	--	--	--	--	89.0	11.0	--	--
1960	--	--	--	--	71.0	29.0	--	--
1970	--	--	--	--	66.0	34.0	--	--
1977	--	--	--	--	68.0	32.0	--	--
China /c								
1950	--	--	--	--	83.5	5.7	10.8	-
1960	--	--	--	--	72.6	10.4	17.0	-
1970	--	--	--	--	79.0	9.4	11.6	-
1980	47.1 (28.7)	32.2 (58.7)	16.3 (9.9)	4.4 (2.7)	67.3	9.0	17.9	5.8

-- Data not available
 - Negligible

/a Excludes ocean shipping, but includes inland water and coastal transport.

/b Percentage shares of ton-kilometers of freight moved do not total 100, due to discrepancies in the original data.

/c Official data concerning ton-kilometers of freight moved on roads does not include own-account trucks for the years prior to 1979. In 1980, own-account trucks accounted for two-thirds of the total ton-kilometers moved on roads, and total ton-kilometers moved on roads prior to 1979 have been estimated assuming a similar share.

All official data concerning the tonnage of freight moved on roads excludes own-account trucks. Figures in parentheses show a modal breakdown which assumes that own-account trucks comprise two-thirds of the total freight tonnage moved on roads.

Sources:
- US: "Transportation in America," July, 1983.
- Japan: Japan Statistical Yearbook, various issues.
- France, USSR, Czechoslovakia, Yugoslavia, Hungary: United Nations Economic Commission for Europe, Annual Bulletin of Transport Statistics (1971, 1980).
- Brazil: The World Bank, Transport Sector of Brazil, May, 1974; GEIPOT, 1979 and 1982.
- Colombia: International Road Federation, World Road Statistics, 1980.
- South Korea: The World Bank, Korea: Transport Sector Issues Survey, April 1983.
- India: Government of India, Report of the National Transport Policy Committee, May 1980.
- China: 1981 Statistical Yearbook of China; 1982 Almanac of China's Economy.

Table B.5: INTERNATIONAL COMPARISONS OF FINAL ENERGY CONSUMPTION PER UNIT GROSS VALUE OF INDUSTRIAL OUTPUT (GVIO), SELECTED COUNTRIES AND YEARS

Country/year	(A) GVIO (1980 $ bln)	(B) Fuel and feedstock	(C) Elec- tricity	(D) Total	Fuel and feedstock intensity B/A	Elec- tricity intensity C/A	Total energy intensity D/A
		(MTCE)			(kgce/$)		
China							
1980	298.9	245.7	70.1	315.8	0.82	0.23	1.06
US							
1973	1,686.6	542.5	258.1	800.6	0.32	0.15	0.47
1980	1,656.7	487.8	284.5	772.3	0.29	0.17	0.47
Japan							
1973	804.1	167.7	120.7	288.4	0.21	0.15	0.36
1980	906.3	140.4	134.2	274.6	0.16	0.15	0.30
France							
1973	296.7	64.7	37.0	101.7	0.22	0.13	0.34
1980	384.8	65.8	48.0	113.8	0.17	0.13	0.30
Germany, F.R.							
1973	498.1	106.5	58.6	165.1	0.21	0.12	0.33
1980	579.7	88.4	64.8	153.2	0.15	0.11	0.26
UK							
1973	415.8	83.7	37.5	121.2	0.20	0.09	0.29
1980	392.2	52.6	35.8	88.5	0.13	0.09	0.23
Brazil /a							
1973	90.9	17.0 (28.0)	12.2	29.2 (40.2)	0.19 (0.31)	0.13	0.32 (0.44)
1978	161.1	28.3 (41.7)	22.6	50.9 (64.3)	0.18 (0.26)	0.14	0.32 (0.40)
India /a							
1973	43.8	34.4 (36.3)	15.4	49.8 (51.7)	0.79 (0.83)	0.35	1.14 (1.18)
1978	65.7	43.4 (46.3)	21.9	65.3 (68.2)	0.66 (0.71)	0.33	0.99 (1.04)
South Korea							
1973	22.9	7.3	3.5	10.8	0.32	0.15	0.47
1980	52.4	15.8	9.1	24.9	0.30	0.17	0.48
Philippines /a							
1973	10.3	2.2 (5.6)	3.3	5.5 (8.9)	0.21 (0.54)	0.32	0.53 (0.86)
1979	14.5	3.2 (7.1)	2.6	5.7 (9.6)	0.22 (0.49)	0.18	0.39 (0.66)
Turkey							
1973	17.8	4.6	3.4	7.9	0.26	0.19	0.44
1979	24.3	5.7	5.0	10.7	0.24	0.21	0.44

Table B.5 (cont'd)

/a Figures in brackets are for total energy consumption, including biomass.

Sources and method:

(1) Industrial gross output value (GVIO) - at factor values or producer prices - was obtained from UN (1983) Yearbook of Industrial Statistics, 1977 and 1981 editions, Volume 1: General Industrial Statistics. In order to achieve as much comparability with energy consumption data as possible, GVIO generally includes ISIC 2 and ISIC 3, minus the following: coal mining (ISIC 210), petroleum and gas production (ISIC 220), petroleum refineries (ISIC 353), and petroleum and coal products (ISIC 354). In other words, GVIO here covers only nonenergy mining and nonenergy manufacturing. In the case of the US, GVIO data for nonenergy mining are not available; it is ascertained from the data available for other years in the UN Yearbook as well as from other sources (such as US Department of Commerce (1984), 1984 US Industrial Outlook) that nonenergy mining accounts for only a small share (less than 1% usually), so that its exclusion does not affect the numbers of interest. For the case of Brazil, however, the GVIO data include the fuel industries. See Table B.6.

(2) Nominal GVIO in individual countries' currencies is converted into comparable 1980 US$ by first deflating by the price index given by the International Financial Statistics Yearbook 1983, line 63 or 63a (where available) for individual countries, and then converting into US$ by the average exchange rate for 1980.

(3) Energy consumption data are from OECD (1984a) Energy Balances of OECD Countries 1970-82, and OECD (1984b), Energy Balances of Developing Countries 1971-82. Energy consumption in "construction," where available (row 26 for the former publication), has been excluded. In the case of the US, energy consumption in the "mining industry," where available, has been excluded (see note 1 above). Neither of these activities account for a substantial proportion of energy consumption.

Table B.6: STRUCTURE OF MINING AND MANUFACTURING GROSS OUTPUT VALUE (EXCLUDING ENERGY INDUSTRIES) IN SELECTED COUNTRIES AND YEARS

Sector:	Food, beverages & tobacco	Tex-tiles	Buildings materials	Chemicals	Metal-lurgy	Machine building	Total gross industrial output value (in current prices) /a
ISIC Number:	31	321	362 + 369	351, 352 355, 356	37	381-385	
	(% shares)						
US /b							($ bln)
1973	17.0	4.4	2.7	10.8	8.0	40.3	845.0
1980	16.2	3.4	2.7	12.8	7.7	41.0	1,656.7
Japan							(¥ trillion)
1973	10.7	7.0	3.6	11.1	12.2	40.2	102.1
1980	12.1	4.4	3.8	12.9	12.0	40.3	205.5
France							(F bln)
1973	20.9	n.a.	n.a.	11.5	8.3/c	34.4	706.0
1980	20.1	3.9	3.0	14.2	8.8	35.4	1,626.1
Germany, F.R.							(DM bln)
1973	13.6	4.4	3.7	13.8	11.3	39.7	628.4
1980	13.5	3.3	3.4	15.7	9.8	42.1	1,053.7
UK							(£ bln)
1973	16.8	5.9	3.1	12.3	9.1	36.5	59.7
1980	22.0	3.4	3.4	13.8	7.2	35.6	168.6
Brazil			/d	/e	/f	/g	(Cr$ bln)/h
1973	20.2	9.0	3.4	18.4	12.0	20.8	322.6
1978	17.6	6.7	4.0	21.3	13.2	21.4	2,638.8
India							(Rs bln)
1973	21.5	19.7	2.9	14.9	11.1	23.0	182.9
1978	20.4	18.6	3.0	17.2	12.7	21.0	385.1
South Korea							(W bln)
1973	20.4	19.4	3.8	11.9	9.1	16.1	3,430.0
1980	15.6	14.3	4.8	17.0	10.6	21.9	31,824.0
Philippines							(₱ bln)
1973 /b	41.7	9.1	3.7	14.6	6.7	12.1	28.7
1979	36.4	9.0	4.3	13.7	4.6	14.7	92.2
Turkey							(LT bln)
1973	28.8	17.2	4.0	10.4	9.8	21.5	127.5
1979	21.6	16.1	4.7	15.5	11.5	22.0	890.3
China							(Y bln)
1980	14.1	16.7	4.5	13.1	10.9	25.9	433.4

Table B.6 (cont'd)

n.a. = Not available

/a Monetary units as shown in parentheses.

/b For the US (1973, 1980) and the Philippines (1973), nonenergy mining excluded; i.e., data are for manufacturing sector minus refineries (ISIC 353) and petroleum/coal products (ISIC 354).

/c Includes metal ore mining.

/d Includes ISIC 361.

/e Includes ISIC 353 and ISIC 354.

/f Includes ISIC 381.

/g Excludes ISIC 381 and ISIC 385.

/h Includes ISIC 210 and ISIC 220, as well as ISIC 353 and ISIC 354.

Note: In some cases the unavailability of disaggregated data has led to deviations from the definition adopted here. Thus, the US data exclude nonenergy mining for both 1973 and 1980; the French data for metallurgy in 1973 includes metal ore mining; and the Philippine data for 1973 exclude nonenergy mining. In none of the cases does this limitation result in a significant bias in the calculations of shares of industrial branches or changes therein or, for that matter, in the calculations of changes in real GVIO (Table B.7) because nonenergy mining usually accounts for a very small proportion of the total GVIO. In the case of Brazil, however, the inclusion of ISIC 353 and 354 in the "Chemicals" and of ISIC 210 and 220 in the total GVIO does introduce a bias both in the calculations of shares of industrial branches and in the calculations of aggregate industrial energy intensities (Tables B.5 and B.7).

Since not all industrial branches are listed in this table, sums of percentages do not equal 100.

Source: The UN Yearbook of Industrial Statistics, 1977 edition (published 1979) and 1981 edition (published 1983), Volume 1 - General Industrial Statistics. "Energy Industries" are defined as coal mining (ISIC 210), petroleum and gas production (ISIC 220), petroleum refineres (ISIC 353), and petroleum and coal products (ISIC 354).

Table B.7: CHANGES IN THE FUEL (INCLUDING FEEDSTOCK), ELECTRICITY AND TOTAL ENERGY INTENSITIES OF INDUSTRIAL OUTPUT IN SELECTED COUNTRIES AND YEARS
(Growth rates per annum)

Country	Period	Fuel and feedstock	Electricity	Total energy
US	1973-80	-1.3	1.7	-0.3
Japan	1973-80	-4.2	-0.2	-2.4
France	1973-80	-3.4	0.0	-2.1
West Germany	1973-80	-4.7	-0.7	-3.2
UK	1973-80	-5.6	0.2	-3.6
Brazil	1973-78 - Commercial	-1.3	0.9	-0.3
	- Total	-3.4	0.9	-2.0
India	1973-78 - Commercial	-3.4	-0.1	-2.7
	- Total	-3.2	-0.1	-2.5
South Korea	1973-80 - Commercial	-0.8	1.8	0.1
Philippines	1973-79 - Commercial	0.6	-9.2	-5.0
	- Total	-1.7	-9.2	-4.3
Turkey	1973-79 - Commercial	-1.6	1.2	-0.1

Source: Table B.5. Changes in intensities were calculated before rounding.

Table B.8: INTERNATIONAL COMPARISON OF KEY INDICATORS IN STEEL PRODUCTION

Market	1980 Steel production (mln tons)	Steel production by process, 1980: Oxygen (%)	Open hearth (%)	Electric (%)	Thomas & other (%)	Continuous casting ratio (% of crude steel)	Energy consumption per ton of crude steel (gcal) /a: 1976	1980
Developed Countries								
Japan	111.4	75.5	-	24.5	-	59.5	5.1	4.5
US	101.7	61.2	27.2	11.6	-	20.3	6.3	6.2
Germany, F.R.	43.8	78.4	6.7	19.9	-	46.0	5.6	5.2
Italy	26.5	45.3	1.7	53.1	-	50.1	4.4	4.2
France	23.2	81.9	0.9	15.9	1.3	41.3	6.0	5.7
UK	21.5*	60.1*	5.4*	34.4*	0.1*	16.9*	6.3	6.4*
Spain	12.7	45.8	5.0	49.2	-	36.7	-	4.4
Developing Countries								
Brazil	15.3	63.4	11.8	24.7	0.1	33.6	-	5.7
Romania	13.3	44.0	36.7	19.3	-	13.1	-	-
India	9.5	20.4	57.9	20.0	1.7	0.0	-	11.0/b
S. Africa	8.9*	64.7*	8.9*	24.2*	2.2*	49.3*	7.9	7.3*
Korea, Rep.	8.6	69.2	1.2	29.7	-	32.4	-	-
Mexico	7.1	37.0	20.8	42.2	-	29.7	-	-
Hungary	3.9	-	90.7	9.3	-	35.0		
Yugoslavia	3.6	31.6	40.1	28.2	-	36.6		
Egypt	0.8	-	-	-	-	-	-	9.5*
China:								
Key plants	28.6/c	-	-	-	-	-	-	8.4/d
Overall	37.1	48.8	32.0	19.2	-	6.6	-	9.1/d

* 1979 data.

/a Energy consumption figures include casting and rolling.

/b According to the source below, specific energy consumption in integrated steel mills during the late 1970s ranged from 9.0 gcal per ton of steel (Bokaro Steel Plant) to 16.0 gcal per ton, with an average of about 12.5 gcal. The same source indicates that electric arc furnace consumption plus steel rolling averages about 4.3 gcal/ton of steel (electricity converted at 3,000 kcal/kWh).

/c Estimate.

/d Figures represent "comparable energy consumption."

Sources: China: Nengyuan (Journal of Energy), No. 3, 1983; 1982 Almanac of China's Economy.
Energy consumption figures for India: Subcommittee II of the Interministerial Working Group, Energy Conservation in Energy-Intensive Industries (India), no date.
All other figures: International Iron and Steel Institute, Steel Statistical Yearbook (1980), World Steel in Figures (1981); the World Bank, "Energy Efficiency in the Steel Industry with Emphasis on Developing Countries," 1983 (draft).

Table B.9: ENERGY CONSUMPTION IN THE CEMENT INDUSTRY IN SELECTED COUNTRIES

	Year	Production (million tons)		% share by wet process	Total energy consumption		Energy consumption per ton	
		Clinker	Cement		Fuel/a (mtoe)	Electricity (GWh)	Fuel /b (mtoe)	Electricity /c (GWh)
Developed Countries								
US	1976	68.6	71.2	59	10.9	11,480/d	0.158	140
Germany, F.R.	1974	31.0	35.6	5	2.8	3,552	0.090	100
UK	1974	17.7	18.4	69	2.6	1,818	0.147	99
France	1973	27.5	31.9	30	2.9	2,935	0.105	92
Developing Countries								
India	1977/78	16.5	19.5	65	2.7	2,400	0.163	123
Turkey	1978	14.8	15.4	10	1.6	n.a.	0.108	n.a.
Portugal	1977	3.8	4.4	30	0.5	578	0.132	131
Tunisia	1981	2.1	2.2	21	0.2	264	0.100	120
Pakistan	1979/80	3.1	3.3	90	0.5	330	0.161	100
Philippines	1979	3.9	4.1	27	0.5	615	0.128	150

/a One toe = 10 million kcal.
/b Per ton of clinker.
/c Per ton of cement.
/d For 1979 corresponding to cement production of 82.0 mt.

Source: Estimated based on data from US Energy R&D Administration, The Cement Industry, 1975; various Bank reports; CEMBUREAU; Turkish Cement Industries Co.; Asian Productivity Organization, Energy Conservation in the Cement Industry, 1982.

Table B.10: INTERNATIONAL COMPARISON OF RATED FUEL CONSUMPTION FOR TRUCKS /a

	Gross vehicle weigth (tons)	Rated payload (tons)	Rated fuel consumption per 100 km (liters)	Fuel consumption per 100 gross ton-km (liters)	Fuel consumption per 100 payload ton-km (liters)	Energy consumption per 100 gross ton-km (1,000 kilocalories)	Energy consumption per 100 payload ton-km (1,000 kilocalories)
New Trucks in Developed Countries /b							
Ford Courer (1981)	1.98	0.69	6.8	3.4	9.9	26.5/c	76.1/c
Isuzu TID25 (1981)	2.74	1.09	8.6	3.1	7.9	24.2/c	60.9/c
International SP2650 (1981)	20.76	11.76	31.1	1.5	2.6	12.0	21.2
Mercedes Benz 1217 (1979)	13.80	6.97	21.3	1.5	3.1	12.4	24.4
Man-VW 9136 (1980)	10.02	5.90	16.9	1.7	2.9	13.5	23.0
Volvo F12F (1981)	38.46	23.32	49.1	1.3	2.1	10.3	16.9
International SF2670 (1981)	37.74	23.86	42.0	1.1	1.8	8.9	14.1
Kenworth K124 (1980)	39.46	23.06	48.7	1.2	2.1	9.9	17.0
Ford Louisville (1981)	36.92	22.87	45.4	1.2	2.0	9.9	15.9
Trucks in India /d							
TATA (1201 SE/42)	11.12	5.0	30.8	2.7	6.2	22.2	49.5
Ashok Leyland Beaver	15.62	7.5	35.5	2.3	4.7	18.3	38.0
Trucks in China							
Haiyan SWH600	n.a.	0.5	8.0	n.a.	16.0	n.a.	123.5
Beijing BJ130	n.a.	2.0	15.0	n.a.	7.5	n.a.	57.5
Shanghai SH130	n.a.	2.0	14.0	n.a.	7.0	n.a.	54.0
Yuejin NJ130	n.a.	2.5	20.0	n.a.	8.0	n.a.	61.8
Jianghuai HF140	n.a.	3.0	25.0	n.a.	8.3	n.a.	64.3
Hongwei GZ140	n.a.	3.5	22.5	n.a.	6.4	n.a.	49.6
Jiefang CA-10B	8.0	4.0	29.0	3.6	7.3	28.0	56.0
Dongfeng EQ140	9.3	5.0	28.0	3.0	5.6	23.2	43.2

/a Energy consumption per ton-km (1,000 kilocalories) is computed in addition to fuel consumption (liters), as the trucks listed for China consume gasoline, while the large trucks in other countries consume diesel oil. Diesel oil is converted at 8,030 kcal/l, while gasoline is converted at 7,720 kcal/l.

/b All fuel consumption figures refer to highway cycle rates under optimal test conditions.

/c Data are unclear as to whether diesel oil or gasoline is consumed. In these figures, it is assumed that gasoline is used.

/d TATA and Beaver trucks often carry payloads higher than the rated payloads given - indeed, Indian laws allow actual payloads to exceed the given rated payloads by as much as 25%. Higher payloads would entail higher energy efficiencies than those given.

Sources: China: Zou, et.al., Qiche yongyou changshi (Common Knowledge Concerning Oil Use in Motor Vehicles), 1977.

Other countries: The World Bank, "India: Increased Energy Efficiency in the Consumption of Petroleum Products," October 1983.

Table B.11: INTERNATIONAL TRENDS IN TOTAL ENERGY CONSUMPTION IN THE CHEMICAL INDUSTRY DURING THE 1970s /a (millions of tons of oil equivalent)/b

	Petroleum products	Natural gas	Solid fuels	Total fuel & feedstock	Electricity /c	Total
Canada						
1970	3.09	1.44	-	4.53	3.10	7.63
1975	2.76	3.41	-	6.17	2.83	9.00
1979	5.18	4.11	0.16	9.45	3.74	13.19
Germany, F.R.						
1970	9.73	2.46	3.78	15.97	10.69	26.66
1975	8.64	4.24	3.04	15.92	11.97	27.89
1979	13.41	4.64	1.97	20.02	14.94	34.96
Italy						
1970	11.21	2.56	0.40	14.17	5.02	19.19
1975	12.51	3.36	0.14	16.01	6.00	22.01
1979	11.11	3.35	0.21	14.67	6.68	21.35
Japan						
1970	27.88	1.25	-	29.13	14.16	43.29
1975	29.67	1.00	0.40	31.07	14.30	45.37
1979	36.91	0.81	0.41	38.13	15.24	53.37
UK						
1970	8.99	0.60	2.86	12.45	5.77	18.22
1975	8.00	4.48	0.53	13.01	5.40	18.41
1979	7.44	5.24	0.18	12.86	6.17	19.03
China						
1980 (est.)	8.65	5.32	24.01	37.98	15.23	53.21

/a Includes petrochemicals.

/b One ton of oil equivalent = 10 million kcal.

/c Calculated at a thermal replacement value of 2,900 kcal/kWh.

Sources (excluding China): OECD, IEA, Energy Balances for OECD Countries, 1970-82; Energy Statistics, 1981/82, Paris, 1984.

Table B.12: SHARE OF DIFFERENT ENERGY SOURCES IN TOTAL ENERGY CONSUMPTION IN THE CHEMICAL INDUSTRY IN SELECTED COUNTRIES, 1980s
(% shares)

	Petroluem products	Natural gas	Solid fuels	Total fuel & feedstock	Electricity /a
Canada					
1970	40.5	18.9	0.0	59.4	40.6
1975	30.7	37.9	0.0	68.6	31.4
1979	39.3	31.2	1.2	71.7	28.3
Germany, F.R.					
1970	36.5	9.2	14.2	59.9	40.1
1975	31.0	15.2	10.9	57.1	42.9
1979	38.4	13.3	5.6	57.3	42.7
Italy					
1970	58.4	13.3	2.1	73.8	26.2
1975	56.8	15.3	0.6	72.7	27.3
1979	52.0	15.7	1.0	68.7	31.3
Japan					
1970	64.4	2.9	-	67.3	32.7
1975	65.4	2.2	0.9	68.5	31.5
1979	69.2	1.5	0.8	71.4	28.6
UK					
1970	49.3	3.3	15.7	68.3	31.7
1975	43.5	24.3	2.9	70.7	29.3
1979	39.1	27.5	1.0	67.6	32.4
China					
1980	16.3	10.0	45.1	71.4	28.6

/a Calculated at a thermal replacement value of 2,900 kcal/kWh.

Source: Table B.11.

Table B.13: AVERAGE ANNUAL PERCENTAGE CHANGE IN ENERGY CONSUMPTION PER UNIT GROSS OUTPUT VALUE IN THE CHEMICAL INDUSTRY IN SELECTED COUNTRIES

	Feedstock and fuel			Electricity			Total		
	1970-75	1975-79	1970-79	1970-75	1975-79	1970-79	1970-75	1975-79	1970-79
Canada	+1.9	+3.7	+2.7	-5.9	0.0	-3.4	-1.0	+2.6	+0.6
Germany	-2.6	-2.8	-2.7	-0.3	-3.0	-1.5	-1.6	-2.9	-2.2
Italy	-4.8	-5.2	-5.0	-3.7	-0.4	-2.3	-4.5	-3.8	-4.2
Japan	-2.7	-2.2	-2.5	-3.8	-5.6	-4.6	-3.1	-3.2	-3.1
UK	-2.6	-3.6	-3.0	-4.8	0.0	-2.7	-3.3	-2.5	-2.9

Sources: Energy consumption: Table B.11.

Gross chemical industry output value: Statistical Office of the United Nations, Yearbook of Industrial Statistics, 1980, 1977 and 1974 editions.

Industrial price series used to convert to constant prices: International Monetary Fund, International Financial Statistics, 1982 Yearbook (line 63).

Table B.14: TRENDS IN ELECTRICITY INTENSITY IN THE MACHINE-BUILDING INDUSTRIES IN SELECTED COUNTRIES

Country	Year	Industry classification
China		Machine-building Unit: GWh/billion 1980 Yuan
	1977	171.6
	1980	179.7
	1982	178.3
Japan		Machinery (including transportation equipment but excluding fabricated metal products) Unit: GWh/output index, base 1975=100
	1974	146.14
	1975	175.17
	1976	173.36
	1977	174.53
	1978	172.54
	1979	164.48
	1980	147.78
	1981	141.17
	1982	145.45
France		Machinery and metal products (ISIC 381-385) Unit: GWh/billion 1980 French francs
	1972	427.3
	1973	431.1
	1974	397.9
	1975	465.6
	1976	513.5
	1977	526.6
	1978	556.2
	1979	551.6
	1980	576.2
	1981	562.5
Germany, F.R.		Machinery and metal products (ISIC 381-385) Unit: GWh/billion 1980 DM
	1972	54.8
	1973	57.1
	1974	58.5
	1975	57.3
	1976	57.6
	1977	54.0
	1978	53.4
	1979	54.7
	1980	55.5
	1981	57.3
UK		Machinery and metal products, excluding professional equipment (ISIC 381-384) Unit: GWh/billion 1980 £
	1972	289.9
	1973	288.2
	1974	258.7
	1975	271.1
	1977	290.4
	1978	289.4
	1979	293.7
	1980	304.1
S. Korea		Machinery and metal products, excluding professional equipment (ISIC 381-384) Unit: GWh/billion 1980 Won
	1972	0.39
	1973	0.31
	1974	0.32
	1975	0.35
	1976	0.31
	1977	0.27
	1978	0.25
	1979	0.27
	1980	0.34

Sources: For Japan, the Bank of Japan (1984), Economic Statistics Annual. For France, Germany F.R., the UK, and S. Korea the UN, Yearbook of Industrial Staistics, 1981 edition.

Table B.15: SHARE OF ELECTRICITY IN TOTAL ENERGY CONSUMPTION IN THE MACHINE-BUILDING INDUSTRIES IN SELECTED COUNTRIES

Country	Year	Industry classification			
China		Machine building			
	1980	33.6			
US		SIC 34	SIC 35	SIC 36	SIC (34+35+36)
	1958	33.2	32.2	43.6	35.7
	1968	40.8	44.7	57.0	47.3
	1973	43.2	48.8	59.3	49.6
	1978	49.5	58.3	64.4	56.7
	1981	52.6	62.6	69.8	61.2
France		Machinery (ISIC 381-385)			
	1973	77.1			
	1978	80.2			
Germany, F.R.		Machinery (ISIC 381-385)			
	1976	56.3			
	1978	59.3			
	1980	55.7			
	1982	58.2			
Italy		Machinery (ISIC 381-385)			
	1973	49.6			
	1978	51.4			
	1980	52.0			
	1982	57.4			
UK		Machinery (ISIC 381-385)			
	1973	44.3			
	1978	42.8			
	1980	44.9			
	1982	47.2			

Sources: US: 1958-78 - David Reister (1983), Aggregate Energy Demand Patterns in the Manufacturing Sector (Institute for Energy Analysis, Oak Ridge); 1981 - US Department of Commerce, Bureau of the Census (1983), 1982 Census of Manufacturers, Fuel and Electric Energy Consumed.

Others (excl. China): OECD.

For US nomenclature of industries, see Table B.16.

Table B.16: LONG-TERM TRENDS IN FUEL AND ELECTRICITY INTENSITIES IN THE MACHINE-BUILDNG INDUSTRIES, US

Annual average growth rates	1958-68	1968-73	1973-78	1978-81
A. SIC-34: Fabricated metal products industry:				
Fuel intensity	-0.4	4.4	-6.8	-4.0
Electricity intensity	2.9	6.6	-2.0	0.2
Total energy intensity	0.8	5.3	-4.6	-1.9
B. SIC-35: Nonelectrical machinery industry:				
Fuel intensity	-3.9	-1.1	-7.7	-7.7
Electricity intensity	1.3	2.2	-0.3	-2.0
Total energy intensity	-2.0	0.5	-3.8	-4.3
C. SIC-36: Electrical machinery industry:				
Fuel intensity	-5.2	-3.5	-6.2	-9.1
Electricity intensity	0.4	-1.7	-2.0	-1.3
Total energy intensity	-2.6	-2.4	-3.6	-4.0

Sources: Energy consumption data are from Reister (1983) for 1958-78 and from the US Department of Commerce for 1981. Output data for 1958-78 are from Reister (1983), and for 1981, from the US Board of Governors of the Federal Reserve System, Statistical Release G.12.3. Electricity is calculated at 2,900 kcal/kWh.

Table B.17: TRENDS IN FUEL AND ELECTRICITY INTENSITIES IN THE FOOD AND RELATED PRODUCTS INDUSTRY IN SELECTED COUNTRIES

			Annual average growth rates of intensities		
Country	Industry coverage	Period	Fuel	Electricity	Total energy
China	Food, beverages & tobacco	1977-82	n.a.	4.9	n.a.
Japan	Food, beverages & tobacco	1976-80	4.8	3.2	4.1
France	Food, beverages & tobacco	1973-78	-4.0	2.2	-1.8
		1978-82	-0.2	3.3	1.2
Germany, F.R.	Food, beverages & tobacco	1973-78	-2.7	2.2	-1.0
		1978-82	-2.2	2.6	-0.3
India	Food products	1974-78	n.a.	13.8	n.a.
Brazil	Food products	1973-78(a)	-4.6	4.3	-3.3
		1973-78(b)	-0.2	4.3	1.8
S. Korea	Food & beverages	1973-80	n.a.	2.8	n.a.
	of which food products	1973-80	n.a.	0.4	n.a.
	beverages	1973-80	n.a.	18.5	n.a.

Sources and notes:

1. Energy consumption data for Japan, France, and the Federal Republic of Germany are from OECD (1984a), Energy Balances of OECD Countries, 1970-82. Energy consumption data for India and Brazil are from OECD (1984b), Energy Balances of Developing Countries, 1971-82. Complete fuel consumption data are not available for India. Electricity consumption data for South Korea are from the UN (1983), Yearbook of Industrial Statistics, 1981 edition, vol. 1 - General Industrial Statistics. Data are also available for the UK (1973-80), but both output in real terms and energy consumption fell during this period; hence energy/electricity intensity calculations are likely to be misleading and have been excluded. In the case of Brazil, (a) refers to total (including biomass) energy consumption, and (b) to only commercial energy consumption.

2. Output statistics in all cases are from the UN (1983), Yearbook of Industrial Statistics 1981 edition, vol. 1 - General Industrial Statistics. These data gives output at current producers' prices or factor values, converted to 1980 prices using the price index line 63 or 63a from the IMF (1983), International Financial Statistics, 1983 Yearbook.

3. Electricity converted at the thermal replacement value of 2900 kcal/kWh.

Table B.18: SHARE OF ELECTRICITY IN TOTAL ENERGY CONSUMPTION IN THE FOOD AND RELATED PRODUCTS INDUSTRY IN SELECTED COUNTRIES

Country	Year	Industry classification	
China		Food, beverage, and tobacco	
	1980	19.1	
US		Food and kindred products (SIC 20) (excl. tobacco)	
	1958	20.3	
	1968	24.2	
	1973	30.0	
	1978	35.6	
	1981	39.3	
Japan		Food , beverage and tobacco	
	1976	40.3	
	1980	38.8	
	1982	40.1	
France		Food, beverage and tobacco	
	1973	32.7	
	1976	38.4	
	1980	41.5	
	1982	43.4	
Germany, F.R.		Food, beverage and tobacco	
	1973	32.4	
	1976	34.2	
	1980	38.8	
	1982	42.6	
UK		Food, beverage and tobacco	
	1973	30.9	
	1976	36.1	
	1980	37.0	
	1982	40.9	
Brazil		Food products	
		(a) Commercial energy	(b) Total energy
	1973	41.6	12.1
	1978	46.9	17.6
	1980	46.0	20.8
	1982	66.9	26.5

Sources and notes:

1. For the US, data up to 1978 are from David Reistar (1983), Aggregate Energy Demand Patterns in the Manufacturing Sector (Institute for Energy Analysis, Oak Ridge) and for 1981 from the US Department of Commerce, Bureau of the Census (1983), 1982 Census of Manufactures, Fuels and Electric Energy Consumed (MC 82-S-4, part 1). Data for Japan, France, Federal Republic of Germany and the UK are from OECD (1984), Energy Balances of OECD Countries 1970-82. Data for Brazil are from OECD (1984), Energy Balances of Developing Countries, 1971-82.

2. Electricity converted at the thermal replacement value of 2900 kcal/kWh.

Table B.19: LONG-TERM TRENDS IN FUEL AND ELECTRICITY INTENSITIES IN THE FOOD AND RELATED PRODUCTS INDUSTRY (SIC 20), US

Annual average growth rates	1958-68	1968-73	1973-78	1978-81
Fuel intensity	3.1	-0.2	-2.5	-2.9
Electricity intensity	5.5	5.8	2.6	2.4
Total energy intensity	3.6	1.4	-0.9	-0.9

Sources and notes:

1. Energy data up to 1978 from Reister (1983), and for 1981 from US Department of Commerce (1983).

2. Output data, in terms of indexes (base 1967 = 100), up to 1978 are from Reister (1983) and for 1981 from the US Board of Governors of the Federal Reserve System, Statistical Release g.12.3, "Industrial Production" (December 15, 1982 issue).

3. Electricity converted at the thermal replacement value of 2900 kcal/kWh.

Table B.20: ENERGY AND ELECTRICITY INTENSITIES IN THE FOOD AND RELATED PRODUCTS INDUSTRY, US, 1981

SIC/Name		Electricity intensity (kWh/1000$)	Total energy intensity (1000 Btu/$)
20	Food and kindred products, total	160	4.68
201	Meat products, subtotal	101	2.39
2011	Meat packing plants	69	1.94
2013	Sausages and other prepared meats	134	2.70
202	Dairy products, subtotal	135	3.46
2022	Cheese, natural and processed	86	3.09
2023	Condensed and evaporated milk	119	5.65
2024	Ice cream and frozen desserts	288	4.46
2026	Fluid milk	147	2.97
203	Preserved fruits and vegetables, subtotal	212	5.81
2033	Canned fruits and vegetables	154	5.99
2037	Frozen fruits and vegetables	467	10.08
204	Grain mill products, subtotal	243	6.83
2041	Flour and other grain mill products	288	4.22
2046	Wet corn milling	741	30.57
205	Bakery products, subtotal	148	4.18
2051	Bread, cake and related products	150	4.32
206	Sugar and confectionary, subtotal	192	9.63
2062	Cane sugar refining	/a	/a
2063	Beet sugar	390	42.46
207	Fats and oils, subtotal	200	7.71
2075	Soybean oil mills	162	6.21
2077	Animal and marine fats, oils	375	18.68
2079	Shortening and cooking oils	126	5.73
208	Beverages, subtotal	160	4.42
2082	Malt beverages	216	6.96
2086	Bottled and soft drinks	99	2.35

/a Data on self-generated electricity consumption are not reported; it could be as high as 250-300 GWh, implying electricity intensity of 100-114 kWh/1000$ and a total energy intensity of 9,000-9,100 Btu/$.

Sources and notes:

1. For fuels and electricity, US Department of Commerce (1983). Electricity is converted at 11505.6 Btu/kWh (equivalent to 2900 kcal/kWh). Output data (value of industry shipments) are from US Department of Commerce, 1984 US Industrial Outlook.

2. Fuel consumption data are for purchased fuels only; no information was available on the extent of nonpurchased fuel consumption in the industry. Electricity consumption data cover both purchased and net self-generated electricity.

Table B.21: TRENDS IN ELECTRICITY INTENSITY IN THE TEXTILE INDUSTRY IN SELECTED COUNTRIES

Country	Year	
China		Unit: GWh/billion 1980 Yuan
	1977	171.2
	1980	168.1
	1982	175.7
Japan		Unit: GWh/output index base 1975=100
	1974	55.99
	1975	63.97
	1976	62.33
	1977	60.69
	1978	61.35
	1979	62.09
	1980	59.64
	1981	59.44
	1982	59.57
S. Korea		Unit: GWh/billion 1980 won
	1972	0.668
	1973	0.541
	1974	0.748
	1975	0.764
	1976	0.735
	1977	0.787
	1978	0.806
	1979	0.897
	1980	0.950
Brazil		Unit: GWh/billion 1980 cruzeiros
	1972	4.821
	1973	3.516
	1974	3.201
	1977	5.333
	1978	6.059
Philippines		Unit: GWh/billion 1980 pesos
	1972	59.30
	1973	60.35
	1974	81.65
	1975	75.50
	1977	102.51

Sources: For S. Korea, Brazil and the Philippines, data are from the UN, Yearbook of Industrial Statistics, 1981 edition. For Japan both electricity and output (in terms of production index) data are from the Bank of Japan (1984), Economic Statistics Annual.

Table B.22: SHARE OF ELECTRICITY IN TOTAL ENERGY CONSUMPTION IN THE TEXTILE INDUSTRY IN SELECTED COUNTRIES

Country	Year	Industry classification	
China		Textiles	
	1980	24.8	
US		Textile mill products (SIC 22)	
	1958	42.4	
	1968	48.8	
	1973	54.3	
	1978	56.9	
	1981	59.8	
Japan		Textile and leather	
	1980	43.0	
	1981	30.3	
	1982	30.6	
France		Textile and leather	
	1982	66.9	
Germany, F.R.		Textile and leather	
	1980	61.2	
	1982	66.0	
UK		Textiles	
	1980	45.7	
	1982	47.1	
Brazil /a		Textiles	
		(A)	(B)
	1973	57.6	52.2
	1978	60.0	55.8
	1980	64.5	60.3
	1982	75.4	69.3
India		Textiles	
	1973	46.9	
	1978	54.1	
	1980	57.3	
	1982	59.6	

/a (A) refers to the share of commercial energy consumption; (B) refers to the share of total (including biomass) energy consumption

Source: OECD.

Table B.23: LONG-TERM TRENDS IN FUEL AND ELECTRICITY INTENSITIES IN THE TEXTILE MILL PRODUCTS INDUSTRY (SIC 22), US

	Annual average rates of change			
	1958-68	1968-73	1973-78	1978-81
Fuel intensity	-2.0	-4.1	-3.0	-4.0
Electricity intensity	0.6	0.3	-1.0	-1.7
Total energy intensity	-0.8	-1.8	-1.9	-1.7

Sources: As for Table B.16.

ENERGY DEMAND SCENARIOS, YEAR 2000

1. This appendix provides further details on projections of energy demand, by fuel and by major economic sector, corresponding to the different scenarios discussed in Chapter 2. Tables C.2, C.3, and C.4 give projections for the QUADRUPLE, MODERATE and BALANCE macroeconomic scenarios with LOW, BASE and HIGH unit energy consumption assumptions, and with energy production at targeted levels. Tables C.5 and C.6 provide projections for the INITIAL and BALANCE macro scenarios, assuming coal production levels of 1,400 million tons in 2000, as opposed to 1,200 million tons -- the macroeconomic assumptions, and hence energy demand projections, are slightly different than for tables C.2 and C.4, due to a need for greater investment and capital and intermediate inputs for faster growth in coal output. A summary of all of the scenarios is provided in Table C.1.

2. For each scenario, surpluses or deficits between production and demand of oil distillates and coal in the year 2000 are illustrated to ease comparisons of different scenarios, based on the following simplistic and arbitrary assumption regarding production and trade in 2000: (1) Net trade in crude and fuel oil amounts to zero; (2) No crude oil is directly burned as fuel outside of the petroleum industry; (3) Gross refinery distillate yields in 2000 are 60%, about the same as today; and (4) The national average calorific value of coal domestically produced remains unchanged. These assumptions were made only to facilitate comparison between scenarios, and in no way represent judgements concerning probable trends, the optimal refinery output balance, or the optimal trade pattern for the future. In analyzing the figures, the potential impact of large-scale fuel oil exports on surpluses or deficits in coal in particular should be considered (see Table C.1). The breakdown of fuel oil consumption among the power and manufacturing sectors given in the various scenarios is also only arbitrary.

3. Figures for oil consumed as fuel in 1980 include crude oil directly consumed as fuel. In each scenario, a figure for thermal power production, calculated at the 1980 net thermal replacement value (0.413 kgCE/kwh), is subtracted from total energy consumption in the power sector, as in an energy balance. However, in order to facilitate comparisons in electricity consumption figures, the same thermal replacement value for electricity was used for 2000, while actual net energy requirements for thermal power production are projected to decrease. This causes substantial discrepancies in power sector figures for 2000 between energy inputs for thermal power production and the output of thermal power, calculated in tons of standard coal equivalent.

Table C.1: SUMMARY OF ENERGY DEMAND SCENARIOS, YEAR 2000

Macroeconomic case (targeted coal production) /a	Growth in GVIAO, 1980-2000	Growth in GDP, 1980-2000	Growth in gross manufacturing output value, 1980-2000	Primary commercial energy demand, year 2000			Electricity demand, year 2000			Appendix table with details
				Low	Base	High	Low	Base	High	
	(% p.a.)			(million TCE)			(TWh)			
Quadruple	7.1	6.6	8.2	1,385	1,555	1,765	1,060	1,180	1,285	C.2
Moderate	5.9	5.4	6.8	1,180	1,320	1,500	885	985	1,070	C.3
Balance	6.4	6.6	7.2	1,270	1,420	1,610	955	1,060	1,150	C.4

Macroeconomic case	Coal production, year 2000 (million tons)	Surplus (deficit) in fuel supply in year 2000 /b (million TCE)			Appendix table with details
		Low	Base	High	
Quadruple	1,200	(115-180)	(265-325)	(435-495)	C.2
Moderate	1,200	5-65	(60-120)	(205-265)	C.3
Balance	1,200	(10-75)	(140-205)	(295-360)	C.4
Quadruple	1,400	(40)-20	(130-190)	(295-360)	C.5
Balance	1,400	65-130	(65)-5	(160-220)	C.6

/a In Tables C.5 and C.6, where coal production is assumed to reach 1,400 million tons in 2000, as opposed to 1,200 million tons, macroeconomic assumptions and scenarios of future energy demand are slightly different.

/b Fuel is defined to include coal, natural gas, fuel oil and solid petroleum products, and crude oil lost or directly consumed. Domestic coal supply is assumed to equal production, and natural gas supply is assumed to reach 25 billion cu m (about 33 million TCE). Ranges portray different fuel oil supply levels, ranging from about 32 million tons (about 46 million TCE, and the same level as 1980) to about 75 million tons (109 million TCE), depending upon export levels.

Table C.2: ENERGY DEMAND: MACRO QUADRUPLE CASE, TARGETED COAL PRODUCTION
MACROECONOMIC ASSUMPTIONS

	Billion 1981 yuan		Average annual growth rates, 1980-2000 (%)
	1980	2000	
GVIAO	719.9	2,836.8	7.10
GDP	432.2	1,537.3	6.55
GDP per capita (Y)	455.2	1,285.2	5.33
Gross Output			
Agriculture	207.1	505.7	4.6
Manufacturing	448.3	2,153.2	8.2
Metallurgy	47.4	166.9	6.5
Chemicals	57.9	301.6	8.6
Building materials	23.5	92.2	7.1
Machine building	117.8	604.6	8.5
Food, beverages, tobacco	62.4	342.9	8.9
Textiles	92.7	411.0	7.7
Other manufacturing	46.6	234.0	8.4
Construction	78.2	281.4	6.6
Commerce and services	124.3	372.8	5.6
Transport (billion units)			
Ton-kilometers	849	3,133	6.7
Passenger-kilometers	228	1,171	8.5

	1980 (million TCE)							2000: BASE consumption case (million TCE)						
	Oil							Oil						
	Distillate	Fuel	Total	Coal	Gas	Power	Total	Distillate	Fuel	Total	Coal	Gas	Power	Total
Agriculture	13.1	0.0	13.1	21.5	0.0	10.8	45.4	28.8	0.0	28.8	47.2	0.0	21.9	97.9
Transportation	19.5	1.5	21.0	19.0	0.0	0.6	40.6	79.8	5.5	85.3	21.3	0.0	9.0	115.6
Residential & commercial	1.9	0.0	1.9	90.2	0.3	10.6	103.0	4.5	0.0	4.5	172.9	1.0	45.1	223.5
Manufacturing	10.0	32.4	42.4	189.4	13.9	70.1	315.9	35.0	78.0	113.0	496.0	29.5	304.1	942.5
Other	5.5	1.5	7.0	9.0	0.0	2.1	18.1	17.3	2.6	19.9	22.4	0.0	6.7	49.0
Total Final Consumption	50.0	35.4	85.4	329.1	14.2	94.2	523.0	165.4	86.1	251.5	759.8	30.5	386.8	1,428.5
Energy industry														
Uses and losses														
Coal	0.1	0.6	0.7	29.0	0.0	7.9	37.6	0.4	0.4	0.8	63.9	0.0	20.6	85.3
Petroleum	0.5	3.8	19.1	0.4	2.1	3.6	25.2	0.9	5.7	26.5	0.7	2.8	7.5	37.4
Power														
Uses and losses	0.7	22.9	23.6	74.3	2.7	18.4	119.0	1.3	16.5	17.8	297.5	0.0	73.2	388.5
Thermal power production							-100.1							-382.8
Total Consumption	51.3	62.7	128.8	432.8	19.0	124.1		168.0	108.6	296.5	1,121.9	33.3	488.1	
Primary energy consumption			128.8	432.8	19.0	24.0	604.6			296.5	1,121.9	33.3	105.3	1,556.9
Original units	MT	MT	MT	MT	bln cu m	TWh		MT	MT	MT	MT	bln cu m	TWh	
Total consumption	35.2	43.0	88.4	605.9	14.3	300.6		115.3	74.5	203.5	1,570.7	25.0	1,182.2	
Primary consumption			88.4	605.9	14.3	58.2				203.5	1,570.7	25.0	255.0	

	Production		Surplus (deficit) for BASE consumption case	
	1980	2000	1980	2000
	(original units)		(original units)	
Crude oil (MT)	105.9	200.0	13.3	0.0
Oil products (MT)				
Fuel oil	33.3	74.5	1.1	0.0
Oil distillates	38.3	111.8	3.1	(3.5)
Subtotal	71.6	186.4	4.2	(3.5)
Natural gas (bln cu m)	14.3	25.0	0.0	0.0
Coal (MT)	620.2	1,200.0	6.4	(370.7)
Electricity (TWh)				
Primary	58.2	255.0	0.0	0.0
Thermal	242.4	927.2	0.0	0.0
Subtotal	300.6	1,182.2	0.0	0.0

	Production		Surplus (deficit) for BASE consumption case	
	1980	2000	1980	2000
	(million TCE)		(million TCE)	
Crude oil	154.3	291.4	19.4	0.0
Oil products				
Fuel oil	48.5	108.6	1.6	0.0
Oil distillates	55.8	162.9	4.5	(5.0)
Subtotal	104.3	271.6	6.1	(5.0)
Natural gas	19.0	33.3	0.0	0.0
Coal	443.0	857.1	5.9	(264.8)
Electricity				
Primary	24.0	105.3	0.0	0.0
Thermal	100.1	382.8	0.0	0.0
Subtotal	124.1	488.1	0.0	0.0
Total Primary Energy	640.3	1,287.1	31.4	(269.8)

	2000: LOW consumption case (million TCE)						
	Oil						
	Distillate	Fuel	Total	Coal	Gas	Power	Total
Agriculture	25.6	0.0	25.6	47.2	0.0	21.9	94.7
Transportation	71.0	5.5	76.5	21.3	0.0	9.0	106.8
Residential & commercial	4.5	0.0	4.5	147.8	1.3	39.4	193.0
Manufacturing	27.5	78.8	106.3	430.5	29.2	267.1	833.0
Other	15.6	2.5	18.1	21.1	0.0	6.7	46.0
Total Final Consumption	144.2	86.8	231.0	667.9	30.5	344.0	1,273.5
Energy industry							
Uses and losses							
Coal	0.3	0.2	0.5	57.4	0.0	19.9	77.8
Petroleum	0.9	5.1	25.0	0.7	2.8	7.5	36.0
Power							
Uses and losses	1.3	16.9	18.2	247.0	0.0	65.5	330.7
Thermal power production							-331.7
Total Consumption	146.7	109.0	274.7	973.1	33.3	436.9	
Primary energy consumption			274.7	973.1	33.3	105.2	1,386.3
Original units	MT	MT	MT	MT	bln cu m	TWh	
Total consumption	100.7	74.8	188.5	1,362.3	25.0	1,058.3	
Primary consumption			188.5	1,362.3	25.0	254.9	

	2000: HIGH consumption case (million TCE)						
	Oil						
	Distillate	Fuel	Total	Coal	Gas	Power	Total
Agriculture	32.0	0.0	32.0	47.2	0.0	21.9	101.1
Transportation	97.7	5.5	103.2	21.3	0.0	9.0	133.5
Residential & commercial	5.5	0.0	5.5	217.3	0.7	47.9	271.4
Manufacturing	47.5	76.3	123.8	559.5	29.8	336.2	1,049.2
Other	20.4	2.8	23.2	25.4	0.0	6.7	55.3
Total Final Consumption	203.0	84.6	287.6	870.8	30.5	421.7	1,610.6
Energy industry							
Uses and losses							
Coal	0.5	0.6	1.1	74.6	0.0	22.2	97.8
Petroleum	0.9	7.1	29.3	0.7	2.8	7.5	40.3
Power							
Uses and losses	1.3	15.8	17.1	343.8	0.0	79.7	440.6
Thermal power production							-425.7
Total Consumption	205.7	108.1	335.1	1,290.0	33.3	531.0	
Primary energy consumption			335.1	1,290.0	33.3	105.2	1,763.5
Original units	MT	MT	MT	MT	bln cu m	TWh	
Total consumption	141.2	74.2	229.9	1,805.9	25.0	1,286.1	
Primary consumption			229.9	1,805.9	25.0	254.9	

	Surplus (deficit), Year 2000	
	LOW case	HIGH case
	(original units)	
Crude oil (MT)	0.0	0.0
Oil products (MT)		
Fuel oil	0.0	0.0
Oil distillates	11.5	(29.9)
Subtotal	11.5	(29.9)
Natural gas (bln cu m)	0.0	0.0
Coal (MT)	(162.3)	(605.9)
Electricity (TWh)		
Primary	0.0	0.0
Thermal	0.0	0.0
Subtotal	0.0	0.0

	Surplus (deficit), Year 2000	
	LOW case	HIGH case
	(million TCE)	
Crude oil	0.0	0.0
Oil products		
Fuel oil	0.0	0.0
Oil distillates	16.7	(43.6)
Subtotal	16.7	(43.6)
Natural gas	0.0	0.0
Coal	(115.9)	(432.8)
Electricity		
Primary	0.0	0.0
Thermal	0.0	0.0
Subtotal	0.0	0.0
Total Primary Energy	(99.2)	(476.5)

Table C.3: ENERGY DEMAND: MACRO MODERATE CASE, TARGETED COAL PRODUCTION MACROECONOMIC ASSUMPTIONS

	Billion 1981 yuan		Average annual growth
	1980	2000	rates, 1980-2000 (%)
GVIAO	719.9	2,266.5	5.90
GDP	432.2	1,233.7	5.38
GDP per capita (Y)	455.2	1,031.4	4.17
Gross Output			
Agriculture	207.1	429.6	3.7
Manufacturing	448.3	1,674.0	6.8
Metallurgy	47.4	129.8	5.2
Chemicals	57.9	252.7	7.6
Building materials	23.5	74.8	6.0
Machine building	117.8	459.9	7.0
Food, beverages, tobacco	62.4	262.0	7.4
Textiles	92.7	317.6	6.4
Other manufacturing	46.6	177.2	6.9
Construction	78.2	230.4	5.6
Commerce and services	124.3	306.0	4.6
Transport (billion units)			
Ton-kilometers	849	2,531	5.6
Passenger-kilometers	228	832	6.7

Appendix C
Table C.3
Page 2 of 3

	1980 (million TCE)							2000: BASE consumption case (million TCE)						
	Oil							Oil						
	Distillate	Fuel	Total	Coal	Gas	Power	Total	Distillate	Fuel	Total	Coal	Gas	Power	Total
Agriculture	13.1	0.0	13.1	21.5	0.0	10.8	45.4	24.5	0.0	24.5	40.1	0.0	21.9	86.5
Transportation	19.5	1.5	21.0	19.0	0.0	0.6	40.6	64.5	4.5	69.0	16.8	0.0	7.2	93.0
Residential & commercial	1.9	0.0	1.9	90.2	0.3	10.6	103.0	4.5	0.0	4.5	167.6	1.0	42.0	215.1
Manufacturing	10.0	32.4	42.4	189.4	13.9	70.1	315.9	28.7	78.8	107.5	377.0	29.5	241.7	755.7
Other	5.5	1.5	7.0	9.0	0.0	2.1	18.1	14.3	2.4	16.7	19.0	0.0	5.6	41.4
Total Final Consumption	50.0	35.4	85.4	329.1	14.2	94.2	523.0	136.5	85.7	222.2	620.5	30.5	318.4	1,191.6
Energy industry														
Uses and losses														
Coal	0.1	0.6	0.7	29.0	0.0	7.9	37.6	0.4	0.4	0.8	63.9	0.0	20.6	85.3
Petroleum	0.5	3.8	19.1	0.4	2.1	3.6	25.2	0.9	5.7	26.5	0.7	2.8	7.5	37.4
Power														
Uses and losses	0.7	22.9	23.6	74.3	2.7	18.4	119.0	1.3	16.8	18.1	230.9	0.0	61.1	310.2
Thermal power production							-100.1							-302.4
Total Consumption	51.3	62.7	128.8	432.8	19.0	124.1		139.1	108.6	267.6	916.0	33.3	407.7	
Primary energy consumption			128.8	432.8	19.0	24.0	604.6			267.6	916.0	33.3	105.3	1,322.1
Original units	MT	MT	MT	MT	bln cu m	TWh		MT	MT	MT	MT	bln cu m	TWh	
Total consumption	35.2	43.0	88.4	605.9	14.3	300.6		95.4	74.5	183.6	1,282.4	25.0	987.4	
Primary consumption			88.4	605.9	14.3	58.2				183.6	1,282.4	25.0	255.0	

	Production (original units)		Surplus (deficit) for BASE consumption case (original units)	
	1980	2000	1980	2000
Crude oil (MT)	105.9	200.0	13.3	0.0
Oil products (MT)				
Fuel oil	33.3	74.5	1.1	0.0
Oil distillates	38.3	111.8	3.1	16.4
Subtotal	71.6	186.4	4.2	16.4
Natural gas (bln cu m)	14.3	25.0	0.0	0.0
Coal (MT)	620.2	1,200.0	6.4	(82.4)
Electricity (TWh)				
Primary	58.2	255.0	0.0	0.0
Thermal	242.4	732.4	0.0	0.0
Subtotal	300.6	987.4	0.0	0.0

	Production (million TCE)		Surplus (deficit) for BASE consumption case (million TCE)	
	1980	2000	1980	2000
Crude oil	154.3	291.4	19.4	0.0
Oil products				
Fuel oil	48.5	108.6	1.6	0.0
Oil distillates	55.8	162.9	4.5	23.9
Subtotal	104.3	271.6	6.1	23.9
Natural gas	19.0	33.3	0.0	0.0
Coal	443.0	857.1	5.9	(58.9)
Electricity				
Primary	24.0	105.3	0.0	0.0
Thermal	100.1	302.4	0.0	0.0
Subtotal	124.1	407.6	0.0	0.0
Total Primary Energy	640.3	1,287.1	31.4	(35.0)

	2000: LOW consumption case (million TCE)							2000: HIGH consumption case (million TCE)						
	Oil							Oil						
	Distillate	Fuel	Total	Coal	Gas	Power	Total	Distillate	Fuel	Total	Coal	Gas	Power	Total
Agriculture	21.7	0.0	21.7	40.1	0.0	21.9	83.7	27.2	0.0	27.2	40.1	0.0	21.9	89.2
Transportation	57.4	4.5	61.9	16.8	0.0	7.2	85.9	79.0	4.5	83.5	16.8	0.0	7.2	107.5
Residential & commercial	4.5	0.0	4.5	142.9	1.3	36.3	185.0	5.5	0.0	5.5	210.9	0.7	44.8	261.9
Manufacturing	22.6	79.6	102.2	325.7	29.2	212.6	669.7	39.0	77.1	116.1	427.4	29.8	266.9	840.2
Other	12.9	2.3	15.3	17.9	0.0	5.6	38.9	16.8	2.6	19.4	21.5	0.0	5.6	46.5
Total Final Consumption	119.1	86.5	205.6	543.5	30.5	283.6	1,063.2	167.5	84.2	251.7	716.7	30.5	346.4	1,345.3
Energy industry														
Uses and losses														
Coal	0.3	0.2	0.5	57.4	0.0	19.9	77.8	0.5	0.6	1.1	74.6	0.0	22.2	97.8
Petroleum	0.9	5.1	25.0	0.7	2.8	7.5	36.0	0.9	7.1	29.3	0.7	2.8	7.5	40.3
Power														
Uses and losses	1.3	17.2	18.5	189.8	0.0	54.9	263.6	1.3	16.2	17.5	268.4	0.0	66.4	352.2
Thermal power production							-260.6							-337.2
Total Consumption	121.7	109.0	249.6	791.5	33.3	365.8		170.2	108.1	299.5	1,060.4	33.3	442.4	
Primary energy consumption			249.6	791.5	33.3	105.2	1,179.6			299.5	1,060.4	33.3	105.2	1,498.4
Original units	MT	MT	MT	MT	bln cu m	TWh		MT	MT	MT	MT	bln cu m	TWh	
Total consumption	83.5	74.8	171.3	1,108.1	25.0	886.1		116.8	74.2	205.6	1,484.6	25.0	1,071.6	
Primary consumption			171.3	1,108.1	25.0	254.9				205.6	1,484.6	25.0	254.9	

	Surplus (deficit), Year 2000 LOW case (original units)	Surplus (deficit), Year 2000 HIGH case (original units)
Crude oil (MT)	0.0	0.0
Oil products (MT)		
Fuel oil	0.0	0.0
Oil distillates	28.7	(5.6)
Subtotal	28.7	(5.6)
Natural gas (bln cu m)	0.0	0.0
Coal (MT)	91.9	(284.6)
Electricity (TWh)		
Primary	0.0	0.0
Thermal	0.0	0.0
Subtotal	0.0	0.0

	Surplus (deficit), Year 2000 LOW case (million TCE)	Surplus (deficit), Year 2000 HIGH case (million TCE)
Crude oil	0.0	0.0
Oil products		
Fuel oil	0.0	0.0
Oil distillates	41.8	(8.1)
Subtotal	41.8	(8.1)
Natural gas	0.0	0.0
Coal	65.7	(203.3)
Electricity		
Primary	0.0	0.0
Thermal	0.0	0.0
Subtotal	0.0	0.0
Total Primary Energy	107.4	(211.4)

Table C.4: ENERGY DEMAND: MACRO BALANCE CASE, TARGETED COAL PRODUCTION
MACROECONOMIC ASSUMPTIONS

	Billion 1981 yuan		Average annual growth rates, 1980-2000 (%)
	1980	2000	
GVIAO	719.9	2,475.8	6.37
GDP	432.2	1,554.3	6.61
GDP per capita (Y)	455.2	1,299.4	5.38
Gross Output			
Agriculture	207.1	507.6	4.6
Manufacturing	448.3	1,796.8	7.2
Metallurgy	47.4	123.7	4.9
Chemicals	57.9	248.9	7.6
Building materials	23.5	78.3	6.2
Machine building	117.8	486.6	7.3
Food, beverages, tobacco	62.4	338.4	8.8
Textiles	92.7	339.2	6.7
Other manufacturing	46.6	181.7	7.0
Construction	78.2	271.6	6.4
Commerce and services	124.3	594.3	8.1
Transport (billion units)			
Ton-kilometers	849	2,754	6.1
Passenger-kilometers	228	1,191	8.6

	1980 (million TCE)							2000: BASE consumption case (million TCE)						
	Oil							Oil						
	Distillate	Fuel	Total	Coal	Gas	Power	Total	Distillate	Fuel	Total	Coal	Gas	Power	Total
Agriculture	13.1	0.0	13.1	21.5	0.0	10.8	45.4	28.9	0.0	28.9	47.4	0.0	21.9	98.2
Transportation	19.5	1.5	21.0	19.0	0.0	0.6	40.6	72.3	4.9	77.2	19.2	0.0	8.2	104.6
Residential & commercial	1.9	0.0	1.9	90.2	0.3	10.6	103.0	4.5	0.0	4.5	190.4	1.0	55.3	251.2
Manufacturing	10.0	32.4	42.4	189.4	13.9	70.1	315.9	28.8	77.9	106.8	394.4	29.5	250.8	781.4
Other	5.5	1.5	7.0	9.0	0.0	2.1	18.1	16.2	3.2	19.4	25.9	0.0	7.8	53.1
Total Final Consumption	50.0	35.4	85.4	329.1	14.2	94.2	523.0	150.7	86.0	236.7	677.3	30.5	343.9	1,288.5
Energy industry														
Uses and losses														
Coal	0.1	0.6	0.7	29.0	0.0	7.9	37.6	0.4	0.4	0.8	63.9	0.0	20.6	85.3
Petroleum	0.5	3.8	19.1	0.4	2.1	3.6	25.2	0.9	5.7	26.5	0.7	2.8	7.5	37.4
Power														
Uses and losses	0.7	22.9	23.6	74.3	2.7	18.4	119.0	1.3	16.5	17.8	255.9	0.0	65.7	339.4
Thermal power production							-100.1							-332.4
Total Consumption	51.3	62.7	128.8	432.8	19.0	124.1		153.3	108.6	281.8	997.8	33.3	437.7	
Primary energy consumption			128.8	432.8	19.0	24.0	604.6			281.8	997.8	33.3	105.3	1,418.2
Original units	MT	MT	MT	MT	bln cu m	TWh		MT	MT	MT	MT	bln cu m	TWh	
Total consumption	35.2	43.0	88.4	605.9	14.3	300.6		105.2	74.5	193.4	1,397.0	25.0	1,060.2	
Primary consumption			88.4	605.9	14.3	58.2				193.4	1,397.0	25.0	255.0	

	Production (original units)		Surplus (deficit) for BASE consumption case (original units)	
	1980	2000	1980	2000
Crude oil (MT)	105.9	200.0	13.3	0.0
Oil products (MT)				
Fuel oil	33.3	74.5	1.1	0.0
Oil distillates	38.3	111.8	3.1	6.6
Subtotal	71.6	186.4	4.2	6.6
Natural gas (bln cu m)	14.3	25.0	0.0	0.0
Coal (MT)	620.2	1,200.0	6.4	(197.0)
Electricity (TWh)				
Primary	58.2	255.0	0.0	0.0
Thermal	242.4	805.1	0.0	0.0
Subtotal	300.6	1,060.1	0.0	0.0

	Production (million TCE)		Surplus (deficit) for BASE consumption case (million TCE)	
	1980	2000	1980	2000
Crude oil	154.3	291.4	19.4	0.0
Oil products				
Fuel oil	48.5	108.6	1.6	0.0
Oil distillates	55.8	162.9	4.5	9.6
Subtotal	104.3	271.6	6.1	9.6
Natural gas	19.0	33.3	0.0	0.0
Coal	443.0	857.1	5.9	(140.7)
Electricity				
Primary	24.0	105.3	0.0	0.0
Thermal	100.1	332.4	0.0	0.0
Subtotal	124.1	437.7	0.0	0.0
Total Primary Energy	640.3	1,287.1	31.4	(131.1)

	2000: LOW consumption case (million TCE)							2000: HIGH consumption case (million TCE)						
	Oil							Oil						
	Distillate	Fuel	Total	Coal	Gas	Power	Total	Distillate	Fuel	Total	Coal	Gas	Power	Total
Agriculture	25.7	0.0	25.7	47.4	0.0	21.9	95.0	32.1	0.0	32.1	47.4	0.0	21.9	101.4
Transportation	64.6	4.9	69.5	19.2	0.0	8.2	96.9	88.2	4.9	93.1	19.2	0.0	8.2	120.5
Residential & commercial	4.5	0.0	4.5	164.1	1.3	49.6	219.5	5.5	0.0	5.5	238.6	0.7	58.1	302.9
Manufacturing	22.8	78.7	101.5	341.8	29.2	219.9	692.4	39.1	76.1	115.1	447.6	29.8	278.1	870.6
Other	14.6	3.1	17.7	24.4	0.0	7.8	49.9	18.9	3.6	22.5	29.7	0.0	7.8	60.0
Total Final Consumption	132.2	86.7	218.9	596.8	30.5	307.3	1,153.6	183.7	84.6	268.3	782.6	30.5	374.0	1,455.4
Energy industry														
Uses and losses														
Coal	0.3	0.2	0.5	57.4	0.0	19.9	77.8	0.5	0.6	1.1	74.6	0.0	22.2	97.8
Petroleum	0.9	5.1	25.0	0.7	2.8	7.5	36.0	0.9	7.1	29.3	0.7	2.8	7.5	40.3
Power														
Uses and losses	1.3	16.9	18.2	212.4	0.0	59.1	289.7	1.3	15.8	17.1	296.3	0.0	71.2	384.7
Thermal power production							-288.5							-369.7
Total Consumption	134.7	109.0	262.7	867.4	33.3	393.8		186.5	108.1	315.8	1,154.2	33.3	474.9	
Primary energy consumption			262.7	867.4	33.3	105.2	1,268.6			315.8	1,154.2	33.3	105.2	1,608.5
Original units	MT	MT	MT	MT	bln cu m	TWh		MT	MT	MT	MT	bln cu m	TWh	
Total consumption	92.4	74.8	180.3	1,214.4	25.0	953.8		128.0	74.2	216.7	1,615.9	25.0	1,150.4	
Primary consumption			180.3	1,214.4	25.0	254.9				216.7	1,615.9	25.0	254.9	

	Surplus (deficit), Year 2000 LOW case (original units)	Surplus (deficit), Year 2000 HIGH case (original units)		Surplus (deficit), Year 2000 LOW case (million TCE)	Surplus (deficit), Year 2000 HIGH case (million TCE)
Crude oil (MT)	0.0	0.0	Crude oil	0.0	0.0
Oil products (MT)			Oil products		
Fuel oil	0.0	0.0	Fuel oil	0.0	0.0
Oil distillates	19.7	(16.7)	Oil distillates	28.7	(24.4)
Subtotal	19.7	(16.7)	Subtotal	28.7	(24.4)
Natural gas (bln cu m)	0.0	0.0	Natural gas	0.0	0.0
Coal (MT)	(14.4)	(415.9)	Coal	(10.3)	(297.0)
Electricity (TWh)			Electricity		
Primary	0.0	0.0	Primary	0.0	0.0
Thermal	0.0	0.0	Thermal	0.0	0.0
Subtotal	0.0	0.0	Subtotal	0.0	0.0
			Total Primary Energy	18.5	(321.4)

Table C.5: ENERGY DEMAND: MACRO QUADRUPLE CASE, HIGH COAL PRODUCTION
MACROECONOMIC ASSUMPTIONS

	Billion 1981 yuan		Average annual growth rates, 1980-2000 (%)
	1980	2000	
GVIAO	719.9	2,816.7	7.06
GDP	432.2	1,528.6	6.52
GDP per capita (Y)	455.2	1,277.9	5.30
Gross Output			
Agriculture	207.1	505.2	4.6
Manufacturing	448.3	2,128.3	8.1
Metallurgy	47.4	165.3	6.4
Chemicals	57.9	300.1	8.6
Building materials	23.5	92.3	7.1
Machine building	117.8	594.5	8.4
Food, beverages, tobacco	62.4	342.0	8.9
Textiles	92.7	404.8	7.6
Other manufacturing	46.6	229.3	8.3
Construction	78.2	281.7	6.6
Commerce and services	124.3	370.7	5.6
Transport (billion units)			
Ton-kilometers	849	3,111	6.7
Passenger-kilometers	228	1,161	8.5

	1980 (million TCE)							2000: BASE consumption case (million TCE)						
	Oil							Oil						
	Distillate	Fuel	Total	Coal	Gas	Power	Total	Distillate	Fuel	Total	Coal	Gas	Power	Total
Agriculture	13.1	0.0	13.1	21.5	0.0	10.8	45.4	28.8	0.0	28.8	47.2	0.0	21.9	97.8
Transportation	19.5	1.5	21.0	19.0	0.0	0.6	40.6	79.3	5.5	84.8	21.1	0.0	9.0	114.9
Residential & commercial	1.9	0.0	1.9	90.2	0.3	10.6	103.0	4.5	0.0	4.5	172.7	1.0	45.0	223.2
Manufacturing	10.0	32.4	42.4	189.4	13.9	70.1	315.9	34.7	78.0	112.7	491.2	29.5	300.8	934.2
Other	5.5	1.5	7.0	9.0	0.0	2.1	18.1	17.3	2.6	19.9	22.4	0.0	6.7	48.9
Total Final Consumption	50.0	35.4	85.4	329.1	14.2	94.2	523.0	164.5	86.1	250.6	754.6	30.5	383.4	1,419.1
Energy industry														
Uses and losses														
Coal	0.1	0.6	0.7	29.0	0.0	7.9	37.6	0.5	0.4	0.9	74.5	0.0	24.1	99.4
Petroleum	0.5	3.8	19.1	0.4	2.1	3.6	25.2	0.9	5.7	26.5	0.7	2.8	7.5	37.4
Power														
Uses and losses	0.7	22.9	23.6	74.3	2.7	18.4	119.0	1.3	16.5	17.8	297.6	0.0	73.2	388.6
Thermal power production							-100.1							-383.0
Total Consumption	51.3	62.7	128.8	432.8	19.0	124.1		167.2	108.6	295.7	1,127.5	33.3	488.2	
Primary energy consumption			128.8	432.8	19.0	24.0	604.6			295.7	1,127.5	33.3	105.2	1,561.7
Original units	MT	MT	MT	MT	bln cu m	TWh		MT	MT	MT	MT	bln cu m	TWh	
Total consumption	35.2	43.0	88.4	605.9	14.3	300.6		114.8	74.5	202.9	1,578.5	25.0	1,182.5	
Primary consumption			88.4	605.9	14.3	58.2				202.9	1,578.5	25.0	254.9	

	Production 1980 (original units)	Production 2000 (original units)	Surplus (deficit) for BASE consumption case 1980 (original units)	Surplus (deficit) for BASE consumption case 2000 (original units)
Crude oil (MT)	105.9	200.0	13.3	0.0
Oil products (MT)				
Fuel oil	33.3	74.5	1.1	0.0
Oil distillates	38.3	111.8	3.1	(2.9)
Subtotal	71.6	186.4	4.2	(2.9)
Natural gas (bln cu m)	14.3	25.0	0.0	0.0
Coal (MT)	620.2	1,400.0	6.4	(178.5)
Electricity (TWh)				
Primary	58.2	255.0	0.0	0.0
Thermal	242.4	927.6	0.0	0.0
Subtotal	300.6	1,182.6	0.0	0.0

	Production 1980 (million TCE)	Production 2000 (million TCE)	Surplus (deficit) for BASE consumption case 1980 (million TCE)	Surplus (deficit) for BASE consumption case 2000 (million TCE)
Crude oil	154.3	291.4	19.4	0.0
Oil products				
Fuel oil	48.5	108.6	1.6	0.0
Oil distillates	55.8	162.9	4.5	(4.3)
Subtotal	104.3	271.6	6.1	(4.3)
Natural gas	19.0	33.3	0.0	0.0
Coal	443.0	1,000.0	5.9	(127.5)
Electricity				
Primary	24.0	105.3	0.0	0.0
Thermal	100.1	383.0	0.0	0.0
Subtotal	124.1	488.2	0.0	0.0
Total Primary Energy	640.3	1,430.0	31.4	(131.8)

	2000: LOW consumption case (million TCE)							2000: HIGH consumption case (million TCE)						
	Oil							Oil						
	Distillate	Fuel	Total	Coal	Gas	Power	Total	Distillate	Fuel	Total	Coal	Gas	Power	Total
Agriculture	25.6	0.0	25.6	47.2	0.0	21.9	94.6	32.0	0.0	32.0	47.2	0.0	21.9	101.0
Transportation	70.6	5.5	76.1	21.1	0.0	9.0	106.2	97.1	5.5	102.6	21.1	0.0	9.0	132.7
Residential & commercial	4.5	0.0	4.5	147.7	1.3	39.3	192.7	5.5	0.0	5.5	217.1	0.7	47.8	271.1
Manufacturing	27.3	78.8	106.1	426.3	29.2	264.2	825.8	47.1	76.3	123.4	554.2	29.8	332.6	1,040.0
Other	15.6	2.5	18.1	21.1	0.0	6.7	45.9	20.3	2.8	23.1	25.4	0.0	6.7	55.2
Total Final Consumption	143.5	86.8	230.3	663.3	30.5	341.1	1,265.3	202.0	84.6	286.6	865.0	30.5	418.0	1,600.1
Energy industry														
Uses and losses														
Coal	0.3	0.2	0.5	67.0	0.0	23.2	90.7	0.6	0.6	1.2	87.0	0.0	25.9	114.0
Petroleum	0.9	5.1	25.0	0.7	2.8	7.5	36.0	0.9	7.1	29.3	0.7	2.8	7.5	40.3
Power														
Uses and losses	1.3	16.9	18.2	247.3	0.0	65.6	331.1	1.3	15.8	17.1	343.8	0.0	79.7	440.6
Thermal power production							-332.1							-425.7
Total Consumption	146.1	109.0	274.1	978.4	33.3	437.4		204.8	108.1	334.1	1,296.6	33.3	530.9	
Primary energy consumption			274.1	978.4	33.3	105.2	1,391.0			334.1	1,296.6	33.3	105.2	1,769.2
Original units	MT	MT	MT	MT	bln cu m	TWh		MT	MT	MT	MT	bln cu m	TWh	
Total consumption	100.3	74.8	188.1	1,369.7	25.0	1,059.4		140.5	74.2	229.3	1,815.3	25.0	1,286.0	
Primary consumption			188.1	1,369.7	25.0	254.9				229.3	1,815.3	25.0	254.9	

	Surplus (deficit), Year 2000 (original units)	
	LOW case	HIGH case
Crude oil (MT)	0.0	0.0
Oil products (MT)		
Fuel oil	0.0	0.0
Oil distillates	11.9	(29.3)
Subtotal	11.9	(29.3)
Natural gas (bln cu m)	0.0	0.0
Coal (MT)	30.3	(415.3)
Electricity (TWh)		
Primary	0.0	0.0
Thermal	0.0	0.0
Subtotal	0.0	0.0

	Surplus (deficit), Year 2000 (million TCE)	
	LOW case	HIGH case
Crude oil	0.0	0.0
Oil products		
Fuel oil	0.0	0.0
Oil distillates	17.3	(42.7)
Subtotal	17.3	(42.7)
Natural gas	0.0	0.0
Coal	21.6	(296.6)
Electricity		
Primary	0.0	0.0
Thermal	0.0	0.0
Subtotal	0.0	0.0
Total Primary Energy	38.9	(339.3)

Table C.6: ENERGY DEMAND: MACRO BALANCE CASE, HIGH COAL PRODUCTION MACROECONOMIC ASSUMPTIONS

	Billion 1981 yuan 1980	Billion 1981 yuan 2000	Average annual growth rates, 1980-2000 (%)
GVIAO	719.9	2,454.2	6.32
GDP	432.2	1,543.2	6.57
GDP per capita (Y)	455.2	1,290.1	5.35
Gross Output			
Agriculture	207.1	506.9	4.6
Manufacturing	448.3	1,770.6	7.1
Metallurgy	47.4	122.1	4.8
Chemicals	57.9	247.5	7.5
Building materials	23.5	78.3	6.2
Machine building	117.8	475.8	7.2
Food, beverages, tobacco	62.4	337.0	8.8
Textiles	92.7	333.1	6.6
Other manufacturing	46.6	176.9	6.9
Construction	78.2	271.5	6.4
Commerce and services	124.3	589.9	8.1
Transport (billion units)			
Ton-kilometers	849	2,731	6.0
Passenger-kilometers	228	1,178	8.6

	1980 (million TCE)							2000: BASE consumption case (million TCE)						
	Oil							Oil						
	Distillate	Fuel	Total	Coal	Gas	Power	Total	Distillate	Fuel	Total	Coal	Gas	Power	Total
Agriculture	13.1	0.0	13.1	21.5	0.0	10.8	45.4	28.9	0.0	28.9	47.4	0.0	21.9	98.1
Transportation	19.5	1.5	21.0	19.0	0.0	0.6	40.6	71.6	4.8	76.4	19.0	0.0	8.1	103.5
Residential & commercial	1.9	0.0	1.9	90.2	0.3	10.6	103.0	4.5	0.0	4.5	190.1	1.0	55.1	250.7
Manufacturing	10.0	32.4	42.4	189.4	13.9	70.1	315.9	28.6	78.0	106.6	389.3	29.5	247.4	772.8
Other	5.5	1.5	7.0	9.0	0.0	2.1	18.1	16.1	3.2	19.3	25.8	0.0	7.7	52.9
Total Final Consumption	50.0	35.4	85.4	329.1	14.2	94.2	523.0	149.6	86.0	235.6	671.5	30.5	340.2	1,277.9
Energy industry														
Uses and losses														
Coal	0.1	0.6	0.7	29.0	0.0	7.9	37.6	0.5	0.4	0.9	74.5	0.0	24.1	99.4
Petroleum	0.5	3.8	19.1	0.4	2.1	3.6	25.2	0.9	5.7	26.5	0.7	2.8	7.5	37.4
Power														
Uses and losses	0.7	22.9	23.6	74.3	2.7	18.4	119.0	1.3	16.6	17.9	255.7	0.0	65.6	339.2
Thermal power production							-100.1							-332.2
Total Consumption	51.3	62.7	128.8	432.8	19.0	124.1		152.3	108.6	280.8	1,002.5	33.3	437.4	
Primary energy consumption			128.8	432.8	19.0	24.0	604.6			280.8	1,002.5	33.3	105.2	1,421.8
Original units	MT	MT	MT	MT	bln cu m	TWh		MT	MT	MT	MT	bln cu m	TWh	
Total consumption	35.2	43.0	88.4	605.9	14.3	300.6		104.5	74.5	192.7	1,403.4	25.0	1,059.5	
Primary consumption			88.4	605.9	14.3	58.2				192.7	1,403.4	25.0	254.9	

	Production 1980 (original units)	Production 2000 (original units)	Surplus (deficit) for BASE consumption case 1980 (original units)	Surplus (deficit) for BASE consumption case 2000 (original units)
Crude oil (MT)	105.9	200.0	13.3	0.0
Oil products (MT)				
Fuel oil	33.3	74.5	1.1	0.0
Oil distillates	38.3	111.8	3.1	7.3
Subtotal	71.6	186.4	4.2	7.3
Natural gas (bln cu m)	14.3	25.0	0.0	0.0
Coal (MT)	620.2	1,400.0	6.4	(3.4)
Electricity (TWh)				
Primary	58.2	255.0	0.0	0.0
Thermal	242.4	804.6	0.0	0.0
Subtotal	300.6	1,059.6	0.0	0.0

	Production 1980 (million TCE)	Production 2000 (million TCE)	Surplus (deficit) for BASE consumption case 1980 (million TCE)	Surplus (deficit) for BASE consumption case 2000 (million TCE)
Crude oil	154.3	291.4	19.4	0.0
Oil products				
Fuel oil	48.5	108.6	1.6	0.0
Oil distillates	55.8	162.9	4.5	10.6
Subtotal	104.3	271.6	6.1	10.6
Natural gas	19.0	33.3	0.0	0.0
Coal	443.0	1,000.0	5.9	(2.5)
Electricity				
Primary	24.0	105.3	0.0	0.0
Thermal	100.1	332.2	0.0	0.0
Subtotal	124.1	437.5	0.0	0.0
Total Primary Energy	640.3	1,430.0	31.4	8.2

	2000: LOW consumption case (million TCE)							2000: HIGH consumption case (million TCE)						
	Oil							Oil						
	Distillate	Fuel	Total	Coal	Gas	Power	Total	Distillate	Fuel	Total	Coal	Gas	Power	Total
Agriculture	25.6	0.0	25.6	47.4	0.0	21.9	94.9	32.1	0.0	32.1	47.4	0.0	21.9	101.3
Transportation	64.0	4.8	68.8	19.0	0.0	8.1	95.9	87.3	4.8	92.1	19.0	0.0	8.1	119.2
Residential & commercial	4.5	0.0	4.5	163.8	1.3	49.4	218.9	5.5	0.0	5.5	238.2	0.7	57.9	302.3
Manufacturing	22.5	78.8	101.4	337.3	29.2	217.0	684.8	38.7	76.2	114.9	442.0	29.8	274.4	861.0
Other	14.6	3.1	17.7	24.3	0.0	7.7	49.7	18.8	3.6	22.4	29.6	0.0	7.7	59.7
Total Final Consumption	131.3	86.7	218.0	591.7	30.5	304.1	1,144.2	182.4	84.5	266.9	776.1	30.5	370.0	1,443.5
Energy industry														
Uses and losses														
Coal	0.3	0.2	0.5	67.0	0.0	23.2	90.7	0.6	0.6	1.2	87.0	0.0	25.9	114.0
Petroleum	0.9	5.1	25.0	0.7	2.8	7.5	36.0	0.9	7.1	29.3	0.7	2.8	7.5	40.3
Power														
Uses and losses	1.3	17.0	18.3	212.4	0.0	59.1	289.7	1.3	15.9	17.2	295.9	0.0	71.2	384.3
Thermal power production							-288.6							-369.3
Total Consumption	133.8	109.0	261.8	871.8	33.3	393.8		185.2	108.1	314.5	1,159.8	33.3	474.5	
Primary energy consumption			261.8	871.8	33.3	105.2	1,272.1			314.5	1,159.8	33.3	105.2	1,612.8
Original units	MT	MT	MT	MT	bln cu m	TWh		MT	MT	MT	MT	bln cu m	TWh	
Total consumption	91.8	74.8	179.7	1,220.6	25.0	953.9		127.1	74.2	215.8	1,623.7	25.0	1,149.4	
Primary consumption			179.7	1,220.6	25.0	254.9				215.8	1,623.7	25.0	254.9	

	Surplus (deficit), Year 2000	
	LOW case	HIGH case
	------- (original units) -------	
Crude oil (MT)	0.0	0.0
Oil products (MT)		
Fuel oil	0.0	0.0
Oil distillates	20.3	(15.8)
Subtotal	20.3	(15.8)
Natural gas (bln cu m)	0.0	0.0
Coal (MT)	179.4	(223.7)
Electricity (TWh)		
Primary	0.0	0.0
Thermal	0.0	0.0
Subtotal	0.0	0.0

	Surplus (deficit), Year 2000	
	LOW case	HIGH case
	-------- (million TCE) --------	
Crude oil	0.0	0.0
Oil products		
Fuel oil	0.0	0.0
Oil distillates	29.6	(23.1)
Subtotal	29.6	(23.1)
Natural gas	0.0	0.0
Coal	128.2	(159.8)
Electricity		
Primary	0.0	0.0
Thermal	0.0	0.0
Subtotal	0.0	0.0
Total Primary Energy	157.8	(182.9)

Table D.1: CHINA'S COAL PRODUCTION, 1970-82
(Million tons)

A. By Type and Size of Mine

	1970	1975	1976	1977	1978	1979	1980	1981	1982
Open pit	13.3	15.5	15.7	15.0	17.0	16.6	17.0	17.2	20.1
Underground	340.6	466.5	467.8	535.7	600.0	618.9	603.1	604.4	646.2
Of which:									
over 0.6 mtpy	n.a.	172.5	149.3	173.7	203.2	212.8	163.2	162.5	179.3
0.1-0.6 mtpy	n.a.	181.8	204.6	227.6	256.0	254.9	286.7	273.1	281.0
Less than 0.1 mtpy	n.a.	112.2	113.9	134.4	141.7	151.2	153.2	161.6	186.0
Total	353.9	482.2	483.5	550.7	617.9	635.5	620.1	621.6	666.3

B. By Type of Coal

	1970	1975	1976	1977	1978	1979	1980	1981	1982
Lignite	13.0	20.3	20.6	23.3	24.9	25.3	24.3	23.4	25.0
Anthracite	56.0	97.1	99.6	115.5	126.2	125.8	129.0	131.1	139.0
Bituminous	284.9	364.8	363.3	411.9	466.8	484.4	466.8	467.1	502.3
Of which coking or with coking properties	(179.3)	(238.5)	(235.1)	(276.0)	(317.7)	(327.4)	(308.3)	(304.0)	(331.7)
Total	353.9	482.2	483.5	550.7	617.9	635.5	620.1	621.6	666.3

C. By Region

	1970	1975	1980	1981	1982	Average annual growth rate (%)
North	102.2	145.8	205.3	214.5	230.7	7.0
of which Shanxi	(53.0)	(75.4)	(120.0)	(132.5)	(145.3)	(8.8)
Northwest	23.0	32.3	49.9	49.1	52.0	7.0
Northeast	84.7	93.6	98.8	93.5	100.7	1.5
East	59.3	74.6	105.4	103.5	106.8	5.0
South-Central	50.7	81.4	95.9	95.5	104.7	6.2
Southwest	34.1	54.5	64.8	65.5	71.4	6.4
Total	354.0	482.2	620.1	621.6	666.3	5.4

D. By Province and Municipality, 1981 /a

Beijing	7.9	(6.0)
Shanxi	132.5	(67.6)
Liaoning	33.7	(28.9)
Heilongjiang	41.7	(33.3)
Jiangsu	15.7	(11.5)
Anhui	23.8	(21.9)
Jiangxi	15.5	(6.1)
Henan	58.3	(32.9)
Hunan	19.9	(3.3)
Guangxi	5.6	(0.0)
Guizhou	14.2	(5.9)
Xizang	insig.	
Gansu	7.9	(4.4)
Ningxia	9.5	(7.8)
Hebei	52.4	(38.4)
Nei Monggol	21.8	(14.8)
Jilin	18.1	(12.4)
Shanghai	1.7	(1.7)
Zhejiang	1.3	(0.0)
Fujian	4.2	(0.0)
Shandong	41.3	(23.8)
Hubei	4.3	(0.0)
Guangdong	7.2	(0.0)
Sichuan	39.4	(0.0)
Yunnan	11.9	(0.9)
Shaanxi	18.5	(11.6)
Qinghai	1.9	(0.0)
Xinjiang	11.4	(3.0)

/a Figures in parenthesis refer to production by central mines.

Source: MOCI, China Coal Industry Yearbook, 1982.

LONG-RUN MARGINAL PRODUCTION COSTS AND MINE LOCATION

1. Long-run marginal costs (LRMC) for China's coal industry have been calculated using the average incremental cost (AIC) method. The basis for the calculations is provided below. The AIC method is explained in paras. 7-9 in this Appendix.

2. Coal mining costs vary significantly from mine to mine, except in the North (particularly in Shanxi) where regular geological and mining conditions allow highly representative mining models to be defined. The bulk of incremental production is planned to be concentrated in the North. This region possesses the largest reserves of economically extractable coal in China and could, from the resource endowment point of view, meet all of China's incremental coal requirements (including demand for anthracite and coking and thermal coals) for at least 50 years. The table below presents the development of coal production by region under the low scenario to the year 2000.

Coal Reserves and Production by Region, 1980-2000
(million tons)

Region	Reserves	Production				Contribution to incremental
	%	1980	%	2000	%	production (%)
North	66	205	33	550	46	59.5
Northeast	3	99	16	181	15	14.2
Northwest	9	50	8	85	7	6.0
East	7	105	17	171	14	11.4
South-Central	4	96	15	131	11	6.0
Southwest	11	65	11	82	7	2.9
Total	100	620	100	1,200	100	100.0

Sources: MOCI and Bank estimates.

3. For the North, there is abundant information on average operating and capital costs for various types and sizes of mines. Also available are costs for a series of projects under construction or under design. On this basis, model mines have been developed, for which LRMC have been calculated. Results fall in a rather narrow range of about Y 36-44 per ton of coal produced. This is explained mostly by the fact that smaller mines with lower capital and operating costs have a significantly shorter life or need to be reconstructed several times over their life, which implies a higher rate of reinvestment than is needed for larger mines. LRMC in the North are not expected to increase much over time.

4. Information for other regions is scarcer, but crude LRMC estimates point to costs being a few yuan per ton higher in the Northwest, as much as Y 20-30 higher in the Northeast (on a quality-adjusted basis) and Y 30-50 higher in the South. Development in the latter region is thus going to be very selective despite high transport cost from, say, Shanxi (Y 40 per ton for a distance of 2,000 km, see para. 5 below).

5. Although it is difficult to ascertain whether the relative emphasis on the various regions is consistent with a least-cost development program, 1/ the mission believes that in broad terms the emphasis is well placed. The North (particularly Shanxi) deserves the development priority in mining and related transport infrastructure given to it in the Government's tentative long-term plans. Moreover, total costs would probably change little within rather wide ranges of regional shares in production. This is because when transport is shadow priced (LRMC of transportation are estimated at over Y 0.02 per ton-km as compared to current average railway tariffs for coal of about Y 0.016 per ton-km), there does not seem to be too much difference in total delivered cost to, say, Shenyang whether the coal is mined and brought from nearby or from Shanxi, as seen in the example below:

Cost of Coal Delivered to Consumers in the Northeast
(Y/ton)

Procedure	Coal Production Cost (LRMC) a/	Transport Cost to consumers (LRMC)	Total
Shanxi Province	36-44	25	61-69
Northeast	30-35	5	65-75

a/ On a quality adjusted basis, at 1984 prices.

Source: Mission estimates.

6. However, over the long run, mining costs in the North are believed likely to fall relative to those in other regions, given the comparatively faster depletion of reserves, particularly those that are economically recoverable, in other regions. At the same time, high-volume long-distance transportation from the North will reap economies of scale, thus reducing the relative importance of transport in total delivered costs of coal. Therefore, the North should become increasingly competitive and thus should capture an even larger share of total production.

1/ Even if detailed information on all mining and transport costs were available, a very large and complex model would be necessary to identify ways of minimizing mining plus transport costs to meet set regional demands.

7. The AIC method estimates LRMC by discounting (at the social rate of interest; a 10% rate was used in this exercise) all incremental costs (capital and operating) that will be incurred in the future to provide the estimated additional amounts of coal produced over a specified period, and dividing that by the discounted value of incremental output over the period, i.e.:

$$\text{AIC} = \frac{\text{Present Value of Capital plus Operating Costs Streams}}{\text{Present Value of Production Stream}}$$

There are other methods of calculating LRMC, but for discrete investment projects such as those encountered in coal mining, the AIC provides a convenient way of ironing out the "lumpiness" of investments.

8. The LRMC approach is particularly useful for comparing investment proposals characterized by widely different conditions, such as life of mines (which can vary from a few years for small mines to 100 years for a few very large mines), construction time (from less than one year to eight or nine years) and learning curve (almost immediate achievement of full production rate, to three or four years before production achieves capacity). In these circumstances, the mere comparison of capital costs per ton of coal capacity or of operating costs can be quite misleading.

9. As an example, AIC for a model large-scale mechanized underground mine in Shanxi is presented below. Basic assumptions are as follows: (i) construction time - 6 years; (ii) achievement of full production - year 9; (iii) initial investment Y 140/ton capacity; (iv) replacement costs - Y 2 per year per ton capacity starting in year 7 up to year 10, Y 6 per year per ton capacity thereafter; (v) operating costs - Y 18 per ton; (vi) life of mine - 40 years; (vii) interest rate - 10%.

Year	Capital cost stream (Y)	Operating cost stream (Y)	Production stream (in tons)
1	10	-	-
2	20	-	-
3	30	-	-
4	30	-	-
5	30	4	0.1 a/
6	20	6	0.2
7	2	14	0.6
8	2	18	0.8
9	2	18	1.0
10-40	6	18	1.0
Net present value	138	112	5.83

a/ Production during construction.

Therefore, the AIC is: $\text{AIC} = \frac{\text{Y } 138 + \text{Y } 112}{5.83 \text{ tons}} = \text{Y } 42.9/\text{ton}$

COAL TRANSPORT VERSUS

ELECTRICITY TRANSMISSION

1. The cost of mining Shanxi's abundant coal reserves combined with the cost of transporting it by rail or using the coal for power generation and transporting power to, say, the northeast power load centers, is often less than the cost of mining coal at the load centers themselves. The relative economic attractiveness of these two options for Shanxi coal is considered in this exercise. Alternative A involves transportation, by a new single track rail line, of 5,000 kcal/kg coal from Shanxi to the northeast power grid to generate electricity at the load center. This is a relatively unfavorable assumption since most investments to transport coal out of Shanxi are more likely to be for electrification of existing lines, or for additional double-track electrified lines, both with considerably lower (about one half) investment costs per ton capacity. Alternative B involves mine-mouth electricity generation in Shanxi and transmission of electricity to the northeast.

2. These alternatives will be evaluated under a series of simplifying assumptions:

(a) Distance: Due to different gradient tolerance, alignment of railway and transmission lines results in a 1,100 km railway line and a 1,000 km transmission line;

(b) Type of Lines: A single-track electrified railway line, with a capacity of 30 million tons of coal per year (on the basis of unit train operation); nine 500 KV transmission lines;

(c) Load Factor: Since mine-mouth power plants are generally conceived as base-load plants, a load factor of 70% (6,120 hours/year) is assumed;

(d) Construction Costs:

- Railway line at Y 3.6 million/km, to require 330 locomotives (at Y 1.2 million each) and 14,300 coal cars (at Y 36,000 each);

- Transmission line at Y 300,000/km and substation at Y 120/kVA;

- Power plant: in Northeast China Y 1,200/kW, in Shanxi Y 1,260/kW to account for higher cost of water and transportation of materials and equipment to Shanxi;

(e) Losses: 2% of coal is lost during transportation and 8% of electricity is lost during transmission;

(f) Efficiency: Plants generate at 340 gr of standard coal equivalent (7,000 kcal/kg) per kWh; and

(g) Construction Time: The railway takes 5 years to build and 3 more to achieve full capacity. Transmission lines take 4 years to build and 3 years more to achieve full capacity.

Evaluation

3. Since the benefits of the two alternatives are virtually the same, the evaluation will concentrate on costs, and only on cost items that differ.

4. Alternative A. Given losses in transportation and efficiency, 61.8 billion kWh are generated in the Northeast,[1/] at 6,120 hour/KW/year (70% load factor); capacity is 10,100 MW. The relevant railway capital costs are:

Cost of line (3.6 x 1,100)	=	Y3,960 m
Cost of locos (1.2 x 330)	=	396 m
Cost of cars (0.036 x 14,300)	=	515 m
Total Capital Costs		$4,871 m

Yearly replacement costs are assumed at Y 10 million after the tenth year. Therefore, the yearly capital charge (at 10% opportunity cost of capital) =

$$\frac{\text{Present Value (capital cost)}}{\text{Present Value (tonnage transp.)}} = \text{Y 22.8 per ton transported or about 2 fen per ton-km.}$$

5. Operating costs are 0.7 fen per ton-km. Total long-run marginal cost for the railway is thus 2.70 fen per ton-km or Y 29.7 per ton transported.

6. In addition, the loss of coal during transportation comes to Y 0.8 per ton transported, given an economic price of coal for Shanxi of Y 40/ton.

7. Total cost of Alternative A = Y 29.7 + Y 0.8 = Y 30.5 per ton.

8. Alternative B. In order to make the same amount of power available in the Northeast as under Alternative A, the mine-mouth power plant needs to be 8% larger and must generate 66.7 billion kWh with a capacity of 10,900 MW. Nine 500 kV lines will be required.

Cost of lines (9 x 300,000 x 1,000)	=	Y 2,700 m
Cost of station (120 x 1.2 x 10,900,000)	=	1,570 m

9. To make this alternative comparable with Alternative A, the cost of the 800 MW of additional power generation capacity (Y 1,008 m)[2/] and the extra

---

1/ $30 \text{ m} \times \frac{1,000}{0.68} \times 0.98 \times \frac{5,000}{7,000}$

2/ 1,260 x 800,000

cost of constructing the plant in Shanxi (Y 606 m)[3/] need to be added to capital costs under Alternative B. Total capital cost is therefore 4,270 + 1,008 + 606 = Y 5,884 m. The Present Value of capital costs divided by the Present Value of equivalent coal transportation is Y 25.70 per ton.

10. Operating costs are 1% of the cost of the line and gear per year, or Y 1.42 per equivalent ton of coal transported;[4/] also to be included as cost under Alternative B are the operating costs for generating the additional 4.9 billion kWh lost during transmission, which come to 2% of pertinent initial investment, and the related cost of coal burnt, or Y 0.68 [5/] and Y 3.10[6/] per equivalent ton transported. Total recurrent cost is therefore 1.42 + 0.68 + 3.10 = Y 5.20 per ton transported.

11. Total cost of Alternative B = Y 25.7 + Y 5.2 = Y 30.9 per equivalent ton transported.

12. Under these assumptions the two alternatives are about equal, with a slight edge for Alternative A, even though this represents a rather unfavorable case for the railroads. Aside from the various unit costs used, the relative merits of these alternatives appear to be sensitive to:

(a) calorific value of coal (the higher the calorific value, the better Alternative A looks);

(b) power plant load factor (the higher the load factor, the better Alternative B looks); and

(c) difference in distance due to alignment (the greater the difference, the better Alternative B looks).

13. For the large quantities that need to be transported from Shanxi, not only one but several double-tracked railways will be required over the next 15 years. The capacity of a double-tracked electrified line is about three times that of a single-tracked line, while investment costs are less than twice as high. Transport costs (LRMC) on a double tracked line are only 60-70% of those indicated in Alternative A (i.e. about Y 20/t), and the break-even point with respect to the calorific value of coal declines to about 3,500 kcal/kg, well below virtually every type of coal except coal preparation wastes (middlings). The unit costs of other capacity augmenting investments

---

3/ (1,260 - 1,200 (10,100,000)

4/ $4{,}270 \text{ m} \times \frac{0.01}{30 \text{ m}}$

5/ $1{,}008 \text{ m} \times \frac{0.02}{30 \text{ m}}$

6/ $4.9 \text{ m} \times \frac{0.68}{1{,}000} \times \frac{7{,}000}{5{,}000} \times \frac{1}{30 \text{ m}} \times 20$

(e.g., electrification of existing railways lines) are similar to the costs of new double-track railways per unit of capacity, and systems-wide LRMC are therefore closer to those of new double-tracked rail lines, or about one-third less than long-distance electric power transmission. Mine-mouth power plants are therefore justified mainly for using coal preparation wastes, very low quality fuels, or serving local electric power needs.

14. Other important factors such as the size of the system or the exact location of power plants can also affect the relative merits of the above alternatives. For example, if the size of the system in question is much smaller, then one railway line will not be fully dedicated to coal, making low-cost, high-density unit train transportation difficult to accommodate within the system. Alternative B shows more flexibility in adjusting to various system sizes, but there may be significant constraints to locating power plants exactly at the mine-mouth. Water availability is a common constraint. Thus the cost of transporting coal from the mine to another location in the vicinity might have to be added to Alternative B. More comprehensive analysis should include consideration of a variety of additional costs or benefits, such as land use implications, or, in the case of power transmission, possible additional benefits resulting from increasing grid integration.

APPENDIX F

POWER

Table F.1: INSTALLED CAPACITY, ELECTRICITY GENERATION AND SALES

Year	Installed capacity (MW)			Energy generation (GWh)			Energy sales (GWh)
	Hydro	Thermal	Total	Hydro	Thermal	Total	
1949	163	1,686	1,849	710	3,600	4,310	3,460
1952	188	1,776	1,964	1,260	6,001	7,261	6,277
1957	1,019	3,616	4,635	4,820	14,515	19,335	16,407
1962	2,379	10,686	13,065	9,042	36,753	45,795	n.a.
1965	3,020	12,056	15,076	10,414	57,190	67,604	56,802
1970	6,235	17,535	23,770	20,450	95,420	115,870	n.a.
1971	7,804	18,478	26,282	25,060	113,300	138,360	101,274
1972	8,700	20,801	29,501	28,820	123,630	152,450	123,600
1973	10,299	23,626	33,925	38,900	127,860	166,760	135,106
1974	11,817	26,291	38,108	41,440	127,410	168,850	135,708
1975	13,428	29,978	43,406	47,630	148,210	195,840	156,969
1976	14,655	32,492	47,147	45,640	157,490	203,130	164,698
1977	15,765	35,686	51,451	47,670	175,740	223,410	181,691
1978	17,277	39,845	57,122	44,630	211,920	256,550	210,239
1979	19,110	43,906	63,016	50,120	231,827	281,947	233,577
1980	20,318	45,551	65,869	58,211	242,416	300,627	257,300
1981	21,933	47,069	69,002	65,546	243,723	309,269	263,410
1982	22,959	49,401	72,360	74,399	253,279	327,678	280,080
1983	24,000	52,600	76,600	86,360	265,040	351,400	297,080/a
Average growth rate (% p.a.)			11.6			13.8	14.0

/a Mission estimate.

Table F.2: ELECTRICITY GENERATION BY REGION AND TYPES OF PLANT
(GWh)

	1970	1975	1976	1977	1978	1979	1980	1981	1982	1983	1984
Total	115,870	195,840	203,130	223,410	256,550	281,947	300,627	309,269	327,678	351,400	374,600
Hydro	20,450	47,630	45,640	47,670	44,630	50,120	58,211	65,546	74,399	86,360	85,500
Thermal	95,420	148,210	157,490	175,740	211,920	231,827	242,416	243,723	253,279	265,040	289,100
Northeast	28,820	41,160	43,020	43,610	48,520	51,580	53,995	54,210	56,147		
Hydro	3,350	5,350	3,560	3,850	2,690	4,746	5,072	6,343	4,509		
Thermal	25,470	35,810	39,460	39,760	45,830	46,834	48,923	47,867	51,638		
North	20,870	34,950	35,480	38,640	45,830	50,559	53,556	55,071	57,527		
Hydro	680	710	560	800	970	1,376	1,313	873	962		
Thermal	20,190	34,240	34,920	37,840	44,860	49,183	52,243	54,198	56,565		
East	29,710	49,490	54,670	60,860	70,140	77,535	83,816	87,429	92,149		
Hydro	4,320	7,920	7,150	7,900	6,450	5,996	9,018	11,109	11,337		
Thermal	25,390	41,570	47,520	52,960	63,690	71,539	74,798	76,320	80,812		
Central-South	18,360	35,410	35,000	39,930	46,150	52,534	57,592	60,883	65,922		
Hydro	6,950	17,020	17,170	16,030	15,630	17,178	20,245	23,327	30,256		
Thermal	11,410	18,390	17,830	23,900	30,520	35,356	37,347	37,556	35,666		
Northwest	8,340	17,010	18,660	20,790	22,460	23,928	24,989	24,774	26,501		
Hydro	2,670	8,580	10,060	10,440	9,750	10,416	10,560	11,060	12,525		
Thermal	5,670	8,430	8,600	10,350	12,710	13,512	14,429	13,714	13,976		
Southwest	9,770	17,820	16,300	19,580	23,450	25,811	26,679	26,902	29,432		
Hydro	2,480	8,050	7,140	8,650	91,50	10,408	12,003	12,834	14,810		
Thermal	7,290	9,770	9,160	10,930	14,300	15,403	14,676	14,068	14,622		

Table F.3: ELECTRICITY DEVELOPMENT SCENARIOS /a

	1981-85	1986-90 Low scenario	1986-90 High scenario	1991-2000 Low scenario	1991-2000 High scenario
Capital Construction Investment (Y million)	23,000	64,600/b	75,800/b	221,000/b	290,000/b
Generating plant	17,250	46,500	54,600	159,400	209,000
Of which: Hydro	7,000	17,600	18,200	55,000	65,000
Fossil-fired	10,250	25,900	31,400	92,400	125,000
Nuclear	-	3,000	5,000	12,000	19,000
Transmission and substations	4,370	14,200	16,700	48,340	63,600
Other	1,380	3,900	4,500	13,260	17,400
New Generating Capacity Added (MW)	14,000	25,900	30,800	96,000	135,000
Of which: Hydro	3,000	7,300	7,600	24,000	33,000
Fossil-fired	11,000	18,600	23,200	67,000	94,000
Nuclear	-	-	-	5,000	8,000
	1985	1990		2000	
Installed Capacity (MW)	74,470	100,370	105,270	196,370	240,270
Of which: Hydro	19,880	27,180	27,480	51,180	60,480
Fossil-fired	54,590	73,190	77,790	140,190	171,790
Nuclear	-	-	-	5,000	8,000
Energy Generated (GWh)	375,000	500,000	520,000	1,000,000	1,200,000
Of which: Hydro	79,000	97,000	97,000	190,000	220,000
Fossil-fired	296,000	403,000	423,000	784,000	936,000
Nuclear	-	-	-	26,000	44,000
Energy Sold (GWh)	322,500	430,000	447,200	860,000	1,032,000
Gross Fuel Requirements (million TCE):/c	133	173	182	288	339

/a Scenarios were developed in conjunction with MWREP in early 1984. All figures exclude small hydro plants with capacities of less than 500 MW and thermal plants with capacities of less than 6 MW.

/b To improve fuel efficiency, existing medium- and low-pressure thermal units (with a total capacity of about 13,000 MW) should be progressively replaced by larger, higher-pressure units. It is assumed that replacement of 3,000 MW and 10,000 MW by the new additions in generating capacity would be undertaken during 1986-90 and 1991-2000, respectively. The investment cost for replacement is included.

/c Includes heat supplied to consumers outside the power industry, totaling 11.85 million TCE in 1980 and 21.6 million TCE in 2000. Plant utilization factors were assumed to remain stable after 1986: 40% for hydro, 63% for fossil-fired thermal and 59-63% for nuclear.

Table F.4: INTERNATIONAL COMPARISON OF POWER SECTOR INVESTMENT LEVELS

Philippines /a					1978	1979	1980	1981
Share of gross domestic investment					3.6	7.6	7.6	9.8
Share of GDP					1.4	2.3	2.3	2.1
Thailand		1970-77			1978	1979	1980	
Share of gross domestic investment		3.9			4.7	2.7	6.5	
Share of GDP		1.0			0.9	0.8	1.8	
Brazil	1974	1975	1976	1977	1978			
Share of gross domestic investment	7.8	8.1	8.7	10.2	9.2			
Share of GDP	1.9	2.0	2.0	2.2	2.0			
India	1974	1975	1976	1977	1978			
Share of gross domestic investment	6.2	6.2	7.9	9.1	8.7			
Share of GDP	1.4	1.4	1.8	1.9	2.0			
China					1978	1979	1980	1981
Share of gross domestic investment					4.1	3.8	3.2	2.7
Share of GDP					1.4	1.2	1.0	0.8

/a Excludes geothermal power development.

Source: World Bank.

ELECTRICITY DEVELOPMENT PROGRAMS AND PROJECTS IN EARLY 1984

A. Major Generation Projects Under Construction

1. Hydro Projects

Projects	Location	Installed capacity	Present status
Gezhouba	Hubei on the Changjiang	2,715	965 MW in operation
Longyangxia	Qinghai on the Huanghe	1,280	
Baishan	Jilin on the Songhuajiang	900 (3 x 300)	
Ankang	Shaanxi on the Hanshui	800 (4 x 200)	
Tongjiezi	Sichuan on the Dadu River	600	
Dahua	Guangxi on the Hongshui	400 (4 x 125)	Civil works completed Equipment under installation
Dongjiang	Hunan on the Leishui	500 (4 x 125)	
Wanan	Jiangxi on the Gangjiang	500	
Yantan	Guangxi on the Hongshui	1,100 (5 x 220) 880 (4 x220)	Construction preparation
Tianshengqiao	Guizhou on the Hongshui River	600	Construction preparation
Lubuge	Yunnan on the Huangni River	(4 x 150)	Construction preparation
	Total	10,275	

2. Thermal Projects

(a) New Stations under Construction

Datong	Shanxi	1,200	200 MW in operation
Jinzhou	Liaoning	1,200	
Huainan	Jiangsu	1,200	
Guixi	Jiangxi	500	
Zouxian	Shandong	1,200	
Dawukou	Ningxia	400	
Fulaerji	Heilongjiang	1,200	
	Total	6,900	

(b) Station Being Expanded

Douhe	Hebei	1,550	800 MW being added
Yuanbaoshan	Nei Monggol	900	600 MW being added
Jianbi	Jiangsu	1,020	600 MW being added
Xuzhou	Jiangsu	1,300	800 MW being added
Qinling	Shaanxi	1,050	800 MW being added
	Total	5,820	3,600 MW being added

B. Large-Scale Hydro Development Plans

Upper Huanghe

From Qinghai to Ningxia, scores of hydroelectric stations are planned with total capacity of 12,600 MW. During the next two decades, seven projects (Longyangxia, Liujiaxia, Heisanxia, Daxia, Gongbuoxia, Jishixia, Laxiwa) with a total installed capacity of 9,000 MW will be constructed. Of the total, 4,000-6,000 MW will be commissioned by 2000. They will supply northwest China and be linked to the power grid supplying Beijing and Tianjin.

Hongshui

In the upper reaches of the Hongshui, there are ten hydroelectric sites with a total capacity of 10,400 MW under planning. Dahua (400 MW) is nearly completed. Tianshengqiao No. 2 is under construction. Five other projects (Tianshengqiao No. 1, Yentang, Longtang, Datanxia, Etang), with a total installed capacity of about 8,700 MW, will be eventually implemented. Of the total, 5,000-6,000 MW will be commissioned before the year 2000. They will supply the Guizhou, Guangxi and Guangdong power grids.

Middle and Upper Changjiang

During the next decade, construction will begin on 14 projects (Gezhouba, Three Gorges, Wuqiangqi, Geheyan, Dongjiang, Wanan, Panshi, Goupitang, Dongfeng, Tongjiezi, Pubugou, Ertan, Baozhuxi and Jinping), with a total installed capacity of 40,000 MW. Of the total, 15,000-22,000 MW are expected to be commissioned before the year 2000.

Middle and Lower Lancang River

Three projects (Manwan, Xiaowang, and Xiajiakou), with a total installed capacity of 6,000 MW, will be started, of which 2,000-3,000 MW will be commissioned by the year 2000 and will supply the Southwest China power grid.

C. Thermal Power Development Program

Shanxi coal and power base

Three groups of thermal power plants, with a total output of 20,000-25,000 MW, are being constructed near the coal pits in north, central and southeast Shanxi. They will mainly supply the North and Central China power grids.

Northeast coal and power base

The base comprises three large open pits (Heling, Iming and Yuanbaoshan) producing lignite and a system of thermal power plants with a possible total capacity of 10,000-12,000 MW. They will help supply the Northeast China power grid.

Nei Monggol coal and power base

Two groups of thermal power plants, with a total output of 5,000-10,000 MW, will be constructed at the mine mouths of Junggar and Dongshang. They will mainly supply North China.

Central coal and power base

Two groups of thermal power plants, with a total output of 3,000 MW and 5,000 MW, are being constructed at mining centers in Henan and western Anhui. They will supply central China.

Northwest coal and power base

Four groups of thermal power plants, with a total output of 5,000-10,000 MW, will be constructed near the Weibei, Shaanbei, Ningxia and Huating coal pits.

Southwest coal and power base

A system of thermal power plants, with a total output of 2,000-3,000 MW, will be constructed near the mining center of Liu-Pan-Sui in Guizhou.

East China load center and port area power plants

Four major thermal projects (Shidongkou, Beilungang, Sunan and Fuzhou) with a total capacity of 8,000-10,000 MW, will be constructed using coal mainly supplied from Shanxi.

Northeast China load center and port area power plants

Three thermal projects (Gaoling, Yingkou and Dalian) with a total capacity of 4,000-8,000 MW.

North China load and port area power plants

Five thermal projects (Shalingzhi, Shijingshan, Jixian, Qinhuangdao, Tianjin) with a total capacity of 6,000-10,000 MW.

South China load center and port area power plants

Three thermal projects (Shajiao, Maoming and Liaobing) with a total capacity of 2,000-3,000 MW.

APPENDIX G

RURAL

Table G.1:

ESTIMATED CROP BY-PRODUCT PRODUCTION PER RURAL PERSON, BY PROVINCE, 1981

	Kg per rural person		Kg per rural person
Northeast		Central-South	
Heilongjiang	805	Guangdong	315
Jilin	845	Guangxi	345
Liaoning	700	Henan	435
		Hubei	460
North		Hunan	445
Beijing	660		
Hebei	430	Southwest	
Nei Monggol	485	Guizhou	275
Shanxi	475	Sichuan	410
Tianjin	525	Yunnan	350
		Xizang	435
East			
Anhui	460	Northwest	
Fujian	355	Gansu	315
Jiangsu	560	Ningxia	465
Jiangxi	440	Qinghai	340
Shandong	465	Shaanxi	380
Shanghai	510	Xinjiang	520
Zhejiang	490		
		NATIONAL	450

Sources and notes: By-products included are from the following crops: rice, wheat, corn, other grains (primarily millet and sorghum), soybeans, tubers, cotton, peanuts, oilseeds, sesame, hemp, and tobacco. Rural population and crop production data are from the SSB, Statistical Yearbook of China, 1981 (1980 population data were adjusted to allow for increases in 1981). Crop by-product to crop production ratios used are as follows, from the Agricultural Technical and Economic Handbook (1983):

Rice	0.9
Wheat	1.1
Corn	1.2
Soybean	1.6
Tubers	0.5
Other grains	1.6
Cotton	3.4
Peanuts	0.8
Oilseed	1.5
Others	1.8

Table G.2: BIOGAS POPULARIZATION, BY PROVINCE, 1981

Province	Reported number of digestors (1,000 units)	Average utilization per year (months)	Average number of pigs per rural person
Northeast			
Heilongjiang	6	5	0.31
Jilin	4	4	0.40
Liaoning	60	5	0.51
North			
Beijing	31	6	0.66
Hebei	52	5	0.27
Nei Monggol	2	5	0.34
Shanxi	1	6	0.23
Tianjin	3	n.a.	0.34
East			
Anhui	26	7	0.24
Fujian	17	10	0.34
Jiangsu	559	8	0.38
Jiangxi	11	7	0.37
Shandong	256	7	0.32
Shanghai	62	6	0.55
Zhejiang	369	8	0.46
Central-South			
Guangdong	44	11	0.41
Guangxi	36	10	0.35
Henan	22	6	0.21
Hubei	116	8	0.33
Hunan	111	8	0.43
Southwest			
Guizhou	neg.	10	0.39
Sichuan	2,727	n.a.	0.59
Yunnan	10	9	0.48
Xizang	-	-	0.10
Northwest			
Gansu	6	6	0.25
Ningxia	1	7	0.17
Qinghai	neg.	4	0.21
Shaanxi	22	n.a.	0.28
Xinjiang	neg.	5	0.08
NATIONAL	4,554	n.a.	0.37

Sources: Number of digestors: Planning Bureau of the Ministry of Agriculture, Animal Husbandry and Forestry, in The Agricultural Yearbook of China, 1982.

Average utilization period: Agricultural Technical and Economic Handbook (1983).

Rural human and pig populations: SSB, Statistical Yearbook of China, 1981 (1980 human population data were adjusted to allow for increases in 1981).

Table G.3: RURAL ELECTRIFICATION, 1979 AND 1982 /a

Region	Percentage of communes electrified		Percentage of brigades electrified	
	1979	1982	1979	1982
Northeast	98.2	98.3	94.5	95.9
North	88.0	91.3	78.3	84.2
Northwest	70.0	73.9	47.8	53.2
East	90.2	94.8	60.7	73.0
Central-south	93.3	89.7	64.1	68.7
Southwest	82.6	85.2	46.9	56.4
All Regions	87.1	89.0	62.6	70.6

Region	Percentage share of non-electrified brigades, 1982	Percentage share of total brigades electrified during 1980-82
Northeast	0.8	1.0
North	7.7	10.6
Northwest	13.4	5.7
East	30.0	50.4
Central-south	24.5	13.3
Southwest	23.6	19.0
All Regions	100.0	100.0

/a "Communes" are currently referred to as "townships," while "brigades" are currently referred to as "villages."

Source: Ministry of Water Resources and Electric Power.

CHINA
MAJOR COAL FLOWS, 1980
Coal Flows (in million tons):
Less than 10.0
10.0 to 20.0
Greater than 20.0
Provincial Boundaries
Coal Region Boundaries
International Boundaries
U. S. S. R.
MONGOLIA
DEM. PEOPLE'S REP. OF KOREA
REPUBLIC OF KOREA
JAPAN
BURMA
VIET NAM
LAO PEOPLE'S DEM. REP.
THAILAND
HEILONGJIANG
JILIN
LIAONING
NEI MONGGOL
BEIJING SHI
TIANJIN SHI
HEBEI
SHANXI
SHANDONG
NINGXIA
GANSU
QINGHAI
SHAANXI
HENAN
JIANGSU
ANHUI
SHANGHAI SHI
HUBEI
ZHEJIANG
SICHUAN
JIANGXI
HUNAN
FUJIAN
GUIZHOU
YUNNAN
GUANGXI
GUANGDONG
TAIWAN
Northeast
North
Northwest
Southwest
East
South Central
Harbin
Mudanjiang
Changchun
Shenyang
Dalian
Qinhuangdao
BEIJING
Tianjin
Datong
Taiyuan
Qingdao
Yanzhou
Lianyungang
Xuzhou
Zhengzhou
Nanjing
Shanghai
Wuhan
Chongqing
Xichang
Guiyang
Kunming
Guangzhou
HONG KONG, U.K.
MACAO, PORT.
Sea of Japan
Yellow Sea
East China Sea
South China Sea
10.6
7.0
6.0
1.7
0.7
14.5
14.1
6.6
33.2
12.6
9.6
5.2
12.8
5.9
12.0
6.0
6.0
3.0
3.0
18.6
4.5
4.1
8.6
8.2
14.2
30.1
11.0
7.0
6.0
7.6
23.3
9.2
3.0
0.7
1.5
2.1
1.3
3.2
100°
110°
120°
130°
50°
40°
30°
20°
KILOMETERS
0 100 200 300 400 500
0 100 200 300
MILES

AUGUST 1985